The Cook's
KITCHEN
BIBLE

The Cook's
KITCHEN
BIBLE

Norma MacMillan

Photography by AMANDA HEYWOOD

ACROPOLIS
BOOKS

First published in 1994 by Lorenz Books

© Anness Publishing Limited 1994

Lorenz Books is an imprint of
Anness Publishing Limited
1 Boundary Row
London SE1 8HP

This edition distributed in Canada by
Book Express, an imprint of
Raincoast Book Distribution Limited
112 East 3rd Avenue, Vancouver
British Columbia, V5T 1C8

Distributed in Australia by Treasure Press

ISBN 1 85967 012 1

A CIP catalogue record for this book
is available from the British Library.

Editorial Director: Joanna Lorenz
Project Editor: Carole Clements
Copy Editors: Jane Sigal and Penny David
Designer: Sheila Volpe
Photographer: Amanda Heywood
Food Styling: Elizabeth Wolf Cohen,
steps by Marilyn Forbes and Cara Hobday

Printed and bound in Hong Kong

ACKNOWLEDGEMENTS

The author would like to thank Jill Eggleton for her help in testing recipes.

For their assistance in the production of this book the publishers wish to thank:

British Gas North Thames
North Thames House
London Road
Staines, Middlesex TW18 4AE

Kenwood Appliances Plc
New Lane
Havant
Hampshire PO9 2NN

M.C. Typeset Limited
The Barn, Woodbank House
Pilgrim's Way
Wouldham, Kent ME1 3RB

Prestige
Prestige House
22–26 High Street
Egham, Surrey TW20 9DU

CONTENTS

~

~ INTRODUCTION ~

Whether you are a complete novice, an experienced cook or an occasional dabbler, there are times when everyone longs for basic techniques and methods to be laid out clearly and simply. This book does just that.

In addition, there are lots of recipes and recipe ideas too, so you can try out the skills you are learning or brushing up. The recipes are designed to illustrate a particular technique. When you read these recipes, take a moment to assess any additional techniques required. Look them up in the index, if you want to review.

USEFUL EQUIPMENT
To be able to cook efficiently and with pleasure, you need good equipment. That is not to say that you should invest in an extensive and expensive collection of pots, pans, tools and gadgets, but a basic range is essential.

In addition, buy the best equipment you can afford, adding more as your budget allows. Well made equipment lasts and is a sound investment; inexpensive pans and tins are likely to dent, break or develop 'hot spots' where food will stick and burn, so will need replacing. Flimsy tools will make food preparation more time consuming and frustrating.

For the top of the stove
When choosing pots and pans, look for those with heavy bottoms, sturdy insulated handles and knobs and tight-fitting lids. Bear in mind, too, how much the pan will weigh when full – a large pot for pasta or stock must not be too heavy for you to lift.

Copper conducts heat best, but is hard to care for. Aluminium is good, as is cast iron, although the latter needs scrupulous care to prevent rust. A vitreous enamel coating on cast iron is a good compromise. Stainless steel is lightweight and durable, but it conducts heat unevenly. A composite or clad bottom containing another metal can improve heat conduction.
- **Stove top essentials**: At least 3 saucepans with lids (2, 3 and 5 pint/1, 2 and 3 litre); small and large frying pans with lids; large flameproof casserole with lid; stockpot or pasta pan with lid.
- **Helpful equipment**: Omelette pan, double saucepan, wok, pancake pan, sauté pan, ridged grill pan, steamer.

For the oven
Cake and bun tins and baking sheets should be made of shiny metal (aluminium, tin or stainless steel) for even heat distribution. Pie and flan tins should be dull metal, glass or ceramic. Roasting tins can be made of any material, but they must be sturdy.
- **Baking and roasting essentials**: 2 round sandwich tins; 8 in (20 cm) or 9 in (23 cm) round and square cake tins; large baking tin (13 × 9 in/33 × 23 cm); large and small loaf tins; deep bun tin; 9 in (23 cm) pie tin; oval or round pie dish; 9 in (23 cm) flan tin with removable bottom, or flan ring; 9 in (23 cm) springform cake tin; Swiss roll tin; 2 baking sheets; roasting tin with rack; large soufflé dish; shallow and deep baking dishes; grill pan with rack; wire rack; oven gloves; oven and meat thermometers.

- **Helpful equipment**: Sandwich tins, round and square cake tins, pie tins, flan tins, springform tins and tartlet tins in alternative sizes; individual soufflé dishes, gratin dishes, ramekins, metal skewers.

Cutting tools
A good set of knives is the most important tool in food preparation. Yet so many cooks make do with flimsy, dull or nicked knives, which can turn even the chopping of onions into an arduous task.

Knives made of carbon steel can be given the sharpest edge, but they rust and discolour easily so must be washed and dried immediately after use. High-carbon stainless steel knives will take a sharp edge and they resist discoloration, but are more expensive. Ordinary stainless steel knives are very difficult to sharpen efficiently.

Whatever knives you choose, keep them sharp. More accidents occur with blunt knives than sharp ones.
- **Cutting essentials**: Chef's knife with 10 in (25 cm) blade, paring knife with 3 in (7.5 cm) blade, flexible vegetable knife with serrated edge and pointed tip, rigid serrated knife with 10–12 in (25–30 cm) blade, sturdy kitchen scissors, knife block or magnetized bar, several cutting boards in different sizes for different uses.
- **Helpful cutting tools**: Filleting knife with thin flexible 7 in (18 cm) blade and sharp point, boning knife with thin 6 in (15 cm) blade, utility knife with 6 in (15 cm) blade, grapefruit knife with curved serrated blade, poultry shears, carving knife and fork.

Preparation tools

You can do a lot with just a big bowl and a sturdy spoon, but there are many tools that make cooking easier.

● **Preparation essentials**: 4 mixing bowls in varying sizes, wooden spoons, long-handled slotted spoon, ladle, wooden spatula, rubber spatulas in varying sizes, palette knife with flexible 10 in (25 cm) blade, fish slice, tongs, large balloon whisk, hand-held electric mixer, potato masher, lemon squeezer, colander, kitchen scales, jug and measuring spoons, vegetable peeler, grater, 2 sieves (1 metal, 1 nylon), long 2-pronged fork, rolling pin, pastry brush, can and bottle openers, corkscrew, kitchen timer, paper towels, wraps, string.

● **Helpful equipment**: Salad spinner, food processor and/or blender, potato ricer, meat mallet, rotary grater, nutmeg grater, citrus zester, canelle knife, apple corer, melon baller, pastry blender, pastry scraper, trussing needle, cherry stoner, pasta machine, table-top electric mixer, baking parchment.

BUYING AND STORING FOOD

A well-stocked kitchen makes meal preparation easy. The key is planning – planning menus for the next few days or the week ahead, then making a shopping list that includes fresh foods as well as those frequently used foods whose stocks are running low or that are near or past their use-by date. Allow yourself to be a little flexible, though. When shopping, take advantage of fresh seasonal foods and special offers.

Knowing how and where to store food – both fresh and preserved – and how long to keep it will be a great help in shopping to stock the kitchen.

In the refrigerator

All foods in the refrigerator or freezer should be well wrapped or stored in sealed containers. This preserves flavour and moisture, and prevents the flavours and odours of other, stronger foods being transferred. It is essential to keep raw meat and poultry well wrapped as their drippings can transfer bacteria to other foods.

Perishable fresh foods, such as meats, poultry, fish and seafood, eggs, cheese and other dairy products, and many fruits and vegetables must be kept refrigerated at a temperature of 35–40°F (1–5°C). For longer storage, many can also be frozen at 0°F (−18°C) or lower. Cooked leftovers must also be refrigerated or frozen. Check fridge and freezer temperatures with a special thermometer. If temperatures are too high, food will spoil rapidly.

Storing fresh fruits

Those fruits that can be kept at room temperature while still unripe include apricots, kiwi fruits, mangoes, nectarines, papayas, peaches, pears, pineapples and plums. Once ripe, all these should be refrigerated and eaten within 2–3 days.

Fruits that can be stored at cool room temperature include apples (although they will be crisper if refrigerated), bananas, dates, grapefruit and oranges. Apples can be kept at room temperature for a few days, dates for several weeks, and grapefruit and oranges for up to a week; beyond that, refrigerate them.

Unless you intend to eat them on the day of purchase, refrigerate fully ripe and perishable fresh fruits. These include berries, cherries, figs, grapes, lemons, limes, melons, pomegranates and tangerines. They can be kept refrigerated for 2–3 days.

Storing fresh vegetables

Like fruits, there are some vegetables that can stored at room temperature. A dark, cool place (about 50°F/10°C) with good ventilation is ideal. Suitable vegetables are garlic, onions, potatoes and sweet potatoes, swede and pumpkin. All can be kept for about 2 months. Store tomatoes at room temperature until they are ripe. After that, refrigerate.

Perishable vegetables should be refrigerated. Some, such as peas or sweetcorn, should be used quickly, while others, like carrots or cabbage, can be kept for a longer period. In most cases, do not wash the vegetable until just before using. Celery, frisée, escarole, spring greens, herbs, lettuce, spinach and watercress should be washed before storage.

Storing canned and dry foods

Full cupboard shelves are a boon for a busy cook, but canned and dry foods can deteriorate if not stored properly or if left too long on the shelf. Kitchen cupboards should be cool (no more than 65°F/18°C) and dry. Staples such as flour, salt, sugar, pasta and grains are best stored in moisture-proof containers. If necessary, remove them from their wrappings and decant them into canisters or jars. Whole-grain products (wholemeal flour and pasta, brown rice, etc) cannot be kept as long as refined ones.

Dried herbs and spices will keep their flavour and scent best if stored in the dark. Light is their enemy, so store them in a cupboard or drawer, rather than on an open spice rack. Oil, too, should be stored in a cool dark place, in an airtight container. Refrigerate nut oils to preserve them longer.

Herbs and spices

The judicious use of a herb or spice, or both, can transform a dish. It's fun to experiment, once you know what you like and which seasonings go well with what foods.

Whenever possible, use fresh herbs, for their wonderful flavour, scent and colour. They're widely available in supermarkets and are also easy to grow, even in pots on a windowsill. Fresh herbs impart their flavour very quickly, so chop just before using and add to hot dishes towards the end of cooking. If fresh herbs are not available, you can, of course, substitute dried. Use them in a ratio of 1 teaspoon dried to 1 tablespoon fresh.

Most spices, both whole and ground, need time to impart their aroma and flavour to a dish. Some are pungent and spicy-hot, others are sweet and fragrant. If you can, grind spices freshly, using a spice mill, nutmeg grater or mortar and pestle. The difference in flavour and aroma between pre-ground and freshly ground is amazing.

GETTING THE TIMING RIGHT

Successful meal preparation is as much dependent on organization as on culinary skills. The initial planning of a menu – whether for the family supper or a dinner party – must give consideration to many things: a good range of flavours, colours and textures, as well as a balance in protein, fat, fibre and other healthy considerations.

That done, it then becomes a question of what you can prepare ahead, and what remains to be done at the last minute so that all is ready at the same time. For the beginner, this can be daunting.

The first step is to read all the recipes before making a final choice. The main dish, with simple accompaniments such as vegetables or a salad and bread, is a good starting point. Surround that with a cold starter (if there is to be one) and a cold dessert that can be made ahead of time. This way you can concentrate your efforts at each stage.

If you do choose two or more hot dishes, consider their cooking times and oven temperatures. If you have only one oven, and the temperatures required for the two dishes are different, this will present difficulties.

Next, make a shopping list. Check that you have all the equipment you require. Once you have everything to hand, you can start the preparation.

Read each recipe through again so you know what lies ahead, and try to estimate how long each preparation stage will take. Review techniques in the preparation that are unfamiliar, using the index to locate them, if necessary. Set the time you want to serve the meal, and work back from there so you know when to start the preparation. It's not a bad idea to write down all these times, as if you were planning military strategy.

If you are serving a starter, you'll need to plan what can be cooked unattended while you are at the table. If your chosen dessert is frozen, it may need some time out of the freezer before serving, so decide when to transfer it from freezer to refrigerator.

Remember to allow time for the final draining of vegetables, or carving of meat, or seasoning of a sauce. It is usually the case that all of these need to be done at the same time – but you only have one pair of hands. So decide what can wait and what will keep hot. Also allow time for plates to be cleared from the table if you are serving more than one course.

If any recipe requires the oven to be preheated or tins to be prepared, do this first. Pots of boiling salted water for cooking vegetables or pasta can be brought to the boil while you are doing the chopping and slicing.

Set out all the ingredients required and prepare them as specified in the recipe. If more than one dish calls for the same ingredients, say chopped onion or parsley, you can prepare the total amount at the same time.

Now start cooking, following your timetable. Check the recipe as you work, and don't be distracted. Keep tasting and sniffing the food as you go – that's much of the fun!

MEASURING TECHNIQUES

Cooks with years of experience may not need to measure ingredients, but if you are a beginner or are trying a new recipe for the first time, it is best to follow instructions carefully. Also, measuring ingredients precisely will ensure consistent results.

Both imperial and metric measures are given in this book. When preparing a recipe, use all imperial or all metric measures. Eggs are size 3 unless specified otherwise and recipes have been tested using a conventional not fan-assisted oven.

USEFUL CONVERSIONS	
Imperial	*Metric*
1 teaspoon	a 5 ml spoon
3 teaspoons = 1 tablespoon	a 15 ml spoon
¼ pint (5 fl oz)	150 ml
½ pint (10 fl oz)	300 ml
¾ pint (15 fl oz)	450 ml
1 pint (20 fl oz)	600 ml
1½ pints	900 ml
2 pints	1.2 litres
1 oz	30 g
2 oz	55 g
3 oz	85 g
4 oz (¼ lb)	115 g
8 oz (½ lb)	225 g
12 oz (¾ lb)	340 g
1 lb (16 oz)	450 g
1 lb 2 oz	500 g
2¼ lb	1 kg
225°F/Gas ¼	110°C
250°F/Gas ½	130°C
275°F/Gas 1	140°C
300°F/Gas 2	150°C
325°F/Gas 3	170°C
350°F/Gas 4	180°C
375°F/Gas 5	190°C
400°F/Gas 6	200°C
425°F/Gas 7	220°C
450°F/Gas 8	230°C
475°F/Gas 9	240°C

1 ▲ For liquids measured in fl oz or pints (ml or litres): Use a glass or clear plastic measuring jug. Put it on a flat surface and pour in the liquid. Bend down and check that the liquid is level with the marking on the jug, as specified in the recipe.

2 ▲ For liquids measured in spoons: Pour the liquid into the measuring spoon, to the brim, and then pour it into the mixing bowl. Do not hold the spoon over the bowl when measuring because liquid may overflow.

3 ▲ For measuring dry ingredients in a spoon: Fill the spoon, scooping up the ingredient. Level the surface even with the rim of the spoon, using the straight edge of a knife.

4 ▲ For measuring dry ingredients by weight: Scoop or pour on to the scales, watching the dial or reading carefully. Balance scales give more accurate readings than spring scales.

5 ▲ For measuring syrups: Set the mixing bowl on the scales and turn the gauge to zero, or make a note of the weight. Pour in the required weight of syrup.

6 ▲ For measuring butter: Cut with a sharp knife and weigh, or cut off the specified amount following the markings on the wrapping paper.

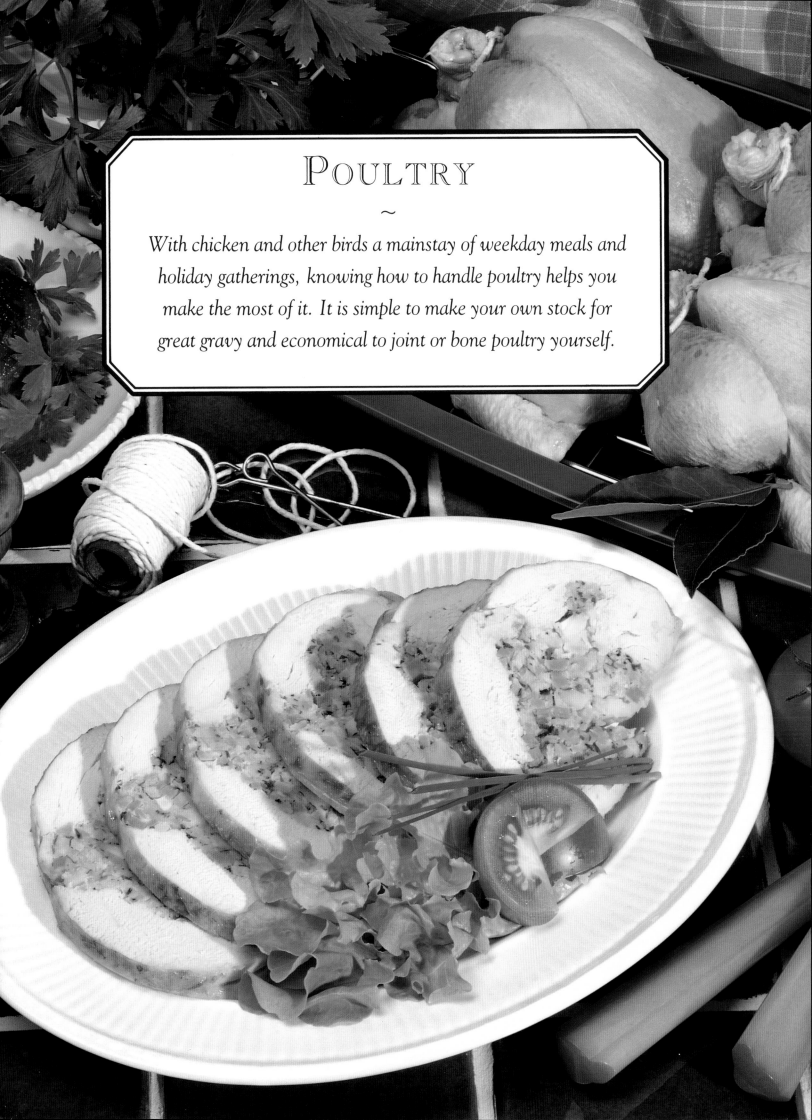

POULTRY

~

*With chicken and other birds a mainstay of weekday meals and
holiday gatherings, knowing how to handle poultry helps you
make the most of it. It is simple to make your own stock for
great gravy and economical to joint or bone poultry yourself.*

TRUSSING POULTRY

Trussing holds a bird together during cooking so that it keeps a neat, attractive shape. If the bird is stuffed, trussing prevents the stuffing falling out. You can truss with strong string or with poultry skewers.

An alternative to the method shown here is to use a long trussing needle and fine cotton string: make 2 passes, in alternate directions, through the body at the open end, from wing to wing, and tie. Then pass the needle through the parson's nose and tie the string around the ends of the drumsticks.

Remove all trussing before serving.

1 ▲ **For an unstuffed bird:** Set it breast down and pull the flap of neck skin over the neck opening. Turn the bird breast up and fold each wing tip back, over the neck skin, to secure firmly behind the shoulder.

2 ▲ Press the legs firmly down and into the breast. If there is a band of skin across the parson's nose, fold back the ends of the drumsticks and tuck them under the skin.

3 ▲ Otherwise, cross the knuckle ends of the drumsticks or bring them tightly together. Loop a length of string several times around the drumstick ends, then tie a knot and trim off excess string.

4 ▲ **For a stuffed bird:** Fold the wing tips back as above. After stuffing the neck end, fold the flap of skin over the opening and secure it with a skewer, then fold over the wing tips.

5 ▲ Put any stuffing or flavourings (herbs, lemon halves, apple quarters and so on) in the body cavity, then secure the ends of the drumsticks as above, tying in the parson's nose, too.

6 ▲ Alternatively, the cavity opening can be closed with skewers: insert 2 or more skewers across the opening, threading them through the skin several times.

7 ▲ Lace the skewers together with string. Tie the drumsticks together over the skewers.

Stuffing tips
When stuffing poultry, the stuffing should be cool, not hot or chilled. Pack it loosely into the bird because it will expand during cooking. Cook any left-over stuffing separately in a baking dish. Do not stuff poultry until just before putting it into the oven or pot. It is not a good idea to stuff the body cavity of a large bird because the stuffing could inhibit heat penetration, and thus not kill all harmful bacteria.

Pot-roast Chicken with Sausage Stuffing

SERVES 6

2 × 2½ lb (1.12 kg) chickens

2 tablespoons vegetable oil

12 fl oz (360 ml) chicken stock or half
   wine and half stock

1 bay leaf

FOR THE STUFFING

1 lb (450 g) pork sausagemeat

1 small onion, chopped

1–2 garlic cloves, finely chopped

1 teaspoon hot paprika

½ teaspoon hot pepper flakes
   (optional)

½ teaspoon dried thyme

¼ teaspoon ground allspice

1½ oz (45 g) coarse fresh breadcrumbs

1 egg, beaten to mix

salt and pepper

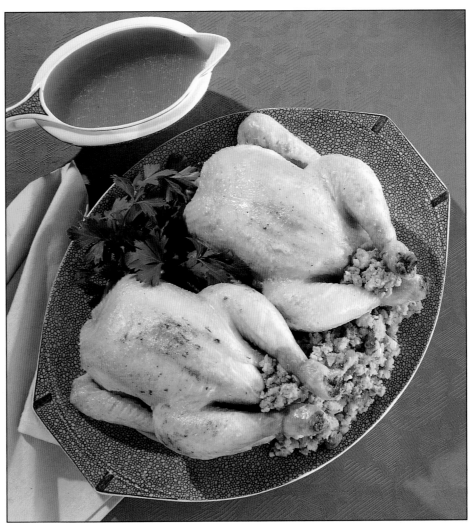

1 Preheat a 350°F/180°C/Gas 4 oven.

2 ▲ For the stuffing, put the
sausagemeat, onion and garlic in a
frying pan and fry over moderate heat
until the sausagemeat is lightly
browned and crumbly, stirring and
turning so it cooks evenly. Remove
from the heat and mix in the
remaining stuffing ingredients with
salt and pepper to taste.

3 Divide the stuffing between the
chickens, packing it into the body
cavities (or, if preferred, stuff the neck
end and bake left-over stuffing
separately). Truss the birds.

4 ▼ Heat the oil in a flameproof
casserole just big enough to hold the
chickens. Brown the birds all over.

~ **VARIATION** ~

For Pot-roast Guinea Fowl, use
2 guinea fowl instead of chickens.

5 ▲ Add the stock and bay leaf and
season. Cover and bring to the boil,
then transfer to the oven. Pot-roast
for 1¼ hours or until the birds are
cooked (the juices will run clear).

6 Untruss the chickens and spoon the
stuffing on to a serving platter.
Arrange the birds and serve with the
strained cooking liquid.

ROASTING POULTRY

Where would family gatherings be without the time-honoured roast bird? But beyond the favourite chicken, all types of poultry can be roasted – from small poussins to large turkeys. However, older tougher birds are better pot-roasted.

1 ▲ Wipe the bird inside and out with damp paper towels. Stuff the bird if the recipe directs and truss it. Spread the breast of chicken with softened or melted butter or oil; bard the breast of a lean game bird; prick the skin of duck and goose.

2 ▲ Set the bird breast up on a rack in a small roasting tin or shallow baking dish. If you are roasting a lean game bird, set the bird in the tin breast down.

Protect and flavour

Before roasting, loosen the skin on the breast by gently easing it away from the flesh with your fingers. Press in softened butter – mixed with herbs or garlic for extra flavour – and smooth back the skin.

3 ▲ Roast the bird, basting it every 10 minutes after the first ½ hour with the accumulated juices and fat in the tin. Turn if directed. If browning too quickly, cover loosely with foil.

4 ▲ Transfer the bird to a carving board and leave to rest for at least 15 minutes before serving. During that time, make a simple sauce or gravy with the juices in the tin (page 38).

Simple Roast Chicken

Squeeze the juice from a halved lemon over a 3–3½ lb (1.35–1.5 kg) chicken, then push the lemon halves into the body cavity. Smear ½ oz (15 g) softened butter over the breast. Roast in a 375°F/190°C/Gas 5 oven for about 1¼ hours. Skim all fat from the roasting juices, then add 4 fl oz (120 ml) water and bring to the boil, stirring well to mix in the browned bits. Season with salt and pepper, and serve this sauce with the chicken. *Serves 4.*

ROASTING TIMES FOR POULTRY

Note: Cooking times given here are for unstuffed birds. For stuffed birds, add 20 minutes to the total roasting time.

Poussin	1–1½ lb (450–700 g)	1–1¼ hours at 350°F/180°C/Gas 4
Chicken	2½–3 lb (1.12–1.35 kg)	1–1¼ hours at 375°F/190°C/Gas 5
	3½–4 lb (1.5–1.8 kg)	1¼–1¾ hours at 375°F/190°C/Gas 5
	4½–5 lb (2–2.25 kg)	1½–2 hours at 375°F/190°C/Gas 5
	5–6 lb (2.25–2.7 kg)	1¾–2½ hours at 375°F/190°C/Gas 5
Capon	5–7 lb (2.25–3 kg)	1¾–2 hours at 325°F/170°C/Gas 3
Duck	3–5 lb (1.35–2.25 kg)	1¾–2¼ hours at 400°F/200°C/Gas 6
Goose	8–10 lb (3.6–4.5 kg)	2½–3 hours at 350°F/180°C/Gas 4
	10–12 lb (4.5–5.4 kg)	3–3½ hours at 350°F/180°C/Gas 4
Turkey (whole bird)	6–8 lb (2.7–3.6 kg)	3–3½ hours at 325°F/170°C/Gas 3
	8–12 lb (3.6–5.4 kg)	3–4 hours at 325°F/170°C/Gas 3
	12–16 lb (5.4–7.2 kg)	4–5 hours at 325°F/170°C/Gas 3
Turkey (whole breast)	4–6 lb (1.8–2.7 kg)	1½–2¼ hours at 325°F/170°C/Gas 3
	6–8 lb (2.7–3.6 kg)	2¼–3¼ hours at 325°F/170°C/Gas 3

Poussins Waldorf

SERVES 6

6 poussins, each weighing about 1¼lb (575g)

salt and pepper

1½–2oz (45–55g) butter, melted

FOR THE STUFFING

1oz (30g) butter

1 onion, finely chopped

10oz (300g) cooked rice

2 celery stalks, finely chopped

2 red apples, cored and finely diced

2oz (55g) walnuts, chopped

5 tablespoons cream sherry or apple juice

2 tablespoons lemon juice

1 Preheat a 350°F/180°C/Gas 4 oven.

2 For the stuffing, melt the butter in a small frying pan and fry the onion, stirring occasionally, until soft. Tip the onion and butter into a bowl and add the remaining stuffing ingredients. Season with salt and pepper and mix well.

3 ◀ Divide the stuffing among the poussins, stuffing the body cavities. Truss. Arrange in a roasting tin. Sprinkle with salt and pepper and drizzle over the melted butter.

4 Roast for about 1¼–1½ hours. Untruss before serving.

CARVING POULTRY

Carving a bird neatly for serving makes the presentation attractive. You will need a sharp long-bladed knife, or an electric knife, plus a long 2-pronged fork and a carving board with a well to catch the juices.

Cut away any trussing string. For a stuffed bird, spoon the stuffing from the cavity into a serving dish. For easier carving, remove the wishbone.

Insert the fork into one breast to hold the bird steady. Cut through the skin to the ball and socket joint on that side of the body, then slice through it to sever the leg from the body. Repeat on the other side.

1 ▲ Slice through the ball and socket joint in each leg to sever the thigh and drumstick. If carving turkey, slice the meat off the thigh and drumstick, parallel to the bone, turning to get even slices; leave chicken thighs and drumsticks whole.

2 ▲ To carve the breast of a turkey or chicken, cut ⅛–¼in (3–5mm) thick slices at an angle, slicing down on both sides of the breastbone. For smaller birds, remove the meat on each side of the breastbone in a single piece, then slice across.

PREPARING DUCK AND GOOSE FOR ROASTING

Duck and goose are bony birds, with most of their rich meat in the breast. There is a thick layer of fat under the skin which could make the birds greasy if it is not removed before cooking or melted out during cooking.

Lean by nature
Wild duck and geese are not as fatty as many farm-raised birds, and should be prepared as you would a game bird so the meat doesn't dry out: bard the breast with rashers of bacon or slices of pork fat.

1 ▲ Pull out any fat from the body and neck cavities. With a skewer or cocktail stick, prick the skin all over the breast of the bird. This will allow the melted fat to run out while the bird is cooking.

2 ▲ Tie the ends of the drumsticks together with string as for a chicken.

Duck with Peach Sauce

SERVES 4

1 × 5–6lb (2.25–2.7kg) duck, prepared for roasting

salt and pepper

5 ripe but firm peaches

8 fl oz (240 ml) orange juice

4 tablespoons peach brandy or Southern Comfort, or peach nectar

1 teaspoon cornflour

2 teaspoons water

2 teaspoons Dijon mustard

fresh parsley or watercress, to garnish

1　Preheat a 400°F/200°C/Gas 6 oven.

2　Rub the duck all over with salt and pepper. Put it breast up on a rack in a roasting tin and roast for 1¼ hours.

3　Meanwhile, peel the peaches: dip in boiling water for 30 seconds, then in iced water to remove the skin. Cut them in half and remove the stones. Purée 2 peach halves with the orange juice in a blender or food processor.

4　Put the remaining peach halves in a saucepan. Sprinkle with the alcohol or peach nectar. Set aside.

5 ▲ Pour off the duck fat from the roasting tin. Place the duck in the tin, without the rack, and pour the orange and peach mixture over it. Roast, basting occasionally with the sauce in the tin, for about 15 minutes more or until the duck is cooked (lift it with a long 2-pronged fork: the juices that run out of the cavity should be clear).

6 ▲ Transfer the duck to a carving board and keep warm. Skim all the fat from the sauce, then set the tin over moderate heat and bring to the boil. Blend the cornflour with the water and stir into the sauce. Simmer, stirring, until thickened.

7　Quarter the duck. Warm the peach halves, then remove with a slotted spoon. Add the mustard to the pan and mix well. Stir this mixture into the sauce and taste. Serve the duck with the peaches, garnished with parsley or watercress. Serve the sauce separately.

SPATCHCOCKING POULTRY

Whole chickens, poussins, guinea fowl and game birds can be split open in half and opened up flat like a book, to resemble the wings of a butterfly. They will then cook evenly under the grill or on a barbecue. A heavy chef's knife can be used to split the bird, but sturdy kitchen scissors or poultry shears are easier to handle.

1 ▲ Set the bird breast down. Cut through the skin and rib cage along one side of the backbone, working from the tail end to the neck. Repeat on the other side of the backbone to cut it free. Keep the backbone for stock, if wished.

2 ▲ Turn the bird breast up. With the heel of your hand, press firmly on the breastbone to break it and flatten the breast.

Testing poultry

Overcooked poultry is dry, tough and tasteless, so knowing when a bird is done is crucial. The most reliable test for a whole bird is to insert an instant-read thermometer deep into the thigh meat (the internal temperature should be 175°F/79°C). Without a thermometer, you can test by piercing the thigh with a skewer or the tip of a knife: the juices that run out should be clear, not pink. Or lift the bird with a long 2-pronged fork and tilt it so that you can check the colour of the juices that run out of the cavity into the roasting tin. Pieces of poultry, particularly breasts, can be tested by pressing them with a finger: the meat should be firm but still slightly springy.

3 ▲ Fold the wing tips back behind the shoulders. Thread a long metal skewer through one wing and the top of the breast and out through the other wing.

4 ▲ Thread a second skewer through the thighs and bottom of the breast. These skewers will keep the bird flat while it is being cooked, and will make it easy to turn over.

GRILLING TIMES FOR POULTRY

Note: Cook 4–6 in (10–15 cm) from the heat; thinner pieces, less than 1 in (2.5 cm), nearer the heat. If the poultry seems to be browning too quickly, turn down the heat slightly.

Poussin, spatchcocked	20–25 minutes
Spring chicken, split in half or spatchcocked	25–30 minutes
Roasting chicken, split in half or spatchcocked	30–40 minutes
Chicken breast, drumstick, thigh	30–35 minutes
Skinless boneless chicken breast	10–12 minutes
Boneless duck breast	10–12 minutes

Grilled Spatchcocked Poussins

SERVES 4

salt and pepper

4 poussins, each weighing about 1 lb (450 g), spatchcocked

olive oil

FOR THE ONION AND HERB SAUCE

2 tablespoons dry sherry

2 tablespoons lemon juice

2 tablespoons olive oil

2 oz (55 g) spring onions, chopped

1 garlic clove, finely chopped

4 tablespoons chopped mixed fresh herbs such as tarragon, parsley, thyme, marjoram, lemon balm

4 ▲ Meanwhile, for the sauce, whisk together the wine, lemon juice, olive oil, spring onions and garlic. Season with salt and pepper.

5 ▼ When the poussins are done, transfer them to a deep serving platter. Whisk the herbs into the sauce, then spoon it over the poussins. Cover tightly with another platter or with foil and leave to rest for 15 minutes before serving.

1 Preheat the grill to high, or prepare a charcoal fire.

2 ▲ Season the birds, then brush them with a little olive oil. Set them on the rack in the grill pan, about 4 in (10 cm) from the heat, or on the barbecue 6 in (15 cm) above the coals.

3 ▲ Cook for 20–25 minutes or until tender. Turn and brush with more oil halfway through the cooking.

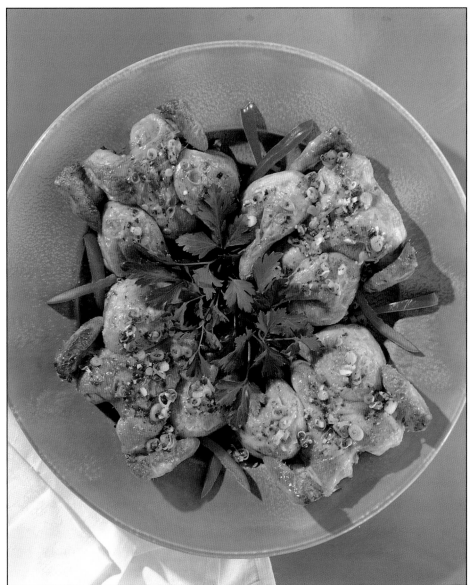

JOINTING POULTRY

Although chickens and other poultry are sold already jointed into halves, quarters, breasts, thighs and drumsticks, sometimes it makes sense to buy a whole bird and to do the job yourself. That way you can prepare 4 larger pieces or 8 smaller ones, depending on the recipe, and you can cut the pieces so the backbone and other bony bits (which can be saved for stock) are not included. In addition, a whole bird is cheaper to buy than pieces.

A sharp knife and sturdy kitchen scissors or poultry shears make the job of jointing poultry very easy.

Safe handling of raw poultry
Raw poultry may harbour potentially harmful organisms, such as salmonella bacteria, so it is vital to take care in its preparation. Always wash your hands, the chopping board, knife and poultry shears in hot soapy water before and after handling the poultry. It is a good idea to use a chopping board that can be washed at high temperature in a dishwasher and, if possible, to keep the chopping board just for the preparation of raw poultry. Thaw frozen poultry completely before cooking.

1 ▲ With the sharp knife, cut through the skin on one side of the body down to where the thigh joins the body. Bend the leg out away from the body and twist it to break the ball and socket joint.

2 ▲ Hold the leg out away from the body and cut through the ball and socket joint, taking the 'oyster meat' from the backbone with the leg. Repeat on the other side.

3 ▲ To separate the breast from the back, cut through the flap of skin just below the rib cage, cutting towards the neck. Pull the breast and back apart and cut through the joints that connect them on each side. Reserve the back for stock.

4 ▲ Turn the whole breast over, skin side down. Take one side of the breast in each hand and bend back firmly so the breastbone pops free. Loosen the bone on both sides with your fingers and, with the help of the knife, remove it.

5 ▲ Cut the breast lengthways in half, cutting through the wishbone. You now have 2 breasts with wings attached and 2 leg portions.

6 ▲ For 8 pieces, cut each breast in half at an angle so that some breast meat is included with a wing portion. Trim off any protruding bones.

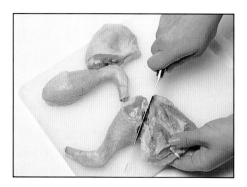

7 ▲ With the knife, cut each leg portion through the ball and socket joint to separate the thigh and drumstick.

Simple Chicken Curry

SERVES 4

2 tablespoons vegetable oil

1 onion, chopped

1 green or red pepper, seeded and diced

1 garlic clove, finely chopped

1½ tablespoons curry powder

½ teaspoon dried thyme

1 lb (450 g) tomatoes, skinned, seeded and chopped, or canned chopped tomatoes

2 tablespoons lemon juice

4 fl oz (120 ml) water

2 oz (55 g) currants or raisins

salt and pepper

1 × 3½ lb (1.5 kg) chicken, cut into 8 pieces and the pieces skinned

cooked rice, to serve

1 Preheat a 350°F/180°C/Gas 4 oven.

2 Heat the oil in a wide, deep frying pan that has an ovenproof handle or in a flameproof casserole. Add the onion, diced pepper and garlic. Cook, stirring occasionally, until the vegetables are soft.

3 ▲ Stir in the curry powder and thyme, then add the tomatoes, lemon juice and water. Bring the sauce to the boil, stirring frequently. Stir in the currants or raisins. Season to taste with salt and pepper.

4 ▲ Put the chicken pieces in the frying pan or casserole, arranging them in one layer. Turn to coat them with the sauce. Cover the pan and transfer to the oven. Cook it for about 40 minutes or until the chicken is tender. Turn the pieces halfway through cooking.

5 Remove the chicken and sauce to a warmed serving platter. Serve with freshly boiled rice.

~ VARIATION ~

For Curried Chicken Casserole, omit the diced pepper and cook 1½ tablespoons finely chopped fresh ginger and 1 green chilli, seeded and finely chopped, with the onion and garlic in a flameproof casserole. In step 3, stir in the curry powder with ¾ pint (450 ml) plain yogurt; omit the tomatoes, lemon juice and water. Add the chicken pieces, cover and cook in a 325°F/170°C/Gas 3 oven for 1–1¼ hours.

MAKING POULTRY SAUTÉS

A sauté combines frying and braising, producing particularly succulent results. It is a method suitable for pieces of poultry as well as for small whole birds such as quails and poussins.

As with frying, the poultry should be dried thoroughly with paper towels before cooking to ensure that it browns quickly and evenly.

1 ▲ Heat a little oil, a mixture of oil and butter, or clarified butter in a heavy frying pan or sauté pan.

2 ▲ Add the poultry and fry it over moderately high heat until it is golden brown, turning to colour evenly.

3 ▲ Add liquid and flavourings called for in the recipe. Bring to the boil, then cover and reduce the heat to moderately low. Continue cooking gently until the poultry is done, turning the pieces or birds over once or twice.

4 ▲ If the recipe instructs, remove the poultry from the pan and keep it warm while finishing the sauce. This can be as simple as boiling the cooking juices to reduce them or adding butter or cream for a richer result.

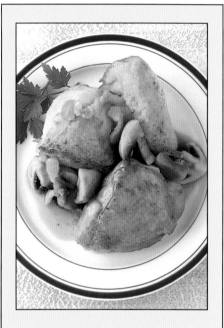

Country Chicken Sauté
Cook 6 oz (175 g) chopped bacon in 2 teaspoons oil over moderately high heat until lightly coloured. Remove and reserve. Dredge a 3½ lb (1.5 kg) chicken, cut into 8 pieces, in seasoned flour. Fry in the bacon fat until evenly browned. Add 3 tablespoons dry white wine and 8 fl oz (240 ml) poultry stock. Bring to the boil and add ½ lb (225 g) quartered mushrooms sautéed in 1 tablespoon of butter and the reserved bacon. Cover and cook over low heat for 20–25 minutes, or until the chicken is tender. *Serves 4.*

5 ▲ Thickening cooking juices: Thicken with equal weights of butter and flour mashed together, called 'beurre manié'. Use 1 oz (30 g) of this paste to 8 fl oz (240 ml) liquid. Whisk small pieces gradually into the boiling sauce until it is smooth and silky.

6 ▲ Another method of thickening cooking juices is to add a mixture of cornflour and water. Use 2 teaspoons cornflour blended with 1 tablespoon water to 8 fl oz (240 ml) liquid. Boil for 2–3 minutes, whisking constantly, until the sauce is syrupy.

Stuffed Chicken Breasts with Cream Sauce

SERVES 4

4 large skinless boneless chicken breasts or chicken suprêmes

2 oz (55 g) butter

3 large leeks, white and pale green parts only, thinly sliced

1 teaspoon grated lime zest

salt and pepper

8 fl oz (240 ml) chicken stock or half stock and half dry white wine

4 fl oz (120 ml) whipping or double cream

1 tablespoon lime juice

1 ▼ Cut horizontally into the thickest part of each breast to make a deep, wide pocket. Take care not to cut all the way through. Set the chicken breasts aside.

2 Melt half the butter in a large heavy frying pan over low heat. Add the leeks and lime zest and cook, stirring occasionally, for 15–20 minutes or until the leeks are very soft but not coloured.

3 Turn the leeks into a bowl and season with salt and pepper. Leave to cool. Clean the frying pan.

~ **VARIATION** ~

For Onion-stuffed Chicken Breasts, use 2 sweet onions, halved and thinly sliced, instead of leeks.

4 ▲ Divide the leeks among the chicken breasts, packing the pockets full. Secure the openings with wooden cocktail sticks.

5 Melt the remaining butter in the frying pan over moderately high heat. Add the stuffed breasts and brown lightly on both sides.

6 Add the stock and bring to the boil. Cover and simmer for about 10 minutes or until the chicken is cooked through. Turn the breasts over halfway through the cooking.

7 With a slotted spatula, remove the breasts from the pan and keep warm. Boil the cooking liquid until it is reduced by half.

8 ▼ Stir the cream into the cooking liquid and boil until reduced by about half again. Stir in the lime juice and season with salt and pepper.

9 Remove the cocktail sticks from the breasts. Cut each breast on the diagonal into ⅜ in (1 cm) slices. Pour the sauce over them and serve.

FRYING CHICKEN

Fried chicken is justifiably popular – crisp and brown outside and tender and juicy within. It's a quick and easy cooking method that can be applied to pieces of rabbit and hare and small turkey joints too.

Dry the pieces thoroughly with paper towels before frying. If they are at all wet, they will not brown properly. If the recipe directs, lightly coat the pieces with egg and crumbs or with a batter.

Succulent Fried Chicken
Mix 8 fl oz (240 ml) milk with 1 beaten egg in a shallow dish. On a sheet of greaseproof paper combine 5 oz (145 g) plain flour, 1 teaspoon paprika, and some salt and pepper. One at a time, dip 8 chicken pieces in the egg mixture and turn them to coat all over. Then dip in the seasoned flour and shake off any excess. Deep-fry for 25–30 minutes, turning the pieces so they brown and cook evenly. Drain on paper towels and serve very hot. *Serves 4.*

1 ▲ **For pan-frying:** Heat oil, a mixture of oil and butter, or clarified butter in a large, heavy-based frying pan over moderately high heat. When the oil is very hot, put in the chicken pieces, skin side down. Do not crowd them or they will not brown evenly; cook in batches if necessary.

3 ▲ **For deep-frying:** Dip the pieces into a mixture of milk and beaten egg, then coat lightly with seasoned flour; allow the coating to set for 20 minutes before frying. (Or coat them with a batter just before frying.)

5 ▲ With a fish slice or tongs, lower the chicken pieces into the oil, a few at a time, without crowding them. Deep-fry until they are golden brown all over and cooked. Turn them so they colour evenly.

2 ▲ Fry until deep golden brown all over, turning the pieces so they colour evenly. Fry until all the chicken pieces are thoroughly cooked. Remove pieces of breast before drumsticks and thighs (dark meat takes longer to cook than white meat). Drain on paper towels.

4 ▲ Half fill a deep pan with vegetable oil. Heat it to 365°F (185°C). You can test the temperature with a cube of bread: if it takes 50 seconds to brown, the oil is at the right temperature.

6 ▲ Drain on paper towels and serve hot. If you want to keep a batch of fried chicken hot while you fry the rest, put it into a low oven, but don't cover it or it will become soggy.

Chicken with Cajun Sauce

SERVES 4

1 × 3½ lb (1.5 kg) chicken, cut into 8 pieces

3½ oz (100 g) plain flour

salt and pepper

8 fl oz (240 ml) buttermilk or milk

vegetable oil, for frying

chopped spring onions, to garnish

FOR THE SAUCE

4 oz (115 g) lard or vegetable oil

scant 2½ oz (70 g) flour

2 onions, chopped

2–3 celery stalks, chopped

1 large green pepper, seeded and chopped

2 garlic cloves, finely chopped

8 fl oz (240 ml) passata

¾ pint (450 ml) red wine or chicken stock

8 oz (225 g) tomatoes, skinned and chopped

2 bay leaves

1 tablespoon soft brown sugar

1 teaspoon grated orange zest

½ teaspoon cayenne pepper

1 For the sauce, heat the lard or oil in a large, heavy pan and stir in the flour. Cook over moderately low heat, stirring constantly, for 15–20 minutes or until the mixture has darkened to the colour of hazelnut shells.

2 ▲ Add the onions, celery, green pepper and garlic and cook, stirring, until the vegetables are softened.

3 Stir in the remaining sauce ingredients with salt and pepper to taste. Bring to the boil, then simmer for 1 hour or until the sauce is rich and thick. Stir from time to time.

4 Meanwhile, prepare the chicken. Put the flour in a plastic bag and season with salt and pepper. Dip each piece of chicken in buttermilk, then dredge in the flour to coat lightly all over. Shake off excess flour. Set the chicken aside for 20 minutes to let the coating set before frying.

5 Heat oil 1 in (2.5 cm) deep in a large frying pan until it is very hot and starting to sizzle. Fry the chicken pieces, turning them once, for about 30 minutes or until deep golden brown all over and cooked through.

6 ▼ Drain the chicken pieces on paper towels. Add them to the sauce and sprinkle with spring onions.

~ **VARIATION** ~

For Pork Chops with Cajun Sauce, substitute 4 large loin chops. The Cajun sauce may also be served with steak, king prawns or fish.

BONING CHICKEN AND TURKEY BREASTS

Boneless poultry breasts, both whole and halves, are widely available, but they tend to be more expensive than breasts with bone. So it is more economical to bone the breasts yourself, and it is really very easy to do. A thin-bladed boning knife is the ideal tool to use.

Terms for chicken breasts
Boneless chicken breasts are often called fillets. If the wing is attached, they are usually known as suprêmes.

---

1 ▲ To take 2 boneless breasts from a whole breast: First pull off the skin and any loose fat. Then with the knife, cut through the breast meat along both sides of the ridged top of the breastbone.

2 ▲ With the knife at an angle, scrape the meat away from the bone down one side of the rib cage. Do this carefully so the breast meat comes away in one neat piece. Repeat on the other side. You now have 2 skinless boneless breasts.

3 ▲ To remove the meat from a breast: If the wing is attached, cut through the ball and socket joint to separate the wing and breast. (Keep the wing for stock or another use.) Pull off the skin, if desired.

4 ▲ Turn the breast over and scrape the meat from the bone, using short strokes and lifting away the bone as it is freed.

5 ▲ Before cooking, remove the tendon next to the long flap or fillet on the underside of the breast. Cut it free of the meat at one end and pull it away, scraping it gently with the knife to remove it neatly.

6 ▲ Trim any fat from the breast. Put it between 2 sheets of cling film or greaseproof paper and pound lightly with a meat mallet, the base of a saucepan or a rolling pin to flatten the breast slightly.

7 ▲ To bone a whole breast for stuffing: You must keep the skin intact. Set the breast skin side down and scrape the meat away from the rib cage, starting at one side and working up to the ridged top of the breastbone. Repeat on the other side.

8 ▲ When the meat has been freed on both sides, lift up the rib cage and scrape the skin gently away from both sides of the top of the breastbone, taking care not to cut through the skin. The whole breast is now boned in one piece.

Stuffed Turkey Breast

SERVES 8

1 × 4½–5 lb (2–2.25 kg) whole turkey breast, skin on, boned

salt and pepper

2 oz (55 g) butter, melted

4 tablespoons dry Madeira or dry white wine

12 fl oz (360 ml) turkey or chicken stock or water

FOR THE STUFFING

1 oz (30 g) butter

1 onion, finely chopped

8 oz (225 g) smoked ham, minced

2 oz (55 g) fresh breadcrumbs

2 tablespoons chopped fresh parsley

½ teaspoon dried thyme

2 oz (55 g) blanched almonds, coarsely chopped

1 egg, beaten to mix

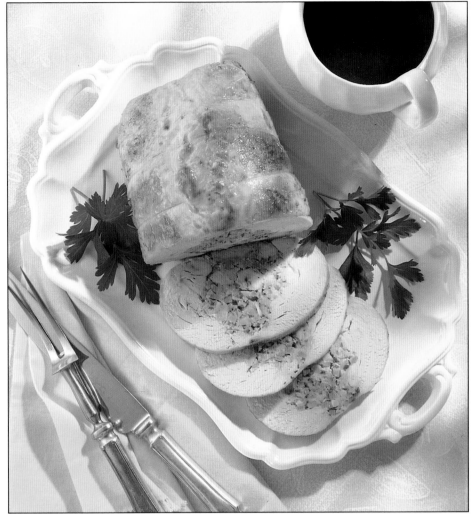

1 Preheat a 325°F/170°C/Gas 3 oven.

2 ▲ For the stuffing, melt the butter in a frying pan and fry the onion, stirring occasionally, until soft. Tip the onion and butter into a bowl and add the ham, breadcrumbs, herbs, almonds and egg. Season to taste with salt and pepper and mix well.

3 Lay the boned turkey breast flat, skin side down. Season with salt and pepper. Spread the stuffing over it in an even layer.

4 ▲ Roll up the breast neatly and tie in several places with string. Use poultry skewers to secure the ends.

5 Place the turkey breast on a rack in a roasting tin. Brush with half of the butter. Mix the remaining butter with the wine. Roast for 2–2½ hours, basting three or four times with the butter mixture. A meat thermometer should register 170°F (77°C).

6 Remove the turkey breast to a carving board. Set aside in a warm place to rest for at least 15 minutes.

7 ▼ Meanwhile, set the roasting tin over high heat. Add the stock or water, bring to the boil and stir to scrape up all the browned bits. Boil for 3–4 minutes. Strain and check the seasoning. Untie the breast and carve into neat slices. Serve with the sauce.

PREPARING TURKEY ESCALOPES

Escalopes are slices cut crossways from the turkey breast. Economical and extremely versatile, they are a lean meat that cooks quickly and can be used as a substitute in most recipes that call for veal escalopes. Turkey escalopes can also be treated in much the same way as thin beef or pork steaks, or used in place of chicken breast fillets.

Slicing across the grain ensures that the escalope won't shrink or curl when it is cooked, and cutting on the diagonal gives good-sized slices.

1 ▲ With a large sharp knife, cut the boned breast across the grain, at a slight angle, into ⅜ in (1 cm) slices.

2 ▲ Put each slice between 2 sheets of greaseproof paper and pound lightly with the base of a pan, a meat mallet, or a rolling pin to flatten to ⅛–¼ in (3–5 mm) thickness. Be careful not to make holes in the meat.

Turkey Rolls with Cranberries

SERVES 4

4 turkey escalopes, prepared for cooking

salt and pepper

2 tablespoons vegetable oil

4 fl oz (120 ml) cranberry juice or fruity red wine

½ teaspoon each arrowroot and water, mixed

FOR THE STUFFING

3½ oz (100 g) cranberries

6 oz (170 g) seedless red grapes

1 large red apple, quartered and cored

1 tablespoon honey

2 teaspoons finely chopped fresh ginger

½ teaspoon ground allspice

1 For the stuffing, work the cranberries, grapes and apple in a food processor until finely chopped.

2 Tip into a sieve placed in a bowl and drain, pressing to extract the juice. Reserve the juice. Mix the fruit with the honey, ginger and allspice.

3 Season the turkey escalopes with salt and pepper. Divide the stuffing among them and spread it over them evenly, almost to the edges.

4 ▲ Roll up each escalope, tucking in the sides, and tie in 2 or 3 places with string, or secure with wooden cocktail sticks.

5 Heat the oil in a frying pan just large enough to accommodate the turkey rolls. Add the rolls and brown them on all sides over moderately high heat for 5–7 minutes.

6 ▲ Add the reserved fruit juice and the cranberry juice or wine to the pan and bring to the boil. Cover and simmer for about 20 minutes or until the turkey is tender and cooked through. Turn the rolls halfway through the cooking.

7 Remove the turkey rolls from the pan and keep warm. Boil the cooking liquid until it has reduced to about 6 fl oz (180 ml). Stir in the arrowroot mixture and boil for 2 minutes. Remove the string or sticks from the turkey rolls and cut into slices. Serve the cooking liquid as a sauce.

MAKING POULTRY STOCK

A good home-made poultry stock is invaluable in the kitchen. It is simple and economical to make, and can be stored in the freezer for up to 6 months. If poultry giblets are available, add them (except the livers) with the wings.

MAKES ABOUT 4 PINTS (2.5 LITRES)

2½–3 lb (1.12–1.35 kg) poultry wings, backs and necks (chicken, turkey, etc)
2 onions, unpeeled, quartered
6½ pints (4 litres) cold water
2 carrots, roughly chopped
2 celery stalks, with leaves if possible, roughly chopped
a small handful of fresh parsley
a few fresh thyme sprigs or ¾ teaspoon dried thyme
1 or 2 bay leaves
10 black peppercorns, lightly crushed

A frugal stock
Stock can be made from the bones and carcasses of roasted poultry, cooked with vegetables and flavourings. Save the carcasses in a plastic bag in the freezer until you have 3 or 4, then make stock. It may not have quite as rich a flavour as stock made from a whole bird or fresh wings, backs and necks, but it will still taste fresher and less salty than stock made from a cube.

1 ▲ Combine the poultry wings, backs and necks and the onions in a stockpot. Cook over moderate heat, stirring occasionally so they colour evenly, until the poultry and onion pieces are lightly browned.

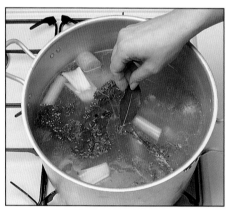

3 ▲ Add the remaining ingredients. Partly cover the stockpot and gently simmer the stock for 3 hours.

5 ▲ When cold, remove the layer of fat that will have set on the surface.

2 ▲ Add the water and stir well to mix in the sediment on the bottom of the pot. Bring to the boil and skim off the impurities as they rise to the surface of the stock.

4 ▲ Strain the stock into a bowl and leave to cool, then refrigerate.

Stock tips
If wished, use a whole bird for making stock instead of wings, backs and necks. A boiling fowl will give wonderful flavour and provide plenty of chicken meat to use in salads, sandwiches, soups and casseroles.

No salt is added to stock because as the stock reduces the flavour becomes concentrated and saltiness increases. Add salt to the dish in which the stock is used.

Cream of Spring Onion Soup

SERVES 4–6

1 oz (30 g) butter
1 small onion, chopped
5 oz (145 g) spring onions, white parts only, chopped
8 oz (225 g) potatoes (2 medium-sized), peeled and chopped
1 pint (600 ml) chicken stock
12 fl oz (360 ml) single cream
salt and white pepper
2 tablespoons lemon juice
chopped spring onion greens or fresh chives, to garnish

1 ▲ Melt the butter in a saucepan and add all the onions. Cover and cook over very low heat for about 10 minutes or until soft.

2 ▲ Add the potatoes and the stock. Bring to the boil, then cover again and simmer over moderately low heat for about 30 minutes. Cool slightly.

3 Purée the soup in a blender or in a food processor.

4 ▼ If serving the soup hot, pour it back into the pan. Add the cream and season with salt and pepper. Reheat gently, stirring frequently. Stir in the lemon juice.

5 ▲ If serving the soup cold, pour it into a bowl. Stir in the cream and lemon juice and season with salt and pepper. Cover the bowl and chill for at least 1 hour.

6 Sprinkle with spring onion greens or chives before serving.

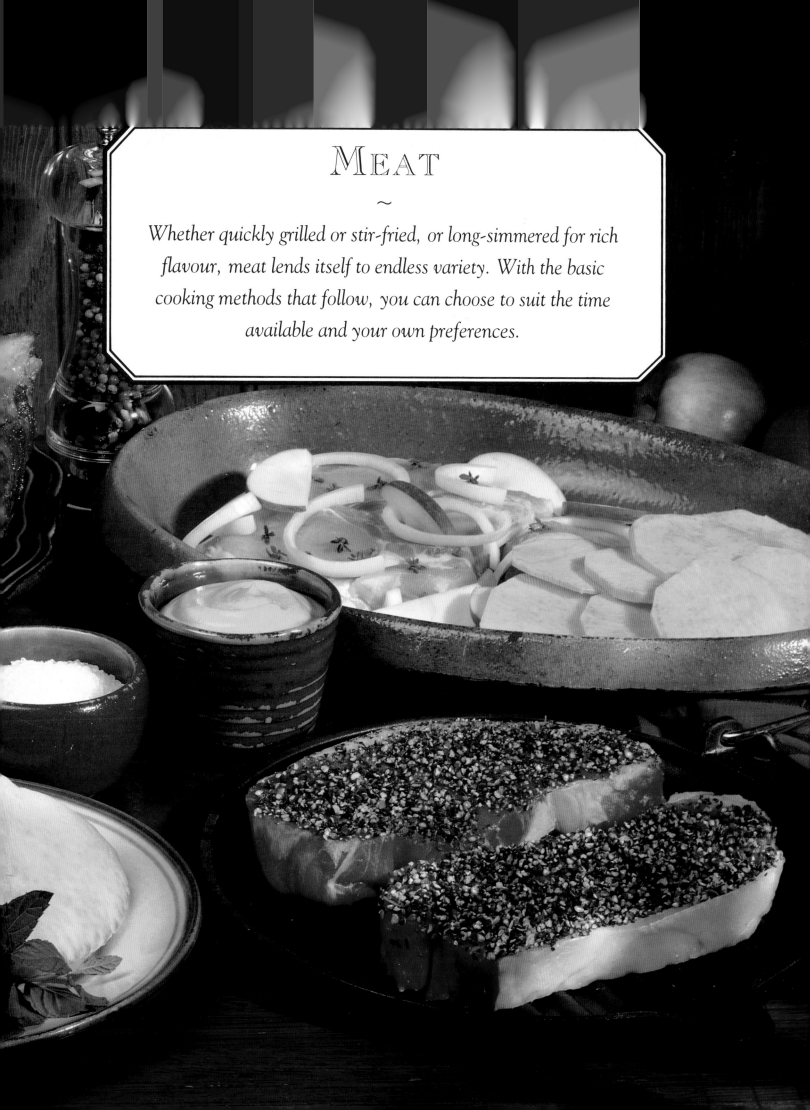

MEAT

~

Whether quickly grilled or stir-fried, or long-simmered for rich flavour, meat lends itself to endless variety. With the basic cooking methods that follow, you can choose to suit the time available and your own preferences.

PREPARING MEAT FOR COOKING

You can buy meat ready for cooking from butchers and supermarkets. However, some cuts need further preparation, depending on how they are to be cooked. After stuffing, for example, a roast will need to be tied.

How much to buy
As a general guide, when buying boneless meat that has little or no fat, allow 5–7oz (145–200g) per serving. For meat with bone that has a little fat at the edge, allow about 8oz (225g) per serving. Very bony cuts such as shin and spareribs have proportionally little meat so you will need 1lb (450g) per serving.

1 ▲ To trim: Use a sharp knife to trim skin or rind and fat from the surface. Leave a little fat on steaks to be grilled, and slash this fat at regular intervals to prevent the steak curling up during cooking. Joints to be roasted should retain a thin layer of fat about ⅛–¼in (3–5mm). Cut away the sinews and tough connective tissue.

2 ▲ If you like, cut and scrape all fat and gristle from the ends of protruding bones (such as on cutlets or joints that contain rib bones). Cover the bone ends with foil to prevent charring.

3 ▲ To chine a joint: For large joints of meat that contain rib bones, such as rib of beef, pork loin and best end of lamb, it is a good idea to cut the chine bone (backbone) where it is joined to the rib bones, to loosen it or to remove it completely before cooking. Do this with a meat saw and sharp knife or ask your butcher to do it. Without the chine bone, the joint will be easy to carve.

4 ▲ To bard a joint: If a very lean piece of meat is to be roasted without a protective crust (a spice mixture, oil and crumbs or pastry, for example), it is a good idea to bard it to keep it moist. Wrap very thin slices of beef fat, pork fat or blanched bacon around the joint and tie them in place. Discard the fat before serving but keep the bacon, if liked.

5 ▲ To tie a boned joint: Joints that have been boned should be tied into a neat shape for roasting or pot roasting. The butcher will do this, but if you want to add a stuffing or seasoning, you will need to retie the joint yourself. Reshape it into a neat roll that is even in circumference. Use butcher's string to make ties around the circumference of the joint at 1in (2.5cm) intervals.

Boned Pork Loin with Apple Cream Sauce

SERVES 6

1 × 3 lb (1.35 kg) boned pork loin, rolled and tied
1 tablespoon fresh thyme leaves or 1 teaspoon dried thyme
salt and pepper
fresh thyme sprigs, watercress and sliced apples, to garnish
FOR THE SAUCE
⅔ oz (20 g) butter
1 onion, chopped
2 apples, such as Granny Smiths, peeled, cored and chopped
¼ pint (150 ml) whipping or double cream
1½ teaspoons Dijon mustard
1 tablespoon creamed horseradish

1 Preheat a 375°F/190°C/Gas 5 oven.

2 ▲ Untie the pork loin. Trim off the skin and most of the fat. Lay the pork out flat, skin side down. Sprinkle it with the thyme, salt and pepper and press into the meat.

~ COOK'S TIP ~

A boned joint will take longer to cook than the same weight joint with bone. This is because the bone conducts heat more readily than the flesh.

---

3 Roll up the loin again and tie it into a neat shape with string.

4 Put the pork loin on a rack in a small roasting tin. Roast for about 1¼–1½ hours or until well cooked.

5 ▼ Meanwhile, for the sauce, melt the butter in a saucepan and add the onion and apples. Cook over low heat for 20–25 minutes, stirring occasionally, until very soft.

6 ▲ Allow the apple mixture to cool slightly, then transfer it to a food processor. Add the cream, mustard and horseradish. Blend until smooth. Season with salt and pepper. Return the sauce to the pan and reheat just before serving.

7 When the pork is cooked, remove it from the oven to rest for about 10 minutes before carving. Garnish with thyme, watercress and apples.

ROASTING MEAT

The dry heat of oven roasting is best suited to tender cuts of meat. If they don't have a natural marbling of fat, bard them. Alternatively, marinate the meat or baste it frequently with the roasting juices during cooking.

Meat should be at room temperature for roasting. Roast on a rack in a tin that is just a little larger than the joint. Without a rack, the base of the joint would stew and not become crisp.

There are two methods of roasting meat. For the first, the joint is seared at a high temperature and then the heat is reduced for the remainder of the cooking time. For the second method, the joint is roasted at a constant temperature throughout. Scientific studies have shown that both methods produce good results, and that it is prolonged cooking, not the method, that affects juiciness and shrinkage. So use whichever method you prefer or follow the recipe.

Suggested roasting times
Following the second roasting method, in a 350°F/180°C/Gas 4 oven, approximate timings in minutes per 1 lb (450 g):
    Beef, rare, 20 + 20 extra*
        medium, 25 + 25 extra
        well done, 30 + 30 extra
    Veal, 25 + 25 extra
    Lamb, 25 + 25 extra
    Pork, 35 + 35 extra
(*Prime cuts such as rib of beef and tenderloin need less time.)

1 ▲ According to the recipe, rub the joint with oil or butter and season. If wished, for extra flavour, with the tip of a sharp knife make little slits in the meat all over the surface. Insert flavourings such as herbs, slivers of garlic, olive slices, shards of fresh ginger and so on.

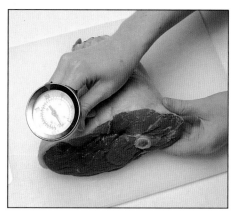

2 ▲ Insert a meat thermometer in the thickest part, not touching a bone. (An instant-read thermometer is sometimes inserted towards the end of roasting.) Roast for the suggested time, basting if necessary.

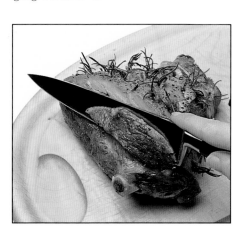

3 ▲ Transfer the cooked meat to a carving board. Leave it to rest for 10–15 minutes before carving. During this time, make a gravy with the roasting juices (page 38), if liked.

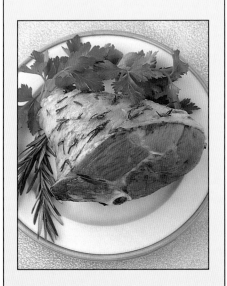

Roast Leg of Lamb
Trim a 5–6 lb (2.25–2.7 kg) leg of lamb, removing almost all the fat. Cut 2–3 garlic cloves into very thin slices. Pull the leaves from 3 sprigs of fresh rosemary. Insert the garlic slices and rosemary leaves into slits in the lamb. Rub the lamb with olive oil and season with salt and pepper. Roast until cooked to your taste. *Serves 8.*

MEAT THERMOMETER READINGS

Beef		Lamb	
rare	125–130°F (52–54°C)	rare	130–135°F (54–57°C)
medium-rare	135°F (57°C)	medium	140–145°F (60–63°C)
medium	140–145°F (60–63°C)	well done	160°F (71°C)
well done	160°F (71°C)		
		Pork	
Veal		medium	150°F (66°C)
well done	160°F (71°C)	well done	160–165°F (71–74°C)

TESTING TO DETERMINE WHEN MEAT IS COOKED

The cooking times given in a recipe are intended to be a guideline. The shape of a cut can affect how long it takes to cook, and people have different preferences for how well cooked they like meat to be. So testing is essential.

Natural law of roasting
A joint will continue to cook in its own retained heat for 5–10 minutes after being removed from oven or pot, so it is a good idea to take it out when it is just below the desired thermometer reading.

1 ▲ Large joints that are roasted or pot-roasted can be tested with a metal skewer. Insert the skewer into the thickest part and leave it for 30 seconds. Withdraw the skewer and feel it: if it is warm, the meat is rare; if it is hot, the meat is well cooked.

2 ▲ The most reliable test is with the use of a meat thermometer, inserted in the centre of the joint, away from bones. Some instant-read thermometers are inserted at the end of cooking. Follow manufacturer's instructions. See the chart for the internal temperatures.

COOKING METHODS AND CHOICE OF CUTS

Roasting
Beef: rib (fore), wing or prime rib, middle rib, fillet, sirloin, topside, aitchbone
Veal: shoulder (oyster), best end of neck, loin, fillet, breast, leg, topside (cushion)
Lamb: shoulder, best end of neck (crown roast), saddle, loin, breast, leg (whole or divided into fillet and knuckle)
Pork: shoulder (spare rib), hand and spring, blade, loin, fillet (tenderloin), leg (whole or divided into fillet and knuckle), fresh belly, spareribs. Also gammon joints and bacon collar and hock

Pot-roasting and braising
Beef: brisket, silverside, top ribs, sirloin, topside, aitchbone, chuck, flank, rump (thick flank), braising steak
Veal: shoulder, best end of neck, middle neck cutlets, breast
Lamb: shoulder, middle neck cutlets, breast, loin, leg

Pork: shoulder (spare rib), loin, fillet (tenderloin). Also gammon joints and bacon collar and hock

Stewing
Beef: neck (clod or sticking), blade, chuck, shin, flank, leg, skirt
Veal: neck, shoulder, scrag, breast, knuckle (osso buco), stewing veal or pie veal
Lamb: middle neck, shoulder, breast, scrag end, chump chops
Pork: spare rib, fillet (tenderloin), loin

Pan-frying
Beef: fillet steak (tournedos), sirloin steak (porterhouse), rump steak, T-bone steak, entrecote, chateaubriand, hamburgers
Veal: cutlets, loin chops, chump chops, escalopes, fillet steaks
Lamb: cutlets, noisettes (boned cutlets), loin chops, chump chops, leg steaks, fillet
Pork: loin chops, spare rib chops, cubes or slices of fillet (tenderloin).

Also streaky and back bacon rashers, gammon rashers, gammon steaks, gammon chops

Grilling
Beef: fillet steak (tournedos), sirloin steak (porterhouse), rump steak, T-bone steak, hamburgers
Veal: cutlets, loin chops, chump chops, fillet steaks
Lamb: cutlets, noisettes (boned cutlets), loin chops, chump chops, leg steaks, cubes of fillet
Pork: loin chops, spare rib chops, cubes or slices of fillet (tenderloin). Also streaky and back bacon rashers, gammon rashers, gammon steaks, gammon chops

Stir-frying
Beef: strips or cubes of rump steak and other steaks
Veal: strips of escalope
Lamb: strips or cubes of shoulder fillet, leg
Pork: strips or cubes of fillet (tenderloin)

MAKING GRAVY

Gravy made from the roasting juices is rich in flavour and colour. It is a traditional accompaniment for roast meat and poultry.

For a thinner sauce, an alternative method to that explained here is deglazing, where liquid is added to skimmed pan juices and boiled to reduce. This is explained on page 48.

Resting a joint before carving
Once a joint is removed from the oven or pot, it should be left in a warm place to 'rest' for 10–15 minutes. During this time, the temperature of the joint evens out, and the flesh reabsorbs most of the juices. Thus, the juices won't leak during carving.

1 ▲ Spoon off most of the fat from the roasting tin. Set the tin over moderately high heat on top of the stove. When the roasting juices begin to sizzle, add flour and stir to combine well.

2 ▲ Cook, scraping the tin well to mix in all the browned bits from the bottom, until the mixture forms a smooth brown paste. Add stock or another liquid as specified in the recipe and bring to the boil, stirring or whisking constantly. Simmer until the gravy has the right consistency, then season with salt and pepper.

Rib of Beef with Shallots

SERVES 8

1 × 10 lb (4.5 kg) fore rib of beef (about 4 ribs), chined

vegetable oil

salt and pepper

1 lb (450 g) plump shallots, unpeeled

1½ tablespoons plain flour

12 fl oz (360 ml) beef stock or 8 fl oz (240 ml) beef stock and 4 fl oz (120 ml) red wine

1 Preheat a 350°F/180°C/Gas 4 oven.

2 If the ends of the rib bones have been left on the joint, scrape them clean, if wished. Rub any exposed bone ends with oil. Season the beef with salt and pepper. Set the joint in a roasting tin, fat side up.

3 Roast the beef until cooked to your taste, basting often with the juices in the tin.

4 ▲ Meanwhile, peel off the outer, papery layers of skin from the shallots, leaving at least 2 layers. Trim the root and stalk ends, if necessary.

5 About 30 minutes before the beef has finished cooking, put the shallots into the roasting tin round the beef.

6 When the beef is ready, transfer it to a carving board and set aside to rest for at least 15 minutes. Remove the shallots from the tin and keep warm.

7 ▼ Spoon off all but about 2 tablespoons of fat from the roasting tin. Make gravy in the tin with the roasting sediments, flour and stock.

8 Carve the rib of beef. Serve with the gravy, the shallots still in their skins (they slip out easily) and roast potatoes, if liked.

BONING A LEG OF LAMB

A boned leg of lamb is much easier to carve than a joint with the bone in. By removing the bones, you can also stuff the pocket left before tying the joint into a neat shape with string.

Boning lamb and leaving the meat opened up flat (called 'butterflying' it) shortens the cooking time by about a third. A butterflied leg can be roasted, grilled or barbecued over charcoal.

Before boning, trim off all fat from the surface of the leg. The pelvic bone comprises the hip bone and the aitchbone.

1 ▲ Set the leg pelvic bone upwards. Working from the fillet end, cut around the ball and socket joint between the hip bone and the main leg bone to free it from the meat. Cut around the pelvic bone to separate it from the meat, then remove it.

2 ▲ Cut through the meat straight down the length of the leg bone, from the hip to the knee.

3 ▲ Using short strokes, cut and scrape the meat away from the bone all around. Cut off the white chip of bone (the knee cap) if it is there.

4 ▲ Continue cutting down the length of the leg bone below the knee (the shank end). Cut and scrape the meat away from the bone as before to free the bone.

5 ▲ Lift the fillet end of the leg bone and cut around the knee to detach it from the meat. To avoid tough meat, cut out the tendons from the meat at the shank end.

6 ▲ To butterfly: Lay the boned leg out flat. Trim off all visible fat, then slash the thick portions of meat and open them so that the whole leg is reasonably even in thickness.

7 ▲ Thread 2 skewers crossways through the meat at its widest part. These will keep the butterflied leg flat during cooking.

Grilling and barbecuing meat
These dry-heat methods of cooking are most suitable for naturally tender cuts of meat or those that have been tenderized. In grilling, meat is cooked under direct heat, either electric or gas powered; in barbecuing, meat is cooked over hot charcoal. The cooking time is determined by the heat and the distance the meat is from the heat source – normally 3 in (7.5 cm) below the grill or 4–6 in (10–15 cm) above the coals.

Mustard-glazed Butterflied Leg of Lamb

SERVES 6–8

4 oz (115 g) Dijon mustard

1–2 garlic cloves, finely chopped

2 tablespoons olive oil

2 tablespoons lemon juice

2 tablespoons chopped fresh rosemary or 1 tablespoon crumbled dried rosemary

salt and pepper

1 × 5 lb (2.25 kg) leg of lamb, boned and butterflied

1 ▲ Combine the mustard, garlic, oil, lemon juice, rosemary, salt and pepper in a shallow glass or ceramic dish. Mix well together.

2 ▲ Add the leg of lamb, secured with skewers, and rub the mustard mixture all over it. Cover the dish and leave to marinate for at least 3 hours. (If the lamb is marinated in the refrigerator, let it return to room temperature before cooking.)

3 Preheat the grill or prepare a charcoal fire.

4 ▲ Place the lamb flat on the rack in the grill pan (lined with foil) or on the barbecue over the charcoal fire. Spread with any mustard mixture left in the bowl.

5 If grilling, set the lamb 4–5 in (10–12.5 cm) from the heat. Cook under the grill or over charcoal until the lamb is crusty and golden brown on the outside, 10–15 minutes on each side for rare meat, 20 minutes for medium and 25 minutes for well done.

6 Transfer the lamb to a carving board and leave it to rest for at least 10 minutes before carving into neat slices (not too thin) for serving.

BROWNING OR SEARING MEAT

Large joints and pieces of meat to be roasted, pot-roasted or stewed are sometimes seared as the first step in their cooking. This may be done either by roasting briefly at a high temperature and then reducing the heat or by frying. The result is a browned crust that adds delicious flavour.

Pot-roasting

This method of cooking tenderizes even the toughest cuts of meat. Prime cuts can also be pot-roasted, but cooking times are cut short – just long enough to reach the degree of cooking you like.

Depending on the desired result, meat to be pot-roasted may or may not have an initial searing.

1 ▲ To sear by frying: Dry the meat well with paper towels. Heat a little oil in a frying pan, flameproof casserole or roasting tin until it is very hot. Put in the meat and fry over high heat until it is well browned on all surfaces. Turn the meat using two spatulas or spoons. (Piercing with a fork would let juices escape, which would be boiled away.)

2 ▲ If roasting, transfer the meat, in its roasting tin, to the oven. If pot-roasting, add a small amount of liquid and cover the pot tightly. If a frying pan has been used for searing, be sure to deglaze it: add some of the liquid called for in the recipe and bring to the boil, scraping up the browned bits from the bottom. Add this flavourful mixture to the pot.

Pot-roast Veal with Herbs

SERVES 6

1 tablespoon vegetable oil
1 × 3 lb (1.35 kg) boned veal shoulder, rolled and tied
4 medium onions, quartered
¼ pint (150 ml) chicken stock
a few sprigs each of fresh thyme, marjoram and rosemary or ¾ teaspoon each dried thyme, oregano and rosemary
salt and pepper

1 Preheat a 300°F/150°C/Gas 2 oven.

2 Heat the oil in a flameproof casserole over high heat (choose a casserole not much larger than the veal joint). Put in the veal joint and brown it, turning frequently to colour it evenly on all sides.

3 ▼ Add the onions, stock and herbs. Season with salt and pepper. Cover tightly and transfer to the oven. Cook for 2½–3 hours.

~ **VARIATION** ~

For Pot-roast Pork with Herbs, substitute a boned pork shoulder or hand and spring.

4 ▲ Remove the veal joint and onions and set aside on a carving board. Leave the veal to rest for at least 10 minutes before carving, discarding the strings.

5 Skim the cooking juices to remove all fat. Bring to the boil, then strain. Taste for seasoning. Serve with the veal and onions.

Chump Chops Braised with Carrots

SERVES 4

2 tablespoons vegetable oil

4 lamb chump chops, weighing about
  5 oz (145 g) each

4 small onions, halved

2 large celery stalks, cut into chunks

8 oz (225 g) baby carrots, halved
  lengthways

½ pint (300 ml) lamb or chicken stock

2 tablespoons tomato purée

1 teaspoon Worcestershire sauce

3 tablespoons chopped fresh parsley

1 bay leaf

salt and pepper

grated zest of 1 lemon

1 Preheat a 350°F/180°C/Gas 4 oven.

2 ▲ Heat the oil in a flameproof casserole that has a tight-fitting lid. Add the chops and brown on both sides. With tongs, remove the chops and set aside.

3 Add the onions and celery to the casserole and cook until they are soft and beginning to brown. Add the carrots, stock, tomato purée and Worcestershire sauce and stir well. Bring to the boil and simmer for 3–4 minutes.

4 ▼ Stir in 2 tablespoons of the parsley and add the bay leaf. Season.

5 Arrange the chops on top of the vegetables. Bring back to the boil, then cover the casserole and transfer to the oven. Cook for 40 minutes.

6 Sprinkle over the lemon zest. Cover again and cook for 10 minutes.

7 Serve immediately, sprinkled with the remaining chopped parsley.

Pot-roast Veal (left), Chump Chops Braised with Carrots

STEWING WITH A FRY START

Fry-start stews have a wonderful rich flavour, due greatly to the initial searing of the meat and vegetables. The long cooking period, in a seasoned liquid, produces a very tender result. Be sure to use a heavy-based pan or casserole.

Saving the flavour
If a different pan is used for searing the meat and vegetables, deglaze it: add wine, stock or water and bring to the boil, scraping up the browned bits from the bottom of the pan. Then add the resulting liquid to the stewpot.

1 ▲ Cut the meat into equal-sized cubes and dry it thoroughly with paper towels. Coat lightly with flour if the recipe instructs.

2 ▲ Heat a little oil in a frying pan or flameproof casserole until it is very hot. Add a few cubes of meat – just enough to cover the bottom of the pan without touching each other. Do not crowd the meat in the pan. If the temperature drops too much, a crisp brown crust will not form.

3 ▲ Fry over moderately high heat until well browned on all sides. Turn the cubes so that they brown evenly, and remove them as they are done.

4 ▲ Add the vegetables and cook, stirring occasionally, until they are well browned. Discard excess oil if the recipe instructs.

5 ▲ Return the meat to the pan. If flour is added now, sprinkle it over the meat and vegetables and cook until it is well combined.

6 ▲ Add liquid barely to cover and stir to mix. Add any flavourings and bring the liquid to the boil. Reduce the heat to a gentle simmer and complete the cooking as specified.

7 ▲ If flour has not been used already, the liquid may be thickened at the end of cooking. One method is adding 'beurre manié', butter and flour paste (page 22), stirred in gradually.

8 ▲ Alternatively, thicken with cornflour mixed with water (page 22). Or remove the meat and vegetables and boil the liquid to reduce it and to concentrate the flavour.

Beef Stew with Dumplings

SERVES 4

1 oz (30 g) plain flour
salt and pepper
1½ lb (700 g) braising steak, cut into 1½ in (4 cm) cubes
3 tablespoons vegetable oil
2 large onions, chopped
2 celery stalks, coarsely chopped
2 large carrots, thickly sliced
2 turnips, cut into cubes
6 oz (170 g) swede, cut into cubes
¾ pint (450 ml) beef stock
1 tablespoon soy sauce
1 bay leaf
1½ teaspoons fresh thyme leaves or ½ teaspoon dried thyme

FOR THE DUMPLINGS

5 oz (145 g) flour
2 teaspoons baking powder
½ teaspoon salt
¼ teaspoon mustard powder
¼ pint (150 ml) milk
2 tablespoons vegetable oil

1 Combine the flour and some salt and pepper in a plastic bag. Add the beef cubes, a few at a time, and toss to coat them. Remove the cubes, shaking off excess flour.

2 ▲ Heat the oil in a flameproof casserole over moderately high heat. Add the cubes of beef, in batches, and brown them well on all sides. Remove them from the casserole as they are browned and set aside.

3 Add the onions, celery, carrots, turnips and swede. Brown them all over, stirring frequently.

4 ▲ Return the beef cubes to the casserole. Add the stock, soy sauce, bay leaf and thyme. Bring to the boil, stirring well to mix in the browned bits from the bottom of the pan.

5 Cover tightly, then reduce the heat to very low. Simmer for about 2 hours or until the beef is very tender.

6 For the dumplings, sift the dry ingredients into a bowl. Add the milk and oil and stir just until the dry ingredients are bound into a soft batter-like dough.

7 ▲ Uncover the casserole and bring the stew liquid back to the boil. Drop the dumpling dough on to the surface of the stew in 8–10 dollops.

8 Cover again and simmer over low heat for 12–15 minutes or until the dumplings are just set and fluffy. Serve immediately.

~ **VARIATION** ~

For Steak Pie, omit the dumplings and put the stew in a baking dish. Cover with puff pastry and bake at 400°F/200°C/Gas 6 for 25 minutes.

STEWING WITH A RAW OR SWEAT START

In stews and pot-roasts where you want to emphasize the natural flavours of the ingredients rather than the flavours that result from browning, the initial searing stage is omitted.

Sweat-start stewing is a combination of two stewing methods. It doesn't use any oil or fat, relying on the fat naturally present in the meat.

1 ▲ Raw-start stewing: Put the meat in a casserole or other pot. Add vegetables, liquid and seasonings as specified in the recipe.

2 ▲ If the recipe instructs, bring the liquid to the boil, then cover the pot. Continue cooking on top of the stove, or transfer to the oven.

3 ▲ Sweat-start stewing: Combine the meat and a little liquid in the stewpot. Cover and cook gently to draw out the meat juices.

4 ▲ Uncover and boil the juices to reduce them to a sticky brown glaze. Continue cooking briskly to brown the meat, then remove it.

5 ▲ Add liquid to deglaze the pot, then add vegetables and flavourings. Return the meat, stir, add more liquid and complete the cooking.

Pork Hot-pot with Apples

SERVES 4

1 oz (30 g) butter
4 large pork loin chops, well trimmed
1 small onion, thinly sliced
2 apples, peeled and thinly sliced
1 teaspoon sweet paprika
½ tablespoon chopped fresh sage or ½ teaspoon dried sage
salt and pepper
4 tablespoons apple juice
1¼–1½ lb (575–700 g) sweet potatoes, thickly sliced

1 Preheat a 350°F/180°C/Gas 4 oven.

2 ▼ Grease a baking dish with one-quarter of the butter. Arrange the chops in one layer.

3 Scatter the onion and apples on top and sprinkle with paprika, sage, salt and pepper. Pour over the juice.

4 ▲ Lay the potato slices over the surface, slightly overlapping them. Cover with foil or a lid. Bake for 1½ hours. Uncover and dot with the remaining butter. Continue baking, uncovered, for 20–30 minutes or until the potatoes are lightly browned.

Lamb Stew with Peas

SERVES 4–6

2–2½ lb (900 g–1.12 kg) boned lamb shoulder, trimmed of excess fat and cut into 1½ in (4 cm) cubes

¾ pint (450 ml) lamb or chicken stock

1 onion, chopped

1 tablespoon chopped fresh rosemary or 1 teaspoon crumbled dried rosemary

salt and pepper

10 oz (300 g) frozen peas, thawed and drained

1 tablespoon mint jelly

1 Put the lamb cubes and 4 fl oz (120 ml) stock in a flameproof casserole. Cover and cook over moderately low heat for about 30 minutes to draw out the juices.

2 Remove the lid and boil the juices, stirring occasionally, until they reduce to a sticky brown glaze.

3 ▼ Continue cooking to brown the cubes of meat well on all sides, turning the cubes so that they colour evenly. With a slotted spoon, remove the lamb cubes from the casserole and set them aside.

4 Skim off as much fat as possible from the remaining juices, then add another 4 fl oz (120 ml) stock. Bring to the boil, stirring thoroughly to mix in all the browned bits from the bottom of the casserole.

5 ▲ Add the onion and rosemary and cook until the onion is soft, stirring occasionally. Return the lamb cubes to the casserole with the remaining stock and season. Bring to the boil. Cover and simmer gently for about 1 hour or until the lamb is tender, adding more stock if needed.

6 Lift out the lamb and keep warm. Skim all fat from the cooking liquid. Add the peas; simmer for 2 minutes. Stir in the mint jelly until melted. Stir in the lamb and serve hot.

Pork Hot-pot with Apples (left), Lamb Stew with Peas

PAN-FRYING AND SAUTÉING

Tender cuts of meat, such as steaks and chops, slices of calf's liver and hamburgers, are ideal for cooking quickly in a heavy frying pan. And the juices left in the pan can be turned into an easy sauce.

Before pan-frying and sautéing, trim excess fat from steaks, chops, escalopes, etc, then dry them very thoroughly with paper towels.

For cooking, use a fat that can be heated to a high temperature. If using butter, an equal amount of vegetable oil will help prevent burning, or use clarified butter.

1 ▲ Heat the fat in the pan over high heat until very hot but not browning. Put in the meat, in one layer. Do not crowd the pan.

2 ▲ Fry until browned on both sides and done to your taste. If pan-frying pork or veal chops, reduce the heat to moderate once they are in the pan.

Testing steak

A reliable way to test steak is by pressing it with your finger. When raw, it is soft and can be squashed. When cooked rare, it will be only slightly springy. When cooked medium, it will offer more resistance and drops of red juice will appear on the surface. When well done, it will be firm to the touch.

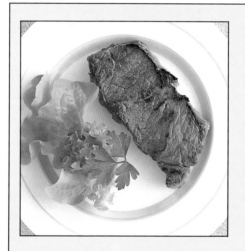

Pan-fried Teriyaki Steak
Combine 3 tablespoons vegetable oil, 1 tablespoon each soy sauce, honey, red wine vinegar and finely chopped onion, 1 crushed garlic clove and ½ teaspoon ground ginger in a plastic bag. Add 4 rump or sirloin steaks and turn to coat well. Put the bag in a dish and marinate for 2 hours. Drain the steaks and pat dry, then pan-fry until cooked to your taste. The steaks can also be grilled. *Serves 4.*

DEGLAZING FOR A PAN SAUCE

After pan-frying or sautéing, a simple yet delicious sauce can be made in the pan. The same method can be used to make gravy for roast meats. It is also a good way to maximize flavour in stews and casseroles.

Before deglazing, remove the meat and keep it warm. Pour or spoon off all the fat from the pan, unless the recipe calls for shallots, garlic, or the like to be softened. In that case, leave 1–2 teaspoons of fat and cook the vegetables in it.

1 ▲ Pour in the liquid called for in the recipe (wine, stock, vinegar, etc). Bring to the boil, stirring well to scrape up all the browned bits from the bottom of the pan and dissolve them in the liquid.

2 ▲ Boil over high heat for 1–2 minutes or until the liquid is almost syrupy. If the recipe instructs, enrich the sauce with cream or butter. Season to taste with salt and pepper and serve.

Pepper Steak with Mushrooms

SERVES 4

2 tablespoons black peppercorns, coarsely crushed
½ teaspoon hot pepper flakes (optional)
4 fillet, sirloin or rump steaks, 6–8 oz (170–225 g) each, well trimmed
3 tablespoons vegetable oil
½ oz (15 g) butter
5 oz (145 g) mushrooms, sliced
2 tablespoons Cognac or whisky
¼ pint (150 ml) whipping or double cream
salt

1 ▲ Combine the peppercorns and hot pepper flakes, if using, and press on to both sides of the steaks.

2 ▲ Heat 1 tablespoon of the oil with the butter in a heavy frying pan that is large enough to accommodate the steaks in one layer. Add the mushrooms and cook over moderate heat, stirring and turning them occasionally, for about 5 minutes or until they are wilted.

3 Increase the heat to moderately high and continue cooking until the liquid from the mushrooms has evaporated and they are lightly browned. With a slotted spoon, remove them from the pan and reserve.

4 Add the remaining oil to the frying pan. When it is very hot, add the steaks. Fry for 2 minutes on each side or until well browned. Continue cooking until done to your taste. (Test by pressing with your finger.) Remove the steaks from the pan and keep them hot.

5 ▲ Pour off all the fat from the pan. Add the Cognac and bring to the boil, stirring and scraping to mix in the browned bits from the bottom of the pan. Add the cream and bring back to the boil. Boil for 1 minute.

6 Stir in the mushrooms and reheat them. Check the seasoning, then pour this sauce over the steaks.

STIR-FRYING

The preparation of ingredients for stir-frying often takes longer than the cooking itself. This is because all ingredients must be cut to uniform sizes so that the cooking can be accomplished quickly and evenly.

A wok is excellent for stir-frying because its high sides let you stir and toss the ingredients briskly. Use long cooking chopsticks or a wooden spatula to keep the ingredients moving around the wok.

Stir-fried Beef with Mange-tout
Cut 1 lb (450 g) lean boneless tender beef into very thin strips. Combine 3 tablespoons soy sauce, 2 tablespoons dry sherry, 1 table-spoon brown sugar and ½ tea-spoon cornflour in a bowl. Heat 1 tablespoon vegetable oil in the hot wok. Add 1 tablespoon each finely chopped fresh ginger and garlic and stir-fry for 30 seconds. Add the beef and stir-fry for 2 minutes or until well browned. Add 8 oz (225 g) mange-tout; stir-fry for 3 minutes. Stir the soy sauce mixture until smooth, then add to the wok. Bring to the boil, stirring and tossing, and simmer just until it is thickened and smooth. Serve immediately, accompanied by freshly boiled rice. *Serves 4.*

1 ▲ Prepare all the ingredients in uniformly sized pieces following recipe instructions.

3 ▲ When the oil is hot (a piece of vegetable should sizzle on contact), add the ingredients in the order specified in the recipe. (Those that take longer to cook are added first.) Do not add too much to the wok at a time or the ingredients will start to steam rather than fry.

2 ▲ Heat a wok or large deep frying pan over moderately high heat. Dribble in the oil down the sides.

4 ▲ Fry, stirring and tossing constantly with chopsticks or a spatula, until the ingredients are just cooked: vegetables should be crisp-tender and meat and poultry tender and juicy.

5 ◄ Push the ingredients to the side of the wok or remove them. Pour liquid or sauce as specified in the recipe into the bottom. Cook and stir, then mix in the ingredients from the side. Serve immediately.

Pork Chop Suey

SERVES 4

12 oz (340 g) pork fillet (tenderloin)
1½ tablespoons cornflour
4 tablespoons soy sauce
1 tablespoon finely chopped fresh ginger
¼ pint (150 ml) beef or chicken stock
4 tablespoons dry sherry
½ teaspoon sugar
salt and pepper
3 tablespoons groundnut or vegetable oil
1 celery stalk, thinly sliced
½ green pepper, seeded and thinly sliced
8 button mushrooms, thinly sliced
1 garlic clove, finely chopped
1 courgette, thinly sliced
4 oz (115 g) canned water chestnuts, sliced
3½ oz (100 g) bean sprouts

1 Trim any fat from the pork, then cut it across the grain into very thin slices. (Freeze the pork for 20–30 minutes so it will be easier to slice.)

2 ▲ Mix 1 tablespoon cornflour, half the soy sauce and the ginger in a bowl. Add the pork and stir well. Cover and marinate for 30 minutes.

3 In another bowl, mix together the remaining cornflour and soy sauce with the stock, sherry, sugar, salt and pepper. Set aside.

4 ▼ Heat the wok, then add half the oil. When it is hot, add the pork mixture and stir-fry over high heat for 1–2 minutes or until all the slices of pork have changed colour. Turn the pork on to a plate.

5 Add the remaining oil to the wok. When hot, add the celery, green pepper, mushrooms and garlic. Stir-fry for 1 minute.

6 ▲ Add the courgette, water chestnuts and bean sprouts. Stir-fry for a further 1–2 minutes or until the vegetables are tender but still crisp.

7 Return the pork to the wok and add the sherry mixture. Cook, stirring, until the sauce boils and thickens. Serve immediately.

PREPARING ESCALOPES

Escalopes are slices of veal from the fillet end of the leg, cut ⅜ in (1 cm) thick. They need to be pounded before cooking, to break the fibres. This tenderizes them and helps to keep them flat during cooking.

Slices of other meat or poultry may also be called escalopes. Beef slices cut from the top of the leg, to be rolled and braised ('birds' or 'olives'), are prepared in the same way.

> **Pounding it out**
> You can also use the base of a heavy saucepan or frying pan to pound and flatten meat escalopes. Choose a pan with a smooth base.

1 ▲ Trim any fat and gristle from around the edge of each escalope. Lay it flat between two sheets of cling film or greaseproof paper.

2 ▲ Using the smooth side of a meat mallet or the long side of a rolling pin, pound gently but firmly all over the escalope to flatten it to ⅛–¼ in (3–5 mm) thickness. It will spread out to almost twice its original size.

Veal Escalopes with Tomato Sauce

SERVES 4

2½ oz (75 g) plain flour

2 tablespoons freshly grated Parmesan cheese, plus more to serve

salt and pepper

1 egg

2 tablespoons milk or water

2½–3 oz (75–85 g) fine fresh breadcrumbs

1 garlic clove, halved (optional)

8 small veal escalopes, weighing 1–1¼ lb (450–575 g), prepared for cooking

½ oz (15 g) butter

3–4 tablespoons olive oil

8 fl oz (240 ml) tomato-herb sauce (page 172)

1 Combine the flour, cheese, salt and pepper on a sheet of greaseproof paper. Lightly beat the egg with the milk or water in a shallow bowl. Spread the crumbs on another sheet of greaseproof paper.

2 If using the garlic, rub the cut sides over the veal escalopes.

3 ▼ One at a time, dip an escalope in the flour mixture to coat both sides lightly; shake off excess flour. Then dip the escalope in the egg mixture. Finally, coat on both sides with crumbs and press them on lightly to help them adhere.

4 ▲ Heat half the butter and oil in a large frying pan over moderately high heat. Add 4 of the prepared escalopes and fry for 1½ minutes on each side or until golden brown and cooked through. Remove from the pan and keep hot while you fry the remaining escalopes.

5 Top each escalope with heated tomato sauce. Serve with additional Parmesan cheese and buttered noodles, if liked.

Beef Birds with Mustard

SERVES 4

8 thin slices of beef topside, weighing about 1¾ lb (800 g), prepared for cooking

3 tablespoons spicy brown mustard

salt and pepper

4 large pickled cucumbers, halved lengthways, or 8 medium-size

2 tablespoons vegetable oil

2 onions, thinly sliced

½ pint (300 ml) Guinness or beef stock

1 bay leaf

1 Preheat a 350°F/180°C/Gas 4 oven. Select a heavy frying pan with an ovenproof handle or a flameproof casserole.

2 Lay the slices of beef out flat on a work surface. Spread each slice with mustard, almost to the edges. Season with salt and pepper.

3 ▼ Place a piece of cucumber along one end of each slice and roll up neatly. Tie the rolls with string or secure with wooden cocktail sticks.

4 Heat the oil in the frying pan or casserole. Add the beef rolls and fry over moderately high heat until they are browned on all sides. Remove them from the pan and set aside.

5 Add the onions to the pan and fry until soft and beginning to brown, stirring frequently.

6 ▲ Return the beef rolls to the pan and add the Guinness and bay leaf. Bring to the boil over high heat.

7 Cover the pan tightly and transfer it to the oven. Cook for 1 hour or until the beef rolls are very tender. Turn them over halfway through cooking to ensure even cooking.

8 Remove the string or sticks and discard the bay leaf before serving. If liked, serve rice or potatoes with the beef birds.

Veal Escalopes with Tomato Sauce (left), Beef Birds with Mustard

MINCING MEAT

Minced meats of all kinds are easily obtainable, but when you want something more unusual for a pâté or you want to use a particular cut of meat, well trimmed of gristle and tendons, you will mince it yourself. Also, if minced meat is to be served raw, as in steak tartare, it must be freshly prepared.

1 ◀ **With a mincer**: This produces the most uniform minced meat, and you can choose coarse or fine textures, according to which blade is used. Trim the meat well and cut it into 1½ in (4 cm) cubes or strips, then feed through the machine.

2 ▲ **With a food processor**: Trim the meat carefully (be sure to remove all gristle because a food processor will chop gristle too) and cut it into cubes. Place in the machine fitted with the metal blade and pulse.

3 ▲ In between turning the machine on and off a few times, stir the meat around so that it is evenly minced. Care must be taken not to overprocess meat to a purée, particularly if making hamburgers (they would be tough).

4 ▲ **By hand**: Trim the meat well. Using a large chef's knife, first cut the meat into cubes, then chop into smaller and smaller cubes. Continue chopping until you have the consistency you want, coarse or fine.

Meat Loaf with Mushroom Stuffing

SERVES 6

8 oz (225 g) mushrooms, coarsely chopped

1 small onion, finely chopped

1 oz (30 g) butter

4½ oz (130 g) fresh breadcrumbs

3 tablespoons chopped fresh parsley

1 teaspoon dried thyme

2 teaspoons bottled brown sauce

salt and pepper

1½ lb (700 g) lean minced beef

8 oz (225 g) lean minced pork

5 tablespoons tomato ketchup

2 eggs, beaten

1 Preheat a 375°F/190°C/Gas 5 oven.

2 Cook the mushrooms and onion in the butter over moderate heat until soft. Turn the mixture into a bowl.

3 ▲ Add the breadcrumbs, parsley, thyme, brown sauce, salt and pepper. Mix well.

4 In another bowl, mix the beef with the pork, tomato ketchup and eggs.

5 ▲ Pack half of the meat mixture into a large loaf tin, pressing it into an even layer. Pack the mushroom mixture on top, then cover with the rest of the meat. Bake for 1¼ hours.

6 Remove from the oven and leave to stand for 15 minutes. Pour off the juices, then turn out the meat loaf on to a serving plate. Serve hot.

Lamb Burgers with Cucumber Sauce

SERVES 4

1½ lb (700 g) lean minced lamb

1 small onion, finely chopped

8 dried apricot halves, finely chopped

4 tablespoons pine nuts

¾ oz (25 g) fine dry breadcrumbs

2 teaspoons mild curry powder

1 egg

salt and pepper

4 pittas (pocket breads), heated and cut in half

FOR THE SAUCE

½ cucumber, peeled and grated

½ pint (300 ml) plain yogurt

2 tablespoons chopped fresh mint

1 ▼ Combine the lamb, onion, apricots, pine nuts, breadcrumbs, curry powder, egg, salt and pepper in a bowl. Mix well together with your fingers until blended.

2 ▲ Divide into 8 portions and shape each into a small burger. Cover and chill for 30 minutes.

3 Meanwhile, for the sauce, squeeze the grated cucumber in a double thickness of paper towels to extract excess water.

4 ▲ Mix together the cucumber, yogurt and mint. Season to taste with salt and pepper.

5 Preheat the grill or prepare a charcoal fire.

6 Grill or barbecue the burgers until they are cooked to your taste, about 10 minutes for medium. Turn them halfway through cooking to ensure that they brown and cook evenly.

7 Serve the burgers in the pitta halves, with the cucumber sauce.

Cottage Pie

SERVES 4

2 oz (55 g) butter
1 large onion, finely chopped
1 celery stalk, finely diced
1 large carrot, finely diced
1 lb (450 g) lean minced beef
1 tablespoon plain flour
8 fl oz (240 ml) hot beef stock
2 tablespoons chopped fresh parsley
1 tablespoon tomato purée
salt and pepper
2 lb (900 g) floury potatoes, peeled
3–4 tablespoons milk
2 teaspoons spicy brown mustard

1 Melt ½ oz (15 g) of the butter in a frying pan over moderate heat. Add the onion, celery and carrot and cook until the onion is soft, stirring occasionally.

2 ▲ Add the beef and fry, stirring, until it is brown and crumbly.

3 ▲ Sprinkle the flour evenly over the surface and stir it into the meat and vegetables.

4 ▲ Gradually add the stock, stirring well. Stir in the parsley and tomato purée. Season with salt and pepper.

5 Bring to a simmer, then cover and cook over very low heat, stirring occasionally, for 45 minutes.

6 Meanwhile, cook the potatoes in boiling salted water until they are tender. Drain well.

7 Put the potatoes in a bowl and mash them. Add the remaining butter and just enough milk to make a soft fluffy texture. Season to taste with salt and pepper.

8 Preheat a 400°F/200°C/Gas 6 oven.

9 Stir the mustard into the beef mixture, then turn it into a baking dish. Cover with a neat layer of potatoes and seal to the sides of the dish. Mark with a fork, if liked. Bake for 20–25 minutes. Serve hot.

COOKING BACON AND SAUSAGES

Bacon is cured meat from the fatty side (or belly) of a pig. Streaky rashers are fattier than back rashers; throughcut or middle rashers combine back and streaky. All three can be used almost interchangeably in recipes. All bacon rashers are available smoked and unsmoked (or green). Trim off rind before cooking, if preferred.

Uncooked sausage – fresh or smoked – must be thoroughly cooked before eating. Test by piercing with a skewer: the juices that run out should be clear. Many precooked sausages are only heated to serving temperature by poaching, braising, frying or grilling.

1 ▲ To fry back bacon or gammon rashers: Heat a little butter or oil, or other fat specified in a recipe, in a heavy frying pan. Arrange the rashers in the pan in one layer and cook over moderate heat until lightly browned, 4–10 minutes, according to the thickness of the rashers.

2 ▲ To fry streaky bacon rashers: Arrange them in a heavy unheated frying pan in one layer. Set the pan over moderately low heat. Cook the bacon, turning it occasionally, until golden brown and cooked, 8–10 minutes, according to the thickness of the rashers. Drain on paper towels.

3 ▲ To bake or grill bacon rashers: Arrange them side by side on a rack in a shallow baking pan. Bake in a 400°F/200°C/Gas 6 oven, turning once, for 10–15 minutes or until golden brown. Or grill under a moderately high heat, turning once, for 3–8 minutes or until crisp and brown on both sides.

4 ▲ To make bacon rolls: Cut off the rind, then cut each rasher across into 2 or 3 pieces. Smooth with the flat side of a knife to flatten. Roll up each piece and secure with a wooden cocktail stick. Cook in the oven around a roasting bird, or grill.

5 ▲ To pan-braise fresh sausages: Arrange in one layer in an unheated frying pan with 3 tablespoons water. Cover and simmer for 5–15 minutes or until cooked through. Drain. Uncover and cook until browned. Or fry, uncovered, in a little fat, turning to brown and cook evenly.

6 ▲ To bake or grill fresh sausages: Arrange them on a rack in a shallow baking tin. Bake in a 400°F/200°C/Gas 6 oven for about 20 minutes until cooked (test with a skewer). Or grill about 4 in (10 cm) from the heat until browned on all sides.

7 ▲ To fry pork sausagemeat: Cook in a frying pan over moderate heat until golden brown and crumbly. Stir constantly while cooking and break up with the side of a spoon or fork. Drain off excess fat.

8 ▲ To poach frankfurters and other cooked sausages: Add them to a saucepan of boiling water. Reduce the heat, cover and simmer for 5–10 minutes or until heated through. To brown poached or fully cooked sausages, grill or fry gently.

Sausage and Bean Casserole

SERVES 4–6

12 oz (340 g) dried white haricot beans, soaked overnight
4 oz (115 g) soft light brown sugar
2 teaspoons mustard powder
3 oz (85 g) light molasses or treacle
1 large onion, chopped
salt and pepper
12 frankfurters or other cooked sausages, cut into 1 in (2.5 cm) pieces

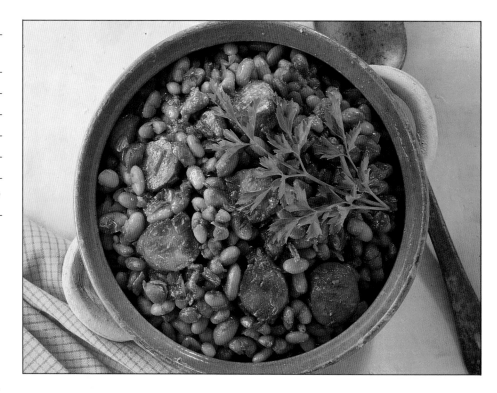

1 Drain the beans and put them in a large saucepan. Cover with plenty of fresh cold water. Bring to the boil, then simmer over low heat for about 1 hour. Drain the beans and reserve the cooking liquid.

2 Preheat a 300°F/150°C/Gas 2 oven.

3 ▲ Mix ¾ pint (450 ml) of the bean cooking liquid with the sugar, mustard and molasses or treacle.

4 ▲ Mix the beans and onion in a casserole. Add the molasses mixture and season. Cover and bake for 3 hours, stirring and adding more liquid occasionally.

5 ◄ Stir in the pieces of frankfurter or other sausage. If the beans seem dry, add a little more of the reserved cooking liquid.

6 Cover the casserole again and continue cooking for a further 1 hour, stirring occasionally. Serve hot, in the casserole.

A selection of sausages

Sausages are available in many forms. Some are ready to eat, but fresh sausages must be cooked thoroughly and those sold as cooked are often heated before serving. All kinds of meats are used and each country has its traditional specialities.

Uncooked sausages include fresh sausages and chipolatas made from pork, beef or other meat (fry, pan-braise, grill or bake); sausagemeat (fry); bockwurst and bratwurst (poach, then fry or grill); boudin blanc (poach or grill); haggis (poach); luganeghe (poach or grill); merguez (grill); Toulouse sausage (essential in cassoulet).

Part or fully cooked sausages include andouillette, sometimes smoked (fry or grill); black pudding (fry or grill); cotechino (poach); frankfurter (poach or grill); kielbasa, sometimes smoked (poach or slice and add to soups and stews); liverwurst (ready to eat cold); saveloy/cervelat (add to soups or bean dishes).

Smoked and dry sausages, all of which are ready to eat cold, include bierwurst, chorizo (which is also sold fresh), mettwurst, mortadella, peperoni (a popular pizza topping) and salami from various parts of Italy, as well as Germany, Hungary, France and Denmark.

MAKING MEAT STOCK

The most delicious meat soups, stews, casseroles, gravies and sauces rely on a good home-made stock for success. Neither a stock cube nor a canned consommé will do if you want the best flavour. Once made, meat stock can be kept in the refrigerator for 4–5 days, or frozen for longer storage (up to 6 months).

On the light side
For a light meat stock, use veal bones and do not roast the bones or vegetables. Put in the pot with cold water and cook as described.

MAKES ABOUT 3½ PINTS (2 LITRES)

4 lb (1.8 kg) beef bones, such as shin, leg, neck and clod, or veal or lamb bones, cut into 2½ in (6 cm) pieces

2 onions, unpeeled, quartered

2 carrots, roughly chopped

2 celery stalks, with leaves if possible, roughly chopped

2 tomatoes, coarsely chopped

7½ pints (4.5 litres) cold water

a handful of parsley stalks

a few fresh thyme sprigs or ¾ teaspoon dried thyme

2 bay leaves

10 black peppercorns, lightly crushed

1 ▲ Preheat a 450°F/230°C/Gas 8 oven. Put the bones in a roasting tin or flameproof casserole and roast, turning occasionally, for 30 minutes or until they start to brown.

2 ▲ Add the onions, carrots, celery and tomatoes and baste with the fat in the tin. Roast for a further 20–30 minutes or until the bones are well browned. Stir and baste occasionally.

3 ▲ Transfer the bones and vegetables to a stockpot. Spoon off the fat from the roasting tin.

4 ▲ Add a little of the water to the roasting tin or casserole and bring to the boil on top of the stove, stirring well to scrape up any browned bits. Pour this liquid into the stockpot.

5 ▲ Add the remaining water. Bring just to the boil, skimming frequently to remove all the foam from the surface. Add the parsley, thyme, bay leaves and peppercorns.

6 ▲ Partly cover the pot and simmer the stock for 4–6 hours. The bones and vegetables should always be covered with liquid, so top up with a little boiling water from time to time if necessary.

7 ▲ Strain the stock through a sieve. Skim as much fat as possible from the surface. If possible, cool the stock and then refrigerate it; the fat will rise to the top and set in a layer that can be removed easily.

Hearty Beef and Vegetable Soup

SERVES 6

8 oz (225 g) braising steak, cut into ½ in (1.5 cm) cubes

8 oz (225 g) lean boned pork shoulder, cut into ½ in (1.5 cm) cubes

3½ pints (2 litres) beef stock

1 bay leaf

12 oz (340 g) tomatoes, skinned, seeded and chopped

1 small red pepper, seeded and chopped

1 small onion, chopped

2 carrots, chopped

1 large boiling potato, peeled and diced

6 oz (170 g) fresh or thawed frozen sweetcorn kernels

1 tablespoon Worcestershire sauce

salt and pepper

1 ▲ Put the beef and pork in a large heavy saucepan and add the stock. Bring to the boil, skimming off all the froth that rises to the surface.

2 ▲ When the liquid is free of froth, add the bay leaf. Partly cover the pan and gently simmer over very low heat for about 1 hour.

3 ▼ Add the tomatoes, red pepper, onion, carrots and potato. Bring back to the boil. Continue simmering, partly covered, for about 45 minutes. Stir from time to time.

4 Add the sweetcorn and simmer for a further 20–30 minutes or until all the vegetables and meat are tender.

5 Discard the bay leaf. Stir in the Worcestershire sauce. Taste and adjust the seasoning before serving.

~ COOK'S TIP ~

This soup can be made 2 or 3 days ahead. The flavour will improve.

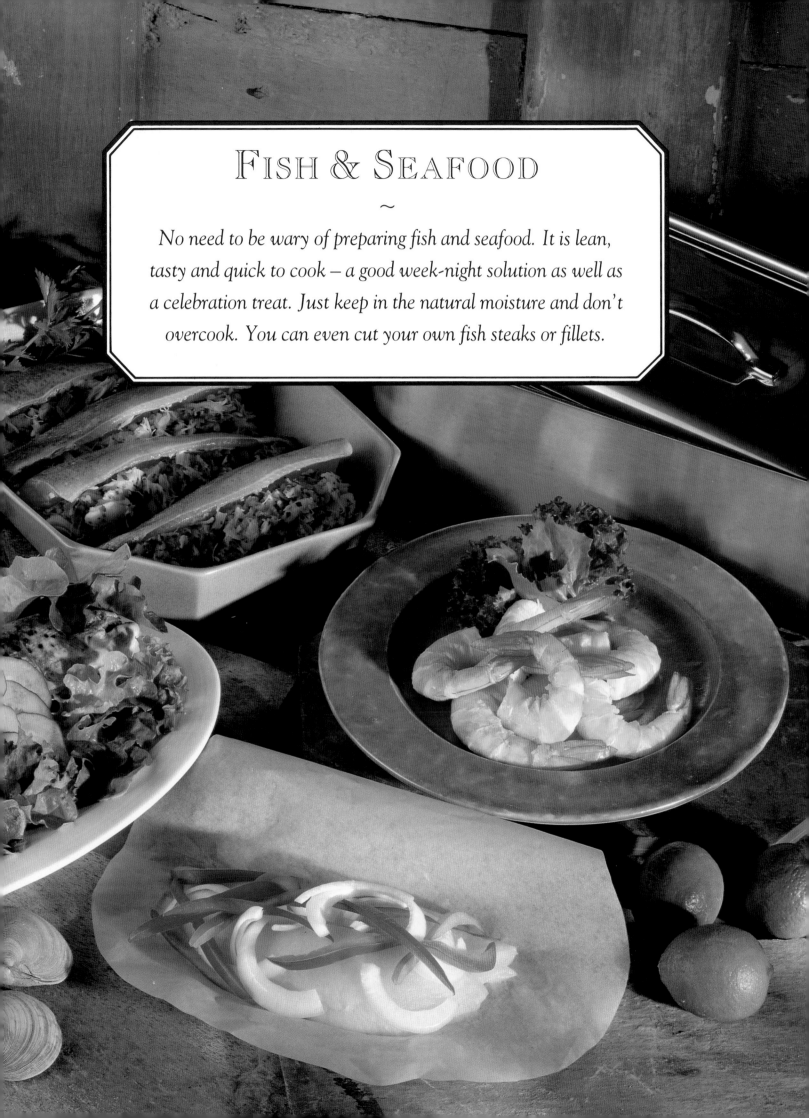

FISH & SEAFOOD

~

No need to be wary of preparing fish and seafood. It is lean, tasty and quick to cook – a good week-night solution as well as a celebration treat. Just keep in the natural moisture and don't overcook. You can even cut your own fish steaks or fillets.

PREPARING WHOLE FISH FOR COOKING

Most fish have scales and these should be removed before cooking unless the fish is to be filleted or the skin is to be removed before serving. Fish sold by fishmongers will normally be scaled as well as cleaned (eviscerated or gutted), but you can do this yourself, if necessary. Trimming the tail gives a whole fish a neat appearance.

All fish preparation is best done in or near the sink, with cool water running. Salt your hands for a good grip on the fish.

1 ▲ **To scale:** Grasp the tail firmly and scrape off the scales using a special fish scaler or a knife, working from the tail towards the head. Rinse the fish well. Repeat on the other side.

2 ▲ **To trim:** For flat fish to be cooked whole, use kitchen scissors to trim off the outer half of the small fin bones all round the fish.

3 ▲ For round fish, cut the flesh on both sides of the anal and dorsal (back) fins and pull them out; the small bones attached will come out too. Trim off the other fins.

4 ▲ If the fish is to be cooked whole, leave the fins on, or just trim them, because they help keep the shape of the fish.

5 ▲ **To trim the tail:** If the tail is to be left on, cut a neat 'V' in the centre with scissors. The fish is now ready for cooking.

A LOOK AT FISH

In terms of shape and structure, most fish fall into one of two general categories: round fish and flat fish.

Round fish have thicker bodies and many of their bones are attached to their fins. They can be filleted or cut into steaks or cutlets, but all will contain small pin bones.

Flat fish have a flat central bone with a row of bones attached on either side. This simple bone structure makes flat fish easy to fillet. Most are too thin to cut into steaks or cutlets.

Large fish such as tuna have a thick bone running down the centre of their bodies; spiking out from this are four rows of bones that divide the flesh into quarters. These boneless 'loins' are usually sliced into steaks.

The fat content of fish is an important consideration in deciding how to cook it. Lean fish can dry out at high temperatures, so a protective coating is a good idea when frying. When grilling, marinate or baste them. Lean and moderately lean fish are best cooked by moist methods such as steaming, poaching and baking in sauce. Oily fish, however, almost baste themselves during cooking, so they are ideal for baking, grilling and pan-frying.

Texture and flavour are also important in choosing how to prepare fish. If the flavour of the flesh is mild, it is important not to overwhelm it. But fish with rich, distinctively flavoured flesh will stand up well to spicy, pungent seasonings.

Fish that are delicate in texture need careful cooking. Pan-frying with a flour coating, steaming and gentle baking are best. However, fish with meaty, dense flesh can be cubed and put on to skewers.

Pan-fried Trout with Olives and Capers

SERVES 4

4 whole trout, ¾–1 lb (340–450 g) each, gutted and trimmed

salt and pepper

flour, for coating

4 tablespoons vegetable oil

3 oz (85 g) butter

3 oz (85 g) black olives, sliced

3 tablespoons capers

2 tablespoons lemon juice

lemon wedges, to serve

1 ▲ Sprinkle the trout with salt and pepper. Coat them lightly with flour, shaking off any excess.

Terms used by fishmongers
Cutlet: Thickish slice cut cross-ways from the middle of a whole gutted fish.
Escalope: Thin slice cut on a slant from a large fillet.
Fillet: Boneless or nearly boneless piece cut lengthways from the sides of the fish. May or may not be skinned.
Gutted: Describes fish that has had its internal organs removed. Other terms used are cleaned and eviscerated.
Steak: Thickish slice cut cross-ways from the tail end of a whole gutted fish.

2 ▲ Heat the oil in a large frying pan over moderate heat. Add the trout and fry for 12–15 minutes or until golden on both sides and cooked.

3 Transfer the trout to a warmed serving platter and keep warm. Pour off all the oil from the pan.

4 ▼ Add the butter to the frying pan and melt it. When it starts to brown and smell nutty, stir in the olives, capers and lemon juice. Cook for 10 seconds, then pour this sauce over the fish. Serve immediately.

BAKING FISH

Most fish are suitable for baking – whole or in fillets, cutlets or steaks. Lean fish, in particular, benefit from some protection to prevent them from drying out: choose recipes that include a stuffing or coating or bake them in a little liquid or sauce, which can also be served with the fish. All of these add extra flavour to the fish too.

Cooking in foil or paper parcels is suitable for many fish, both small whole ones and pieces (fillets, cutlets or steaks). This seals in moisture, so the effect is similar to steaming.

A good rule of thumb to calculate cooking time for fish is 10 minutes in a 425°F/220°C/Gas 7 oven for each 1 in (2.5 cm), measured at the thickest part.

1 ▲ To bake fish with liquid, pour over a small amount of stock, wine, water or other liquid as specified in the recipe, then add seasonings.

2 ▲ To bake fish in foil or paper, wrap tightly with seasonings and flavourings as specified and place the parcel on a baking sheet.

Baked Fish Steaks
Arrange 1½ lb (700 g) white fish steaks in a shallow baking dish. Sprinkle the fish with 2 tablespoons chopped shallot or onion and 3 tablespoons lemon juice or dry white wine. Drizzle with 1 oz (30 g) melted butter and season with salt and pepper. Bake in a 425°F/220°C/Gas 7 oven for about 10 minutes or until the fish is cooked. Pour the cooking juices over the steaks before serving.
Serves 4.

A SELECTION OF FISH VARIETIES

Choose the freshest fish you can find. If necessary, substitute another variety with similar qualities.

Lean fish

Bream
- round fish, saltwater
- firm, moist texture; delicate, sweet flavour
- fry, grill, bake, steam
- substitute red mullet, John Dory

Brill
- flat fish, saltwater
- fine texture, delicate flavour
- fry, grill, bake, steam, poach
- substitute other flat fish, such as turbot, John Dory

Cod
- round fish, saltwater
- flaky, tender texture; mild flavour
- grill, bake, steam, poach
- substitute haddock, halibut

Haddock
- round fish, saltwater
- soft, moist texture; mild flavour
- grill, bake, steam, poach
- substitute cod, halibut

Hake
- round fish, saltwater
- white flesh with good flavour
- grill, bake, steam, poach
- substitute cod, haddock

Halibut
- flat fish, saltwater
- firm, moist texture; mild, sweet flavour
- grill, bake, steam, poach
- substitute plaice, sole

John Dory
- flat fish, saltwater
- flaky texture; nutty sweet flavour
- poach, bake, grill, steam
- substitute brill, halibut

Plaice
- flat fish, saltwater
- fine texture; delicate flavour
- fry, grill, bake, steam
- substitute sole, other flat fish

Sea bass
- round fish, saltwater
- flaky or firm flesh; mild flavour
- grill, fry, bake
- substitute salmon, grey mullet, John Dory

TESTING TO DETERMINE WHEN FISH IS COOKED

All seafood cooks quickly. If overcooked it becomes dry and loses its succulent quality. In the case of meaty fish such as tuna and swordfish, it can be unpleasantly chewy. It is therefore worth knowing how to judge when fish is perfectly cooked.

The flesh of raw fish and crustaceans is translucent; it becomes opaque when it is cooked.

1 ▲ To determine whether a fish is cooked, make a small slit in the thickest part. Lift with the knife to look into the opening.

2 ▲ The fish is ready when still very slightly translucent in the centre or near the bone (it will continue to cook when removed from the heat).

Skate
- flattened body with large fins (wings), saltwater
- flaky, well-flavoured flesh
- fry, grill, poach, steam

Sole (Dover and lemon)
- flat fish, saltwater
- fine texture; delicate flavour
- fry, grill, bake, poach
- substitute plaice

Turbot
- flat fish, saltwater
- succulent; firm yet tender; superb flavour
- bake, grill, poach, steam
- substitute brill, John Dory

Moderately lean fish
Grey mullet
- round fish, saltwater
- delicate, easily digested flesh
- fry, grill, poach, bake

Monkfish
- round, saltwater
- firm texture; sweet, similar to lobster
- fry, grill, bake, poach, stew
- substitute cod, halibut

Red mullet
- round fish, saltwater
- delicate texture with excellent flavour
- grill, bake, fry
- substitute trout

Swordfish
- thick central bone, saltwater
- firm, meaty texture; mild but distinctive flavour
- grill, bake, steam, poach
- substitute dogfish/rock salmon, tuna

Trout
- round fish, freshwater
- tender, flaky texture; delicate, rich
- fry, grill, bake
- substitute sea trout, small salmon

Tuna
- thick central bone, saltwater
- some varieties more oily
- firm, meaty texture; mild to strong flavour
- bake, steam, poach, grill
- substitute swordfish, dogfish/rock salmon

Moderately oily and oily fish
Carp
- round fish, freshwater
- soft, flaky texture; mild flavour
- bake, grill, fry, steam
- substitute cod, haddock

Herring
- round fish, saltwater
- moist and tender; rich flavour
- grill, bake, fry, souse
- substitute mackerel

Mackerel
- round fish, saltwater
- moist and tender or firm texture; rich, distinctive flavour
- grill, bake, fry, souse
- substitute herring

Salmon
- round fish, freshwater/saltwater
- flaky, tender texture; mild to rich
- bake, grill, steam, poach
- substitute large sea trout

Sea trout/salmon trout
- round fish, saltwater
- moist, flaky texture; mild, sweet
- grill, bake, fry
- substitute salmon, rainbow trout

POACHING FISH

Whole fish, large and small, as well as fillets, cutlets and steaks are excellent poached because the gentle cooking gives succulent results. Poached fish can be served hot or cold, with a wide variety of sauces. The poaching liquid may be used as the basis for the sauce.

Poaching containers
A long rectangular fish kettle with a perforated rack enables you to lift the fish out of the liquid after cooking. You could also use a large wire rack set in a deep tin.

1 ▲ To oven-poach small whole fish, fillets, cutlets or steaks: Place the fish in a buttered flameproof dish that is large enough to hold the pieces comfortably. Pour in enough liquid to come two-thirds of the way up the side of the fish.

2 ▲ Add any flavourings called for in the recipe. Press a piece of buttered greaseproof on top to keep in the moisture without sticking to the fish.

3 ▲ Set the dish over moderate heat and bring the liquid just to the boil. Transfer the dish to a 350°F/180°C/Gas 4 oven and poach until the fish is just cooked. To test, with the tip of a sharp knife, make a small cut into the thickest part of the fish (ideally near a bone): the flesh should be slightly translucent.

4 ▲ To poach whole fish, fillets, cutlets or steaks on top of the stove: Put large whole fish on the rack in a fish kettle, or set on a piece of muslin that can be used like a hammock. Small whole fish, fillets, cutlets and steaks may be poached in a fish kettle on a rack, or set directly in a wide saucepan or frying pan.

5 ▲ Prepare the poaching liquid (salted water, milk, wine, stock or court bouillon) in the fish kettle or in a large casserole or roasting tin (or a wide saucepan or frying pan for fillets, cutlets and steaks). Set the rack in the kettle, or the muslin hammock in the casserole or tin. Add more liquid, if necessary, to cover the fish.

6 ▲ Cover the kettle or casserole and bring the liquid just to the boil. Reduce the heat and simmer very gently until the fish is cooked.

Poached Sole Fillets
Oven-poach 8 skinless sole fillets, about 1½lb (700g), each ½in (1.5cm) thick. Use ½pint (300ml) dry white wine or fish stock with 4–6 chopped spring onions, 4–6 lemon slices and a few allspice berries for flavouring. Simmer for 3–5 minutes, then remove the fish. Boil the cooking liquid until reduced to 4 tablespoons, then strain it. Season with salt and pepper. *Serves 4.*

Poached Whole Fish with Green Mayonnaise

SERVES 6 OR MORE

1 whole salmon, sea trout or sea bass, weighing about 5 lb (2.25 kg), scaled if necessary, gutted and trimmed

12 fl oz (360 ml) green mayonnaise (page 180), to serve

FOR THE COURT BOUILLON

¾ pint (450 ml) dry white wine

about 4½ pints (3 litres) water

1 large onion, sliced

2 carrots, thinly sliced

1 celery stalk, thinly sliced

½ lemon, sliced

a few parsley sprigs

1 bay leaf

12 black peppercorns

4 allspice berries (optional)

salt

1 ▲ Combine all the ingredients for the court bouillon in a fish kettle or in a large roasting tin. Bring to the boil, cover and simmer for 20 minutes.

2 Place the fish on the kettle rack, or set it on a piece of muslin. Lower the fish into the court bouillon. The fish should be covered with liquid, so add more water if necessary.

3 Cover and bring back to boiling point, then simmer very gently for 15–20 minutes or until just cooked.

4 ▼ Remove the kettle from the heat and lift the fish, by means of the rack or muslin hammock, out of the court bouillon. Drain well, then transfer the fish to a serving platter and leave to cool slightly.

5 ▲ Gently peel off the skin and pull out the fins. If salmon has been used, gently scrape off the thin layer of greyish flesh. Cool completely.

6 Serve the cooled fish with the green mayonnaise.

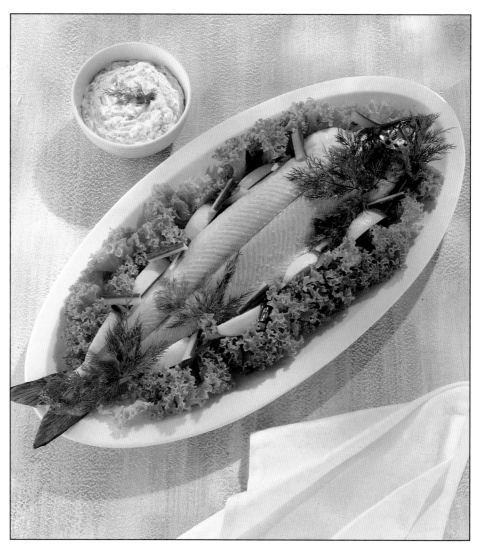

STEAMING FISH

This simple, moist-heat method of cooking is ideal for fish and shellfish. If you don't have a steamer, it is easy to improvise.

Steamed Salmon with Herbs
Line a heatproof plate with fresh herb sprigs (dill, parsley, chives etc). Set 2 portions of seasoned salmon fillet, each 1 in (2.5 cm) thick, on top. Steam Chinese-style for about 10 minutes. If liked, top with a flavoured butter (page 174) or serve with Holland-aise (page 178). *Serves 2.*

1 ▲ Using a steamer: Arrange the fish on the rack in the steamer and set over boiling water. Cover and steam until done.

3 ▲ Steaming larger fish and fillets: Arrange the fish on a rack in a roasting tin of boiling water or on a plate set on the rack. Cover tightly with foil and steam until done.

2 ▲ Chinese-style steaming: Arrange the fish on a heatproof plate that will fit inside a bamboo steamer or wok. Put the plate on the rack in a steamer or wok; set over boiling water. Cover and steam until done.

4 ▲ Steaming in foil: Wrap the fish and seasonings in foil, sealing well, and set on a rack in the steamer or in a large roasting tin of boiling water. Steam until done.

CUTTING FISH STEAKS AND CUTLETS

Round fish and large flat fish such as halibut are often cut into steaks and cutlets for cooking. Steaks are cut from the tail end of the fish, while cutlets are cut from the centre. They are usually cut about 1–1½ in (2.5–4 cm) thick.

1 ▲ With a large, sharp knife, slice the fish across, at a right angle to the backbone, into slices of the desired thickness.

2 ▲ If necessary, cut through the backbone with kitchen scissors or a knife with a serrated blade.

Fish Steaks with Mustard Sauce

SERVES 4–6

4–6 halibut or turbot steaks,
    1 in (2.5 cm) thick

salt and pepper

1½ oz (45 g) butter, melted

lemon wedges, for serving

FOR THE MUSTARD SAUCE

4 tablespoons Dijon mustard

½ pint (300 ml) double or whipping
    cream

½ teaspoon caster sugar

1 tablespoon white wine vinegar or
    lemon juice

1 Preheat the grill. Season the fish steaks with salt and pepper. Arrange them on an oiled rack in the grill pan and brush the tops of the steaks with melted butter.

2 ▼ Grill about 4 in (10 cm) from the heat for 4–5 minutes on each side or until cooked. Brush with more melted butter when you turn the steaks.

3 ▲ Meanwhile, for the sauce, combine the ingredients in a saucepan and bring to the boil, whisking constantly. Simmer, whisking, until the sauce thickens. Remove from the heat and keep warm.

4 Transfer the fish to warmed plates. Spoon over the sauce and serve immediately, with lemon wedges.

CUTTING FISH FILLETS

Fillets are boneless pieces of fish, and for this reason are very popular. A sharp filleting knife, with its thin, flexible blade, is the tool to use for removing the fillets. Be sure to keep all the bones and trimmings for making stock.

Round fish are easy to fillet and they produce a boneless piece from each side. Large flat fish are also easy to deal with, although they are filleted slightly differently from round fish and they yield 4 narrow fillets – 2 from each side.

Filleting small flat fish
You can take 2 fillets from smaller flat fish (one from each side): Cut behind the head and down the sides of the fish as above, but do not make the central cut. Starting from the head end on one side and working down the fish, cut the flesh away from the rib bones until you reach the centre (the backbone). Rotate the fish and repeat on the other side to cut away the whole fillet. Turn the fish over and repeat to cut away the second whole fillet.

1 ▲ To fillet a round fish: Lay the fish flat, on its side. First cut off the head. With the tip of the knife, cut through the skin all along the length of the backbone.

2 ▲ Working from head to tail and holding the knife almost parallel to the fish, use short strokes to cut 1 fillet off the rib bones in one piece. Follow the slit cut along the backbone.

3 ▲ When you reach the tail, cut across to release the fillet. Repeat the procedure on the other side to remove the other fillet.

4 ▲ Run your fingers over the flesh side of each fillet to locate any stray bones. Pull them out with tweezers.

5 ▲ To fillet a flat fish: Lay the fish flat and make a curved cut behind the head, cutting down to but not through the backbone. With the tip of the knife, slit the skin down both sides of the fish where the fin bones meet the rib bones, 'outlining' the fillets, and slit across the tail.

6 ▲ Slit straight down the centre line of the fish, from head to tail, cutting down to the backbone. Working from the centre at the head end, cut 1 fillet neatly away from the rib bones on one side. Hold the knife blade almost parallel to the fish and use short strokes.

7 ▲ Rotate the fish and cut away the second fillet. Turn the fish over and repeat to remove the 2 fillets on the other side. Pull out any stray bones with tweezers.

Fish Fillets with Peppers in Paper Parcels

SERVES 4

2 tablespoons olive oil

1 onion, thinly sliced

1 garlic clove, finely chopped

2 peppers, 1 green and 1 red, seeded and cut into thin strips

8 oz (225 g) tomatoes, coarsely chopped

1 tablespoon chopped fresh mint

2 teaspoons chopped fresh marjoram or ½ teaspoon dried oregano

salt and pepper

4 skinless fish fillets, such as brill, bream or trout

4 oz (115 g) feta cheese, crumbled

4 ▲ Put a spoonful of the pepper mixture on one half of each piece of paper or foil and set a fish fillet on top. Spoon some of the remaining pepper mixture over each portion of fish. Scatter the cheese on top.

5 ▼ Fold the paper or foil over the fish and fold the edges over several times to seal. Set the parcels on a baking sheet.

6 Bake for 20–25 minutes or until the fish is cooked. If you used paper, you can serve the fish in the parcels, but remove fish from foil for serving.

1 Preheat a 350°F/180°C/Gas 4 oven.

2 ▲ Heat the oil in a frying pan and cook the onion, stirring occasionally, for 3–5 minutes or until soft. Add the garlic and peppers and fry until tender but not browned. Stir in the tomatoes and herbs. Season with salt and pepper. Remove from the heat.

3 ▲ Cut 4 rounds of greaseproof paper, baking parchment or foil, each the size to wrap a fillet comfortably.

SKINNING FISH FILLETS

Before cooking, dark or tough skin is usually removed from fish fillets. However, if they are to be grilled, the skin helps keep the shape and should not be removed.

> **Getting a grip on fish**
> If you salt your fingers, you will get a better grip on the tail end so you can hold the skin taut as you cut. This is also a good way to hang on to fish while scaling.

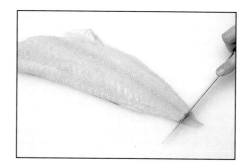

1 ▲ Lay the fillet flat, skin side down, tail end towards you. Make a small crossways cut through the flesh down to the skin at the tail end.

2 ▲ Grip the bit of skin firmly and insert the knife blade so it is almost parallel to the skin, then cut the fillet away. Use a gentle sawing motion and make one continuous cut.

Layered Fish Casserole

SERVES 6–8

1¼ pints (750 ml) milk
1 slice of onion
2–3 sprigs of fresh parsley
1 bay leaf
a few black peppercorns
3 oz (85 g) butter
2½ oz (70 g) plain flour
½ teaspoon grated lemon zest
1 egg, beaten to mix
salt and pepper
5 oz (145 g) water biscuits, coarsely crushed
1½ lb (700 g) skinless white fish fillets, finely diced
8 oz (225 g) skinless smoked haddock or whiting fillet, cut into strips

1 Preheat a 350°F/180°C/Gas 4 oven.

2 Bring the milk to the boil with the onion, herbs and peppercorns. Off the heat, let stand 20 minutes to infuse. Melt 2½ oz (70 g) of the butter, stir in the flour, then strain in the milk. Bring to the boil, whisking constantly, then simmer until thickened.

3 ▲ Remove the pan from the heat. Add the lemon zest and egg and mix well. Season with salt and pepper.

4 ▲ Scatter about one-third of the biscuit crumbs over the bottom of a buttered baking dish. Cover with a layer of half the diced fish. Spoon half the sauce over the fish and arrange the strips of smoked fish on top. Repeat the layers of crumbs, fish and sauce.

5 ▼ Scatter the remaining biscuit crumbs over the surface. Dot the top with the remaining butter.

6 Bake for about 35 minutes or until bubbling round the edges and lightly browned on top. Serve hot.

> **~ VARIATION ~**
>
> For Fish Pie, omit the biscuits and egg. Fold the diced fish into the sauce. Put half in a buttered baking dish and cover with a layer of smoked fish strips. Top with the remaining fish mixture. Cover with mashed potato, dot with butter and bake as above.

BONING FISH FOR STUFFING OR BUTTERFLYING

Round fish, such as trout, mackerel and salmon, are normally cleaned by slitting open the belly. It is a simple step on from here to removing the backbone. This leaves a bone-free fish and a neat shape for stuffing.

When the boned fish is opened out like a book, or 'butterflied', it is approximately the same thickness throughout for even, quick cooking.

1 ▲ If the head has not already been removed, cut it off by slicing just behind the gills. Remove the tail completely, cutting straight across.

2 ▲ Enlarge the belly opening. Set the fish on a board, skin side up, with the belly flaps against the board. Press firmly along the backbone to loosen it. Turn the fish over.

Boning through the back
An alternative boning method to the one shown here is done from the back rather than the belly. Leave the head and tail on the fish. Set the fish belly down on the work surface and use a sharp knife to slit the skin along one side of the backbone, all the way from the head to the tail. Ease the knife through the slit and work it down the side of the rib cage to detach the bones completely from the flesh. Slit the skin on the other side of the backbone and ease the knife down the rib cage to detach the flesh on that side. With scissors, snip the backbone free at head and tail ends, then lift it out along with the gills and the stomach contents.

3 ▲ If it is possible, lift out the backbone and rib cage in one piece after freeing it with the knife. If it is necessary to cut the backbone out, slide the knife under the bones along one side of the rib cage.

4 ▲ Gently ease the knife outwards under the rib bones, away from the backbone. Repeat on the other side.

5 ▲ Lift up the rib cage in one piece and slide the knife under the backbone, to free it from the skin.

6 ▲ Run your fingers over the flesh to locate any other bones and pull them out with tweezers.

7 ▲ After boning, rinse the fish under cool running water and pat dry with paper towels.

Baked Fish Stuffed with Crab

SERVES 4

4 streaky bacon rashers

1 oz (30 g) butter

2 oz (55 g) spring onions, chopped

1 large celery stalk, diced

grated zest of 1 large lemon

1 tablespoon chopped fresh parsley

1 oz (30 g) crumbs made from day-old French or Italian bread

salt and pepper

6–8 oz (170–225 g) white crabmeat

1 egg, beaten to mix

4 whole fish such as trout or red snapper, ¾–1 lb (340–450 g) each, scaled if necessary, gutted and boned for stuffing

1 Preheat a 375°F/190°C/Gas 5 oven.

2 Fry the bacon rashers in the butter in a frying pan until crisp. Drain on paper towels. Chop the bacon.

3 Pour off all but 1 tablespoon of the fat from the frying pan into a small bowl and reserve. Brush a little reserved fat over the bottom of a baking dish or roasting tin that will accommodate the fish comfortably. Set aside.

4 ▲ Heat the fat still in the frying pan and cook the spring onions and celery, stirring occasionally, for 5–7 minutes or until soft.

5 Mix together the vegetables, lemon zest, parsley, breadcrumbs, salt and pepper. Fold in the crabmeat and bacon. Bind with the egg.

6 ▼ Open up each fish like a book, skin side down. Spread the stuffing over one half. Pack it down firmly, then fold over the fish and press down gently. Close the opening with cocktail sticks, if wished.

7 ▲ Set the fish in the prepared baking dish or roasting tin. Brush the tops of the fish with a little of the reserved fat. Bake for 25–30 minutes or until the fish is cooked.

8 Carefully transfer the fish to warmed serving plates and serve immediately.

GRILLING FISH

The intense dry heat of this method of cooking is best used for fish with a lot of natural oil, such as salmon, mackerel and tuna. However, leaner fish can also be grilled, as long as you baste them frequently to keep them moist or cook them in a little liquid.

Always preheat the grill. If liked, line the grill pan with foil to save on washing up.

Fish can also be very successfully grilled over charcoal. Choose full-flavoured fish that will not be overwhelmed by the smoky taste. Thin pieces are easier to handle if placed in a hinged wire fish basket. Be sure to baste well during cooking to prevent the fish from drying out.

Fish Kebabs with Lemon Butter
Combine 2 tablespoons each melted butter and lemon juice with 1 teaspoon mustard powder and 1 finely chopped garlic clove. Cut 1½ lb (700 g) halibut, monk-fish or sea bass steaks into 1 in (2.5 cm) cubes. Thread on to skewers with pieces of red pepper. Brush with the butter mixture and grill, basting frequently and turning to cook evenly, until done. *Serves 4.*

1 ▲ **To grill oilier fish**: For small whole fish, boned and butterflied fish, fillets, cutlets and steaks that are at least ½ in (1.5 cm) thick, or cubes of fish for skewers, rinse the fish and pat it dry with paper towels. Marinate the fish if the recipe instructs.

3 ▲ Set the fish under the grill, 3–4 in (7.5–10 cm) from the heat (thin pieces should be closer to the heat for a shorter time than thicker ones). Grill, basting once or twice and turning if the recipe specifies, until the fish is done.

2 ▲ Preheat the grill with the grill pan in place. When hot, lightly brush the hot pan with oil. If using foil, line it before preheating and then brush with oil when hot. Arrange the fish in the pan, in one layer, skin side down. Brush the fish with butter, oil or a basting mixture, according to the recipe instructions.

4 ▲ **To grill leaner fish**: For small whole fish, and fish steaks, cutlets and fillets that are at least ½ in (1.5 cm) thick and prepared for cooking as above, arrange in a buttered flameproof dish. Add a little liquid (wine, stock etc) just to cover the bottom of the dish. Brush the fish with butter, oil or a basting mixture, according to recipe instructions. Grill as above, without turning the fish.

FILET OF BEEF WITH NIÇOISE

Serves 6 to 8.

Measure filet vertically at thic[k]...
Roast for 15 minutes to the inch f[or]...
minutes for medium rare and 25 for [well]...

- 2 tbsp. Dijon mustard
- 2 tbsp. soy sauce
- 3 cloves garlic, chopped
- 2 tbsp. olive oil
- 3-lb. beef tenderloin

Niçoise sauce:
- ¾ cup mayonnaise
- 4 anchovies, chopped
- 2 tbsp. chopped parsley
- 2 tbsp. chopped chives
- Juice of 1 lime
- Pepper to taste

Preheat oven to 425 F. Combine mustard, soy sauce, garlic and olive oil. Brush on to filet. Place on rack and roast to desired degree of doneness.

Combine Niçoise ingredients. Carve beef into thin slices and serve with sauce on the side. Serves 6 to 8.

ROASTED POTATO SALAD

- 2 lbs. mini red potatoes
- 3 tbsp. olive oil
- 1 tbsp. balsamic vinegar
- ¼ cup mayonnaise
- 1 tbsp. horseradish
- 1 tbsp. lemon juice
- 1 cup finely chopped red onion
- 1 cup finely chopped red pepper
- ¼ cup chopped parsley

Preheat oven to 400 F. Cut potatoes in half, but do not peel. Toss with oil and balsamic vinegar. Season with salt and pepper. Place in baking dish and roast for 45 minutes or until browned and tender.

Combine mayonnaise, horseradish and lemon juice. Toss potatoes with onion, red pepper and mayonnaise mixture. Sprinkle with parsley. Serves 6 to 8.

Lucy Waverman's latest book is Lucy Waverman's Fast and Fresh (Firefly Books).

...ection against disease—heart disease, cancer and infections. According ...t fall by the American Institute for Cancer Research (AICR) and the ...e act of eating 10 servings of fruits and vegetables daily could slash ...ven more powerful strategy: Eating an overall cancer-preventive diet ...g 30 to 40 percent of all cancers worldwide.

...disease protection out of your everyday eating is to use a wider ...ollins, a nutrition consultant to the Washington, D.C.–based ...ase fighters in herbs and spices called phytochemicals," she says. ...ances that plants have developed to guard against insects, fungi ... phytochemicals offer a powerful disease-fighting benefit for

...er, for example," says Collins. Using more herbs and spices often ...sts that excessive salt consumption raises the risk of stomach ...ressure. Reducing sodium can also help in staving off bone-...mmon in women over age 40.

POTENT HERBS, SPICES & FLAVORS

...and flavorings to work into your family's healthy eating plan.

...atic plant ...ount on it ...raw with ...ables.

...for spices ...chemical ...d chavi-...cancerous ...cells.

CUMIN ...ey plant, cumin ...inst liver cancer. Use this Indian spice with turmeric to add an earthy flavor to chicken, pasta dishes or lentil soup.

GARLIC This herb's anticancer (especially stomach, skin, liver, breast, colon, lung, cervical and nasal cancers), heart disease protection and immune-boosting powers stem from its organosulfur compounds. Cook garlic gently to enjoy it most (never use high heat). It's great with just about any meat, fish, poultry, pasta or bean dish.

GINGER This is another anticancer herb. Use the fresh root to reap the most benefit, although the dried, ground version also offers some health advantages. Grate the fresh root (available in the produce section) and sprinkle the juice from the pulp into any type of stir-fry—beef and broccoli, chicken and summer squash or a medley of vegetables.

MINT This anticancer (especially anti-breast cancer) herb is more versatile than you think. Stir chopped fresh mint into cottage cheese, creamed peas and ham, rice, fruit salad or iced tea.

ONIONS These edible bulbs may be the most widely used—and powerful—of all seasonings. Raw or cooked, onions add intense flavor and lots of organosulfur compounds. Onions too strong? Try their milder relatives—leeks and shallots. They go with just about everything.

OREGANO A wonderful staple of Italian cooking, this versatile herb has at least two flavonoids (a category of phytochemicals) thought to disable the carcinogenic substances that form during grilling and high heat preparation. Try oregano with tomato-based recipes, vegetables or chicken.

ROSEMARY This lemon-with-a-touch-of-pine herb fights cancer. Rosemary also may have anti-inflammatory powers. Tastes great with fish, poultry or vegetables.

SAGE This ancient herb's name comes from the Latin word *salvus* meaning "safe," which reflects the herb's healing powers; it's another cancer fighter. Add sage to turkey (of course), pork, cheese and bean dishes.   —*K.N.*

POWER-PACKED RECIPES

Winter Warm Rosemary Orange Pasta

Servings: 4
Preparation time: About 20 minutes
Cooking time: About 25 minutes

This unusual pasta dish warms your soul with a rich combination of rosemary, garlic and onion. The flavoring elements are also what pack the anticancer and immune-boosting power of this dish. The zucchini and orange juice add lots of flavonoids to fight heart disease and cancer and possibly help prevent infections. To make this a complete meal with protein, stir in a box of extra-firm lite tofu (cut into small chunks).

1   tablespoon extra virgin olive oil
1½ tablespoons dried rosemary
1   clove garlic, minced
1   red onion, cut into chunks
½   teaspoon black pepper
1   medium yellow zucchini, thinly sliced
1   medium green zucchini, thinly sliced
½   cup orange juice
3   cups cooked rotini pasta
½   cup orange juice plus 2 teaspoons cornstarch
1   can (7 ounces) mandarin oranges, drained

Heat olive oil with rosemary, garlic and red onion over low heat for 10 minutes, stirring occasionally. Add black pepper, zucchini and ½ cup orange juice; cover and simmer 15 minutes over low heat. Add cooked pasta and toss. Increase heat to medium and stir in orange juice-cornstarch mixture. Stir gently until mixture thickens. Remove from heat and fold in mandarin oranges.
Per serving: About 259 cal, 7 g pro, 48 g carb, 5 g fat, 16% cal from fat, 0 mg chol, 8 mg sod, 5 g fiber.

Gently Spiced Lentil-Vegetable Soup

Servings: 6
Preparation time: About 20 minutes
Cooking time: About 1 hour and 10 minutes

A pleasing blend of herbs and spices—turmeric, cumin, black pepper—add interest to this filling wintertime soup and pack a powerful anticancer punch. The complement of dried beans (lentils), barley, root vegetables and fresh green spinach (washed thoroughly) add yet another array of disease-fighting chemicals, fiber and traditional nutrients that spur you on to great health and well-being. This soup freezes well.

2   tablespoons extra virgin olive oil
2   small onions, chopped
1   clove garlic, minced
1   cup uncooked lentils
1   can (28 ounces) crushed tomatoes
4   cups water
½   cup pearled barley
2   large carrots, peeled and sliced
2   medium parsnips, peeled and sliced
1   teaspoon turmeric
1   teaspoon ground cumin
1   teaspoon ground black pepper
2   teaspoons salt
1   tablespoon lemon juice
1   teaspoon sugar
½   pound young spinach leaves, washed and torn in half

In large, heavy kettle, heat oil over low heat with onions and garlic; cook 5 to 7 minutes. Add remainder of ingredients except spinach. Stir well, cover and simmer over medium heat for 1 hour. Remove from heat; stir in spinach, cover and allow to steam for 5 minutes.
Per serving: About 323 cal, 15 g pro, 57 g carb, 6 g fat, 16% cal from fat, 0 mg chol, 992 mg sod, 19 g fiber.

Hint of Italy Chicken Casserole

Servings: 4
Preparation time: About 20 minutes
Cooking time: About 25 minutes

An easy family-pleasing casserole ready in just minutes, this dish adds to your disease-protection repertoire with Italian seasoning's blend of oregano, rosemary and sage, herbs packed with phytochemicals thought to bolster the body against cancer. Keeping the fat low and stirring in phytochemical-rich broccoli further bumps up the health-promoting power of this mild yet interesting casserole. Stir-frying with canola oil, too, is a healthy choice here, since it's lower in saturated fat than the more commonly used corn oil.

1   tablespoon canola oil
1   pound boneless, skinless chicken breasts, cut into bite-sized pieces
1   tablespoon Italian seasoning
½   teaspoon salt
¼ to ½ teaspoon black pepper
1   can condensed cream of mushroom soup
1   package (10 ounces) frozen chopped broccoli, thawed (do not drain liquid)
3   cups cooked egg noodles

Heat canola oil over medium-high heat in large nonstick skillet. Add chicken; sprinkle with seasonings. Stir-fry until chicken is browned and cooked through. Reduce heat to low. Stir in condensed soup until chicken is well coated. Add broccoli; toss to mix. Gently fold in egg noodles. Cover and allow mixture to heat through for 10 minutes.
Per serving: About 453 cal, 39 g pro, 39 g carb, 15 g fat, 29% cal from fat, 124 mg chol, 917 mg sod, 4 g fiber.
(continued on page 106)

Grilled Butterflied Salmon

SERVES 6–8

1½ tablespoons dried juniper berries

2 teaspoons dried green peppercorns

1 teaspoon caster sugar

⅛ teaspoon salt

3 tablespoons vegetable oil

2 tablespoons lemon juice

1 × 5 lb (2.25 kg) salmon, scaled, gutted and boned for butterflying

lemon wedges, to serve

1 Put the juniper berries and peppercorns in a spice mill or mortar and pestle and grind coarsely. Turn the ground spices into a small bowl and stir in the sugar, salt, oil and lemon juice.

2 ▲ Open the salmon like a book, skin side down. Spread the juniper mixture evenly over the flesh. Fold the salmon closed again and place on a large plate. Cover and marinate in the refrigerator for at least 1 hour.

3 Preheat the grill.

4 ▼ Open up the salmon again and place it, skin side down, on an oiled baking sheet. Spoon any juniper mixture left on the plate over the fish.

5 Grill about 4 in (10 cm) from the heat for 8–10 minutes or until the fish is cooked. Serve the fish immediately, with lemon wedges.

COATING AND FRYING FISH

Fish to be fried is often coated with egg and crumbs, or with a batter. The coating makes a crisp crust to protect the fish and keep it moist. Many other foods – boneless chicken breasts, veal escalopes and vegetables, for example – are also egg-and-crumbed.

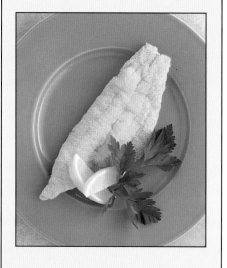

Deep-fried Catfish
Egg-and-crumb 8 catfish (or trout) fillets, using seasoned flour, egg and cornmeal. Deep-fry and serve with tartare sauce. *Serves 4.*

1 ▲ Lightly beat egg in a shallow dish. Spread flour on a plate or sheet of greaseproof paper and season with salt and pepper or as specified. Spread crumbs (fine breadcrumbs, crushed water biscuits, etc) on another.

2 ▲ **To egg-and-crumb large pieces of fish**: Dip the fish first in the seasoned flour, turning to coat both sides lightly and evenly. Shake or brush off excess flour.

3 ▲ Next dip the floured fish in the egg, turning to moisten both sides.

4 ▲ Dip the fish in the crumbs, turning to coat evenly. Press to help the crumbs adhere. Shake or pat off excess crumbs. Refrigerate for at least 20 minutes to set the coating.

5 ▲ **To egg-and-crumb small pieces of fish** (strips of fish fillet or goujons, prawns, etc): Put the crumbs in a plastic bag. After dipping the fish in seasoned flour and egg, toss a few pieces at a time in the bag of crumbs.

6 ▲ **To pan-fry**: Heat oil or a mixture of oil and butter in a frying pan (enough fat to coat the bottom of the pan in a thin layer or as recipe instructs). When it is very hot, put the fish in the pan, in one layer. Fry until golden brown on both sides and the fish is done. Drain on paper towels before serving.

7 ▲ **To deep-fry**: Half fill a deep pan with oil and heat it to 375°F (190°C) on a deep-frying thermometer. Gently lower the coated pieces of fish into the hot oil (frying them only a few at a time). Fry until golden brown, turning them occasionally so that they cook evenly. Remove and drain on paper towels before serving.

Chinese-spiced Fish Fillets

SERVES 4

2½ oz (70 g) plain flour

1 teaspoon Chinese five-spice powder

salt and pepper

8 skinless fillets of fish such as plaice or lemon sole, about 1¾ lb (800 g) in total

1 egg, beaten to mix

1½–2 oz (45–55 g) fine fresh breadcrumbs

groundnut oil, for frying

1 oz (30 g) butter

4 spring onions, cut diagonally into thin slices

12 oz (340 g) tomatoes, seeded and diced

2 tablespoons soy sauce

3 ▼ Drain the fillets on paper towels, then transfer to plates and keep warm. Pour off all the oil from the frying pan and wipe it out with paper towels.

4 ▲ Melt the butter in the pan and add the spring onions and tomatoes. Cook for about 1 minute, stirring well. Stir in the soy sauce.

5 Spoon the tomato mixture over the fish and serve immediately.

1 ▲ Sift the flour together with the Chinese five-spice powder, salt and pepper on to a plate. Egg-and-crumb the fish fillets, dipping them first in the seasoned flour, then in beaten egg and finally in breadcrumbs.

2 Pour oil into a large frying pan to a depth of ½ in (1.5 cm). Heat until it is very hot and starting to sizzle. Add the coated fillets, a few at a time, and fry until just cooked and golden brown on both sides, 2–3 minutes according to the thickness of the fillets. Do not crowd the pan or the temperature of the oil will drop and allow the fish to absorb too much oil.

MAKING FISH STOCK

Fish stock is much quicker to make than meat or poultry stock. Ask your fishmonger for heads, bones and trimmings from white fish.

MAKES ABOUT 2 PINTS (1 LITRE)

1½ lb (700 g) heads, bones and trimmings from white fish
1 onion, sliced
2 celery stalks with leaves, chopped
1 carrot, sliced
½ lemon, sliced (optional)
1 bay leaf
a few fresh parsley sprigs
6 black peppercorns
2¼ pints (1.35 litres) water
¼ pint (150 ml) dry white wine

1 ▲ Rinse the fish heads, bones and trimmings well under cold running water. Put in a stockpot with the vegetables, lemon, if using, the herbs, peppercorns, water and wine. Bring to the boil, skimming the surface frequently, then reduce the heat and simmer for 25 minutes.

2 ▲ Strain the stock without pressing down on the ingredients in the sieve. If not using immediately, leave to cool and then refrigerate. Fish stock should be used within 2 days, or it can be frozen for up to 3 months.

Fisherman's Stew

SERVES 4

6 streaky bacon rashers, cut into strips
½ oz (15 g) butter
1 large onion, chopped
1 garlic clove, finely chopped
2 tablespoons chopped fresh parsley
1 teaspoon fresh thyme leaves or ½ teaspoon dried thyme
1 lb (450 g) tomatoes, skinned, seeded and chopped or canned chopped tomatoes
¼ pint (150 ml) dry vermouth or white wine
¾ pint (450 ml) fish stock
10 oz (300 g) potatoes, diced
1½–2 lb (700–900 g) skinless white fish fillets, cut into large chunks
salt and pepper

1 Fry the bacon in a large saucepan over moderate heat until lightly browned but not crisp, then remove the bacon and drain on paper towels.

2 ▲ Add the butter to the pan and cook the onion, stirring occasionally, for 3–5 minutes or until soft. Add the garlic and herbs and continue cooking for 1 minute, stirring. Add the tomatoes, vermouth or wine and stock and bring to the boil.

3 Reduce the heat, cover and simmer the stew for 15 minutes. Add the potatoes, cover again and simmer for a further 10–12 minutes or until they are almost tender.

4 ▼ Add the chunks of fish and the bacon. Simmer gently, uncovered, for 5 minutes or until the fish is just cooked and the potatoes are tender. Adjust the seasoning and serve.

~ COOK'S TIP ~

For fish stock, use heads, bones and trimmings only from mild, white-fleshed fish, not from strong-flavoured oily fish.

PEELING AND DEVEINING PRAWNS

Prawns can be cooked in their shells, but more often they are peeled first (the shells can be used to make an aromatic stock). The intestinal vein that runs down the back is removed from large prawns mainly because of its appearance, although the vein may contain grit which makes it unpleasant to eat.

Prawns in shell are sold with their heads. These are easily pulled off, and will enhance the flavour of stock made with the shells.

1 ▲ Holding the prawn firmly in one hand, pull off the legs with the fingers of the other hand. Pull off the head above the legs.

2 ▲ Peel the shell away from the body. When you reach the tail, hold the body and pull away the tail; the shell will come off with it. Or, you can leave the tail on the prawn and just remove the body shell.

3 ▲ Make a shallow cut down the centre of the curved back of the prawn. Pull out the black vein with a cocktail stick or your fingers.

4 ▲ To butterfly prawns: Cut along the deveining slit to split open the prawn, without cutting all the way through. Open up the prawn flat.

5 ▲ To devein prawns in the shell: Insert a cocktail stick crossways in several places along the back where the shell overlaps to lift out the vein.

Spicy Butterflied Tiger Prawns

SERVES 4–6

6 tablespoons olive oil
5 tablespoons orange juice
4 tablespoons lime juice
1 large garlic clove, finely chopped
1 teaspoon allspice berries, crushed
¼ teaspoon hot chilli flakes
salt and pepper
2 lb (900 g) raw tiger or king prawns, peeled, deveined and butterflied
lime wedges, to serve

1 ▲ Combine the oil, fruit juices, garlic, allspice, chilli flakes and seasoning in a large shallow baking dish. Add the prawns and turn to coat completely with the spiced oil.

2 Cover the dish and leave to marinate for 1 hour at room temperature or at least 2 hours in the refrigerator.

3 Preheat the grill.

4 Spread out the prawns in one layer in the baking dish, arranging them cut side up as much as possible. Grill about 4 in (10 cm) from the heat for 6–8 minutes or until the flesh becomes opaque. There is no need to turn them.

5 Serve hot, with lime wedges.

Scallops Wrapped in Parma Ham

SERVES 4

24 medium-size scallops, without corals, prepared for cooking

lemon juice

8–12 slices of Parma ham, cut lengthways into 2 or 3 strips

olive oil

pepper

lemon wedges, to serve

1 Preheat the grill or prepare a charcoal fire.

2 Sprinkle the scallops with lemon juice. Wrap a strip of Parma ham around each scallop. Thread on to 8 skewers.

3 ▲ Brush with oil. Arrange on a baking sheet if grilling. Grill about 4 in (10 cm) from the heat, or cook over charcoal, for 3–5 minutes on each side or until the scallops are opaque.

4 Set 2 skewers on each plate. Sprinkle the scallops with freshly ground black pepper and serve with lemon wedges.

Preparing scallops

If they are still in the shell, use a short sturdy knife to pry open, as for clams (page 86). Discard the fringe-like membrane and dark organs. Set the red-orange coral, or roe, aside.

Pull off and discard the small piece of gristle from the side of the white meat. Rinse well.

Spicy Butterflied Tiger Prawns (left), Scallops Wrapped in Parma Ham

PREPARING MUSSELS AND CLAMS

Molluscs such as mussels and clams should be eaten very fresh and must be alive when you buy them and cook them (unless they have been shelled and frozen). You can tell that they are alive if their shells are tightly closed; any shells that are open should close promptly when tapped. Any dead mussels or clams, or any with broken shells, should be discarded.

If you have collected clams yourself, let them stand in a bucket of sea water for several hours, changing the water once or twice. (Do not use fresh water because it will kill the molluscs.) Add a handful or two of cornmeal or flour to the water to help clean the clams' stomachs. Clams bought from the fishmonger will already have been purged of sand.

Sailor's Mussels
Prepare 7 pints (4 litres) live mussels. Steam with ½ pint (300 ml) dry white wine or fish or chicken stock, 1 small chopped onion, 1–2 crushed garlic cloves and ¾ oz (25 g) chopped fresh parsley. With a slotted spoon, transfer the opened mussels to large bowls. Add 1½ oz (45 g) butter to the cooking liquid and stir until melted, then add pepper. Pour over the mussels. *Serves 4.*

1 ▲ Scrub the shells of mussels or clams with a stiff brush and rinse well. This can be done under cool running water.

3 ▲ **To steam**: Put a little dry white wine or water in a large pot, with flavourings as the recipe specifies. Add the mussels or clams, cover tightly and bring to the boil. Steam for 5–10 minutes or until the shells open, shaking the pot occasionally.

5 ▲ **To open a live clam or mussel**: Hold it firmly in one hand, with the hinge in your palm. Insert the side of a clam or oyster knife blade between the shell halves and work it round to cut through the hinge muscle.

2 ▲ Before cooking mussels, pull off their 'beards' (their anchor threads) with the help of a small knife. Rinse the mussels well.

4 ▲ Serve the mussels or clams in their shells, or shell them before using. Strain the cooking liquid (which will include all the delicious liquor from the shells) and spoon it over the mussels or clams, or use it as the basis for a sauce.

6 ▲ Open the shell and cut the clam or mussel free of the shell. Do this over a bowl to catch all the liquor from the shell. (Clams may be eaten raw, but mussels are always cooked.)

Phyllo Clam Puffs

MAKES ABOUT 4½ DOZEN

9 sheets phyllo pastry, each about 12 × 18 in (30 × 45 cm)
12 oz (340 g) full-fat soft cheese
1 egg, beaten to mix
6 oz (170 g) steamed clams, chopped, or well drained canned clams
4 spring onions, chopped
2 tablespoons chopped fresh dill
a few drops of Tabasco sauce
salt and pepper
6–8 oz (170–225 g) butter, melted

1 Preheat a 400°F/200°C/Gas 6 oven.

2 Stack the sheets of phyllo pastry on top of each other. Cover with a sheet of cling film to prevent drying out.

3 ▲ Combine the soft cheese, egg, clams, spring onions, dill, Tabasco and some salt and pepper in a bowl. Mix well.

~ **COOK'S TIP** ~

Phyllo (or filo) pastry dries out very quickly and then can become too brittle to use. So when working with phyllo pastry, keep the sheets you are not using covered with cling film and a damp tea towel, and remove the sheets individually just before brushing with melted butter or oil.

4 Lay one sheet of phyllo pastry on the work surface and brush it lightly and evenly with melted butter. Lay another sheet of phyllo pastry neatly on top and brush it also with butter. Cover with a third sheet of phyllo pastry and brush with butter.

5 ▼ Spoon about one-third of the clam mixture in a line along one long side of the stacked phyllo pastry, about 1 in (2.5 cm) in from the edge.

6 ▲ Fold the nearest long phyllo pastry edge over the clam filling and continue rolling up. Cut the roll across in half and put the two halves on a buttered baking sheet. Brush the rolls with melted butter.

7 Make two more rolls in the same way and put the halves on the baking sheet. Brush them all with melted butter. Bake for 20 minutes or until golden brown and crisp.

8 Using scissors, cut the rolls across into bite-size pieces. Serve as soon as possible, as nibbles with drinks.

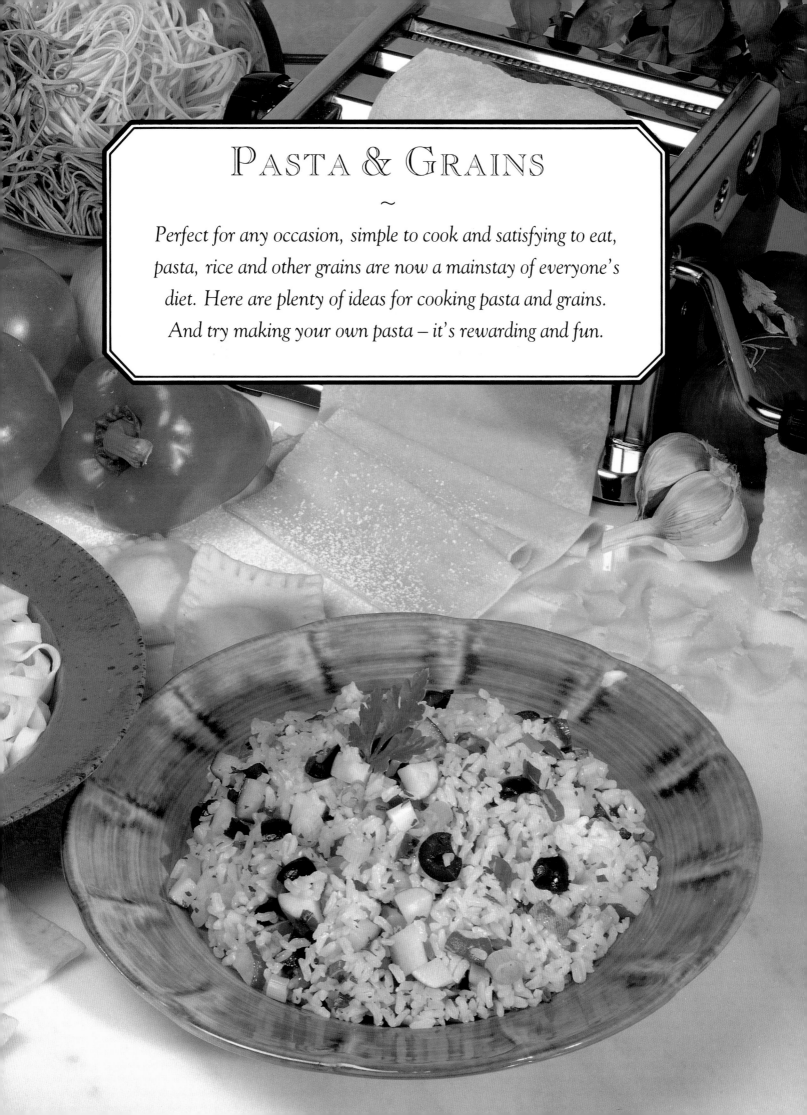

PASTA & GRAINS

~

Perfect for any occasion, simple to cook and satisfying to eat,
pasta, rice and other grains are now a mainstay of everyone's
diet. Here are plenty of ideas for cooking pasta and grains.
And try making your own pasta – it's rewarding and fun.

COOKING PASTA

Both fresh and dried pasta are cooked in the same way. The golden rules for success are: use plenty of water and keep checking the pasta to be sure it does not overcook.

Fresh pasta will cook much more quickly than dried – in 1–4 minutes as opposed to 5 minutes or more.

Buttered Noodles
Cook 1 lb (450 g) fettuccine or tagliatelle (fresh or dried) until 'al dente'. Drain well and return to the pot. Add 1½–2 oz (45–55 g) butter or margarine and a good pinch of grated nutmeg. Season. Toss until the noodles are coated, then serve. *Serves 6.*

Buttered Noodles with Herbs
Omit the nutmeg and add ½ oz (15 g) chopped fresh herbs such as parsley, dill, basil or thyme – singly or a mixture.

Buttered Noodles with Cheese
Add 3 tablespoons freshly grated Parmesan cheese.

1 ▲ Bring a very large pot of salted water to the boil: use at least 6 pints (4 litres) of water and 2 teaspoons salt to 1 lb (450 g) of pasta. Drop in the pasta all at once and stir to separate the shapes or strands.

3 ▲ Bring the water back to the boil, then reduce the heat slightly and boil until the pasta is just done. For dried pasta, follow the packet instructions, but start testing as soon as you reach the minimum time given. To test, lift a piece of pasta out on a wooden fork or slotted spoon. Cut it in half. There should be no sign of opaque, uncooked pasta in the centre. Or bite it – it should be tender but still firm. In Italian, this is when it is 'al dente', or to the tooth.

2 ▲ If you are cooking spaghetti, allow the ends in the water to soften slightly and then gently push in the rest as soon as you can.

4 ▲ Drain the pasta well in a colander, shaking it vigorously to remove all excess water. Serve immediately because the pasta will continue to cook from its own heat.

When to undercook pasta
If you are going to cook the pasta further, by baking it in a lasagne for example, undercook it slightly at this first stage. Pasta for a salad should also be a little under-cooked, so that it will not become soggy when it is mixed with the dressing.

Pasta, Bean and Vegetable Soup

SERVES 4–6

4 oz (115 g) dried borlotti or black-eye beans, soaked overnight

2 pints (1.2 litres) vegetable, poultry or meat stock

1 large onion, chopped

1 large garlic clove, finely chopped

2 celery stalks, chopped

½ red pepper, seeded and chopped

12 oz (340 g) tomatoes, skinned, seeded and chopped or canned chopped tomatoes

8 oz (225 g) piece of smoked bacon loin

3 oz (85 g) tiny pasta shapes for soup

2 courgettes, halved lengthways and sliced

1 tablespoon tomato purée

salt and pepper

shredded fresh basil, to garnish

1 Drain the beans and put them in a large pot. Cover with fresh cold water and bring to the boil. Boil for 10 minutes, then drain and discard the water. Rinse the beans.

2 Return the beans to the rinsed pot, add the stock and bring to the boil. Skim off the foam from the surface.

3 ▲ Add the onion, garlic, celery, red pepper, tomatoes and bacon. Bring back to the boil. Cover and simmer over low heat for 1½ hours or until the beans are just tender.

4 Lift out the bacon. Shred the meat coarsely with two forks and set aside.

5 ▼ Add the pasta shapes, courgettes and tomato purée to the soup. Season to taste with salt and pepper. Simmer the soup, uncovered, for a further 5–8 minutes, stirring occasionally. (Check the suggested pasta cooking time on the packet.)

6 ▲ Stir in the shredded bacon. Taste and adjust the seasoning, then serve the soup hot, sprinkled with shredded fresh basil.

MAKING PASTA DOUGH

Pasta dough is very simple to make and, like most things, the more you do it the better the results will be. As in making pastry and bread doughs, the quantity of liquid needed can vary, according to how absorbent the flour is. The recipe here is for a basic egg pasta, with several variations.

MAKES ABOUT 1 LB (450 G)

10 oz (300 g) plain flour, preferably 'type 00' pasta flour

1 teaspoon salt

3 size-2 eggs, beaten to mix

1 ▲ Put the flour and salt on a work surface and make a well in the centre. Add the eggs to the well.

2 ▲ With fingertips, gradually incorporate the flour into the eggs. When all the flour is mixed in, you should be able to gather up a pliable dough; if too moist, add more flour.

Pasta flavourings
● For *Green Pasta*: Blanch 12 oz (340 g) spinach, Swiss chard or other green leaves, then drain well and squeeze dry. Purée or chop the greens very finely. Add with the eggs.
● For *Fresh Herb Pasta*: Finely chop 1 oz (30 g) fresh herb leaves, such as basil, flat-leaf parsley and coriander. Add with the eggs.
● For *Tomato Pasta*: Add 1½ tablespoons tomato purée with the eggs.
● For *Lemon Pasta*: Add 1½ tablespoons grated lemon zest with the eggs.
● For *Herb and Garlic Pasta*: Add ½ oz (15 g) finely chopped mixed parsley and oregano or marjoram and 1–2 finely chopped garlic cloves with the beaten eggs.
● For *Saffron Pasta*: Add ½ teaspoon ground saffron to the flour and salt or steep ½ teaspoon saffron threads in 1 tablespoon very hot water and add with the eggs through a small sieve.
● For *Wholemeal Pasta*: Substitute 2½ oz (75 g) wholemeal flour for the same quantity of plain flour.

3 ▲ Flour the work surface. Knead the dough by pushing it away with the heel of your hand and then folding it back. Continue kneading for 8–10 minutes or until it is smooth and elastic. (Or use a pasta machine for kneading – see page 94.)

4 ▲ Shape the dough into a ball and put it in a bowl. Cover with cling film. Leave to rest for at least 15 minutes before rolling and cutting.

Food processor pasta dough
To mix the pasta dough in a food processor, put the flour and salt in the container. Pulse to blend. With the machine running, gradually add the eggs through the feed tube. Continue processing for 3–5 minutes or until the ingredients come together into a smooth ball of dough that is elastic.

ROLLING AND CUTTING PASTA DOUGH BY HAND

You can roll pasta dough by hand, but it is hard work. If you intend to make pasta frequently, it may be worth buying a machine.

Divide the dough into 3 or 4 pieces. Roll and cut one piece at a time. Keep the remaining dough tightly wrapped in cling film to prevent it from drying out while you work.

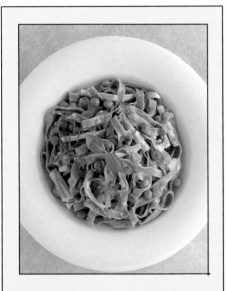

Pasta with Ham and Peas
Cook 2 finely chopped garlic cloves in 1 oz (30 g) of butter in a saucepan for 1 minute or until softened. Add 5 oz (145 g) thawed frozen peas, 8 oz (225 g) cooked ham cut into matchstick strips, ½ pint (300 ml) whipping cream and seasoning and bring to the boil. Toss with 12 oz (340 g) fresh fettuccine, cooked and drained, and 2 oz (55 g) freshly grated Parmesan cheese. Serve at once, with additional Parmesan cheese if wished. *Serves 4.*

Keeping fresh pasta
If fresh noodles are not to be cooked the day they are made, allow them to dry completely. Then wrap loosely and store at room temperature for up to 4 days.

1 ▲ Put a piece of dough on a lightly floured surface and pat it into a flat disc. Using a long rolling pin, roll out the dough in all directions, starting from the centre each time.

3 ▲ For stuffed pasta shapes, use the dough immediately, while it is still malleable. If cutting noodles, sprinkle the rolled out dough with flour and leave to dry for 10–15 minutes.

5 ▲ Uncoil the noodles with your fingers and scatter them on a floured tea towel. Leave to dry for about 5 minutes before cooking. Or wrap in cling film and refrigerate for later cooking.

2 ▲ Continue rolling, with long even strokes, until you have a large sheet of dough that is about ⅛ in (3 mm) thick, or less for thinner noodles.

4 ▲ To cut, roll up the sheet of dough like a flat Swiss roll. With a knife, cut across into noodles of the required width: ⅛ in (3 mm) for fettuccine, ¼ in (5 mm) for tagliatelle.

6 ▲ To dry, leave them on the floured towel, or hang them over a broom handle, and dry for 2–3 hours. Sprinkle them with semolina to prevent them sticking together and pack loosely in a plastic bag or in a box with each layer separated.

USING A PASTA MACHINE

A pasta machine – hand-cranked or electric – takes all the drudgery out of making fresh pasta. You are able to roll the dough paper-thin and to cut very fine noodles such as tagliolini and tagliarini – impossible by hand.

The smooth rollers on a pasta machine can be set wide apart or very close together, normally with the use of a dial. You start at the widest setting to knead the dough and then reduce the space gradually until the dough reaches the right thickness. Then a roller with blades cuts noodles of the desired width.

1 ▲ **To knead dough:** Flatten a piece of the dough slightly and then feed it through the machine's rollers on their widest setting.

2 ▲ Fold the resulting strip of dough in half and feed it through again. Continue folding the dough and feeding it through until smooth and elastic, 8–10 times. (If it feels sticky, dust it with flour before continuing.)

Lemon Pasta with Clam Sauce
Cook 2–3 finely chopped garlic cloves in 5 tablespoons olive oil for 1 minute or until softened. Add 8 oz (225 g) steamed shelled clams, chopped if large, with 3 tablespoons of their cooking liquid, or canned baby clams (*vongole*), drained. Heat the clams through, then add 4 tablespoons chopped parsley and 2–3 tablespoons lemon juice. Toss the sauce with 12 oz (340 g) fresh lemon pasta (page 92), cooked and drained, and freshly ground pepper. Serve immediately. *Serves 4.*

3 ▲ **To roll dough:** Adjust the rollers to the next narrower setting and feed the strip of dough through again, without folding it. Narrow the rollers again and feed the strip of dough through. Continue feeding the dough through the rollers at increasingly narrow settings until it is the desired thinness. Sprinkle with flour and dry for 10–15 minutes.

4 ▲ **To cut noodles:** Set the blades on the machine to the desired width. Feed the strip of dough through the blades, letting it fall on to a floured tea towel. Dry for about 5 minutes before cooking. (Or dry completely for longer storage – see page 93.)

Drying out
It is important to leave the pasta dough to dry before cutting it into noodles, or they will tend to stick together. If the day is humid, this initial drying can take up to 30 minutes.

Noodles with Tomato and Mushroom Sauce

SERVES 2–4

1 oz (30 g) dried Italian mushrooms (porcini)
6 fl oz (180 ml) warm water
2 lb (900 g) tomatoes, peeled, seeded and chopped or drained canned tomatoes
¼ teaspoon dried hot chilli flakes
salt and pepper
3 tablespoons olive oil
4 slices of pancetta or unsmoked back bacon, cut into thin strips
1 large garlic clove, finely chopped
12 oz (340 g) tagliatelle or fettuccine
freshly grated Parmesan cheese, to serve

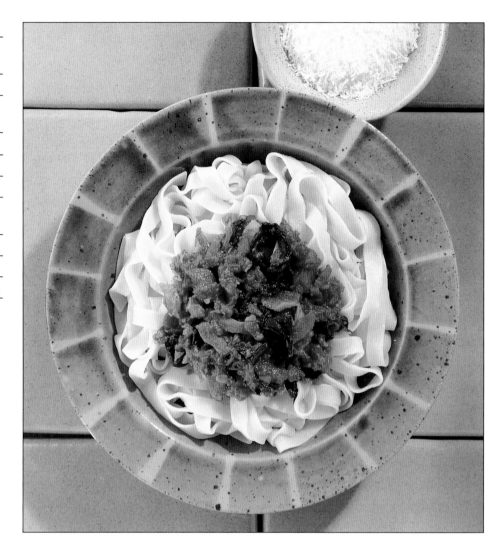

1 Put the mushrooms in a bowl and cover them with the warm water. Leave to soak for 20 minutes.

2 Meanwhile, put the tomatoes in a saucepan with the chilli flakes and seasoning. If using canned tomatoes, crush them coarsely with a fork or potato masher. Bring to the boil, reduce the heat and simmer for 30–40 minutes or until reduced to about 1¼ pints (750 ml). Stir from time to time to prevent sticking.

3 ▲ When the mushrooms have finished soaking, lift them out and squeeze over the bowl; set aside. Carefully pour the soaking liquid into the tomatoes through a muslin-lined sieve, leaving the sandy grit in the bottom of the bowl. Simmer the tomatoes for a further 15 minutes.

4 ▼ Meanwhile, heat 2 tablespoons of the oil in a frying pan. Add the strips of pancetta or bacon and fry until golden but not crisp. Add the garlic and mushrooms and fry for 3 minutes, stirring. Set aside.

5 Cook the pasta in a large pot of boiling salted water until it is just tender to the bite, or 'al dente'.

6 ▲ Add the bacon and mushroom mixture to the tomato sauce and mix well. Season with salt and pepper.

7 Drain the pasta and return it to the pot. Add the remaining oil and toss to coat the strands. Divide among hot plates, spoon the sauce on top and serve with Parmesan cheese.

CUTTING FLAT PASTA SHAPES

For wide noodles, like pappardelle, and for pasta for layering or rolling up, such as lasagne and cannelloni, roll the dough by hand or machine to about ⅛ in (3 mm) thickness. Lay the rolled dough strip, which will be about 4–5 in (10–12.5 cm) wide, on a lightly floured surface. Trim the sides to make them straight and square, using a sharp knife or, for pappardelle, a fluted pasta wheel. Lasagne may also be cut with a wheel for a decorative fluted edge.

1 ▲ To make lasagne or cannelloni: For lasagne, cut the dough strip into rectangles about 10–12 in (25–30 cm) long, or to fit your baking dish. For cannelloni, cut into rectangles about 5 × 3 in (12.5 × 7.5 cm).

2 ▲ For pappardelle: Cut the strip of dough into long noodles about ⅝ in (1.5 cm) wide. These noodles are traditionally cut with a fluted pasta wheel, and need not be uniform as they are meant to be rustic.

Tuna Lasagne

SERVES 6

1 quantity fresh pasta dough (pages 92–94), cut for lasagne, or 12 oz (340 g) oven-ready dried lasagne
½ oz (15 g) butter
1 small onion, finely chopped
1 garlic clove, finely chopped
4 oz (115 g) mushrooms, thinly sliced
4 tablespoons dry white wine (optional)
1 pint (600 ml) white sauce (page 170)
¼ pint (150 ml) whipping cream
3 tablespoons chopped parsley
salt and pepper
2 × 7 oz (200 g) cans tuna, drained
2 canned pimientos, cut into strips
2½ oz (75 g) thawed frozen peas
4 oz (115 g) mozzarella, grated
1 oz (30 g) freshly grated Parmesan cheese

1 For fresh lasagne noodles, bring a large pot of salted water to the boil. Cook the noodles, in small batches, until almost tender to the bite. For dried noodles, soak in a bowl of hot water for 3–5 minutes.

2 ▲ Lift out noodles into a colander and rinse with cold water. Lay them on a tea towel, in one layer, to drain.

3 Preheat a 350°F/180°C/Gas 4 oven.

4 ▲ Melt the butter in a saucepan. Cook the onion until soft. Add the garlic and mushrooms. Cook until they are soft, stirring occasionally.

5 Pour in the wine, if using. Boil for 1 minute. Add the white sauce, cream and parsley. Season to taste.

6 Spoon a thin layer of sauce over the bottom of a 12 × 9 in (30 × 23 cm) baking dish. Cover with a layer of lasagne noodles. Flake the tuna. Strew half of the tuna, pimiento strips, peas and mozzarella over the noodles. Spoon one-third of the remaining sauce evenly over the top and cover with another layer of lasagne noodles.

7 ▲ Repeat the layers, ending with noodles and sauce. Sprinkle with the Parmesan. Bake for 30–40 minutes or until bubbling hot and the top is lightly browned. Cut into squares and serve from the baking dish.

MAKING RAVIOLI

The variety of stuffings for these pasta shapes is endless, and they can be dressed simply with butter, oil or cream, or with a rich sauce. Roll the dough, divided into 2 or 4 portions, as thinly as possible – no more than $\frac{1}{16}$ in (1.5 mm) if you can.

Making individual ravioli
If making ravioli with hand-rolled pasta, it is easier to cut out squares or rounds from the dough rather than making them in strips. Put a mound of stuffing in the centre of each pasta shape, moisten the edges and set another one on top. Or, fold rounds into half moons.

---

1 ▲ Lay the rolled strip of dough on a lightly floured surface. Spoon mounds of the stuffing, $\frac{1}{2}$–$\frac{3}{4}$ teaspoon each, in neat rows over the dough, spacing the mounds evenly about $1\frac{1}{2}$ in (4 cm) apart (or according to recipe instructions).

2 ▲ Using your fingers or a pastry brush, moisten the dough around the mounds with cold water.

3 ▲ Lay another strip of dough carefully on top.

4 ▲ With your fingers, press the sheets of dough together between the mounds of stuffing.

5 ▲ Using a pasta wheel, pizza cutter or knife, cut neatly between the mounds to make squares.

6 ▲ Crimp the edges of each ravioli with a fork or your fingers to ensure they are completely sealed.

7 ▲ Alternatively, cut out ravioli with special cutters that are available in different shapes, or with round pastry cutters.

8 ▲ Sprinkle the ravioli with semolina, coating them all over, to prevent them from sticking together.

Ravioli with Cheese and Herbs

SERVES 4–6

8 oz (225 g) full-fat soft cheese, softened

1 garlic clove, finely chopped

1 oz (30 g) mixed herbs such as thyme, basil, chives, parsley, finely chopped

salt and pepper

1 quantity fresh pasta dough (pages 92–94), rolled by machine into 2 12 in (30 cm) strips, or divided into 4 and rolled by hand as thinly as possible

semolina, to coat

4 oz (115 g) butter

1 ▲ Mix together the soft cheese, garlic and most of the herbs. Season with salt and pepper.

2 Make the ravioli, filling them with the cheese and herb mixture. Toss the ravioli in a little semolina to coat lightly and leave to rest at room temperature for about 15 minutes.

3 ▼ Bring a large pot of salted water to the boil. Drop in the ravioli and cook for 7–9 minutes or until they are just tender to the bite. Drain well.

4 ▲ Melt the butter. Toss the ravioli with the melted butter. Sprinkle with the remaining herbs and serve.

~ **VARIATION** ~

For Ravioli with Gorgonzola and Pine Nuts, fill the ravioli with a mixture of 4 oz (115 g) each full-fat soft cheese and crumbled gorgonzola cheese; omit the garlic and herbs. Sprinkle the cooked ravioli with 1 oz (30 g) toasted pine nuts instead of herbs.

COOKING RICE

There are many different ways to cook rice, and each has its adherents. The simplest is to cook rice in a large quantity of boiling water, then drain. However, valuable nutrients will be discarded in the water. The ways given here retain the rice's nutrients. Timings are for long-grain white rice (one part rice to two parts water).

1 ◀ To steam rice: Put the measured quantity of salted water in a saucepan and bring to the boil. Add the rice and stir. Bring back to the boil, then cover the pan and steam over very low heat until the rice has absorbed all the water and is tender, 15–18 minutes for white rice and 35–40 minutes for brown rice. Remove the pan from the heat and leave for 5 minutes, covered. To serve, fluff the rice with a fork.

2 ▲ To sauté and steam rice (pilaf): Heat oil, butter or a mixture of the two in a saucepan over moderate heat. Add the rice and stir to coat the grains. Sauté for 2–3 minutes, stirring constantly. Add the measured quantity of boiling salted water. Bring back to the boil, then cover and steam over very low heat until the water has been absorbed and the rice is tender.

3 ▲ To bake rice: Put the rice in a baking dish and add the measured quantity of boiling salted water. Cover tightly with foil or a lid and bake in a preheated 350°F/180°C/Gas 4 oven until the water has been absorbed and the rice is tender, 20–30 minutes for white rice and 35–45 for brown. Cooking time depends on many factors, including the seal of the dish.

Rice Salad
Steam or bake 6oz (170g) long-grain rice. While hot, dress with 6 tablespoons vinaigrette (page 182). Cool. Add 2oz (55g) each chopped spring onions, celery, radishes, cucumber and quartered black olives with another 4floz (120ml) vinaigrette. Combine well and sprinkle with chopped parsley. *Serves 4–6.*

A LOOK AT RICE

There are thousands of varieties of rice grown all over the world, with differing flavours and aromas. But for the cook, the choice of which rice to use in a dish is based mainly on the length of the rice grain.

Long-grain rice has grains that are four to five times as long as they are wide. It is dry and fluffy after cooking, with the grains remaining separate. Examples of long-grain rice include: Basmati (aromatic, with a rich nutty flavour; much used in Indian cooking), brown long-grain rice (husk removed but nutritious bran layer left; texture is slightly chewy, mild nutty flavour), and white or polished long-grain rice (most widely used; mild in flavour). Long-grain rice is excellent steamed or baked, in pilafs and salads.

Short-grain rice, with an almost round shape, is very starchy and tends to cling together after cooking. Examples of short-grain rice include: Arborio and Carnaroli rice (used in creamy textured dishes) and glutinous or sweet rice (very sticky after cooking; used in Oriental desserts and snacks). Short-grain rice is the one to use for puddings, risotto, croquettes, sushi, stir-fried rice and moulded rice dishes.

Medium-grain rice, in between the other two, is more tender than long-grain rice but less moist than short-grain. It is fluffy and separate if served hot, but clumps as it cools.

Raisin and Almond Pilaf

SERVES 4

1½ oz (45 g) butter

¾ oz (25 g) flaked almonds

1 small onion, finely chopped

2 oz (60 g) raisins or sultanas

8 oz (225 g) long-grain rice

1 pint (600 ml) chicken stock or water

salt and pepper

1 Melt the butter in a saucepan. Add the almonds and fry over moderate heat, stirring, until they are golden brown. Remove the almonds with a slotted spoon, drain on paper towels and set aside.

2 Add the onion to the saucepan and cook until soft, stirring occasionally.

3 ▼ Stir in the raisins and rice and sauté for 2–3 minutes or until the rice looks slightly translucent.

4 ▲ Add the stock or water. Bring to the boil, then cover the pan and steam over very low heat for 20–25 minutes or until the rice is tender and all liquid has been absorbed.

5 Season with salt and pepper. Stir in the almonds and serve.

MAKING RISOTTO

This Italian favourite lends itself to so many variations and, depending on the flavourings and additions, it can be served as a first course, a main dish or an accompaniment.

If possible, use a special risotto rice such as Arborio or Carnaroli, because it retains its nutty texture while giving the essential creaminess to the risotto. For best results, use well-flavoured homemade stock.

Risotto with Parmesan
Make the risotto with 2¼ pints (1.3 litres) chicken stock, 1 oz (30 g) butter, 3 tablespoons chopped onion, 1 crushed garlic clove and 12 oz (340 g) Arborio rice. Just before the risotto is ready, stir in another 1 oz (30 g) butter and 2 oz (55 g) freshly grated Parmesan cheese. Season and serve. *Serves 6.*

Regulating the temperature
During cooking, adjust the heat so that the risotto bubbles merrily, but don't let it boil fiercely or the stock will evaporate before it can be absorbed by the rice.

1 ▲ In a saucepan, bring the measured quantity of stock to the boil, then reduce the heat so the liquid is kept at a gentle simmer.

3 ▲ Add the rice and stir to coat it with the fat. Sauté for 1–2 minutes over moderate heat, stirring.

2 ▲ Heat butter, oil or a mixture of the two in a wide, heavy pan. Add chopped onion (plus garlic and/or other flavourings specified in the recipe) and cook over low heat until soft, stirring occasionally.

4 ▲ Add a ladleful of the simmering stock (or an initial quantity of wine, vermouth etc, if the recipe specifies) and stir well. Simmer, stirring frequently, until the rice has absorbed almost all the liquid.

5 ◄ Add another ladleful of simmering stock and cook, stirring, until it is almost all absorbed. Continue adding the stock in this way until the grains of rice are tender but still firm to the bite ('al dente', like pasta) and the risotto is creamy but not runny. You may not need to add all the stock. Total cooking time will be about 30 minutes.

Risotto with Chicken

SERVES 4

2 tablespoons olive oil

8 oz (225 g) skinless boneless chicken breast, cut into 1 in (2.5 cm) cubes

1 onion, finely chopped

1 garlic clove, finely chopped

¼ teaspoon saffron strands

2 oz (55 g) Parma ham, cut into thin strips

1 lb (450 g) risotto rice, preferably Arborio

4 fl oz (120 ml) dry white wine

3 pints (1.8 litres) simmering chicken stock

1 oz (30 g) butter (optional)

1 oz (30 g) freshly grated Parmesan cheese, plus more to serve

salt and pepper

1 ▲ Heat the oil in a wide heavy-based pan over moderately high heat. Add the chicken cubes and cook, stirring, until they start to turn white.

2 ▲ Reduce the heat to low and add the onion, garlic, saffron and Parma ham. Cook, stirring, until the onion is soft. Stir in the rice. Sauté for 1–2 minutes, stirring constantly.

3 ▲ Add the wine and bring to the boil. Simmer gently until almost all the wine is absorbed.

4 Add the simmering stock, a ladleful at a time, and cook until the rice is just tender and the risotto creamy.

5 ▼ Add the butter, if using, and Parmesan cheese and stir in well. Season with salt and pepper to taste. Serve the risotto hot, sprinkled with more Parmesan.

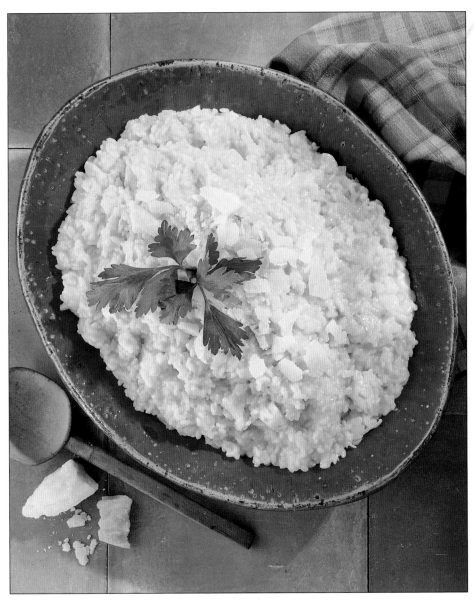

COOKING WILD RICE

Although called 'rice', this is actually an aquatic grass. Its deliciously nutty flavour and firm chewy texture make it a perfect complement to many meat and poultry dishes. It is also an excellent partner for vegetables such as courgettes, patty pan squash and mushrooms. It can be cooked like rice, by boiling or steaming, needing only a longer cooking time.

1 ▲ **To boil wild rice**: Add the rice to a large pot of boiling salted water (about four parts water to each one of rice). Bring back to a gentle boil and cook for 45–50 minutes or until the rice is tender but still firm and has begun to split open. Drain well.

2 ▲ **To steam wild rice**: Put the rice in a saucepan with the measured quantity of salted water. Bring to the boil, cover and steam over very low heat for 45–50 minutes or until tender. Cook uncovered for the last 5 minutes to evaporate excess water.

Wild Rice and Turkey Salad

SERVES 4

6 oz (170 g) wild rice, boiled or steamed

2 celery stalks, thinly sliced

2 oz (55 g) spring onions, chopped

4 oz (115 g) small button mushrooms, quartered

1 lb (450 g) cooked turkey breast, diced

4 fl oz (120 ml) vinaigrette dressing, made with walnut oil (page 182)

1 teaspoon fresh thyme leaves

2 pears, peeled, halved and cored

1 oz (30 g) walnut pieces, toasted

1 ▲ Combine cooled cooked wild rice with the celery, spring onions, mushrooms and turkey in a bowl.

2 ◀ Add the dressing and thyme and toss well together.

3 Thinly slice the pear halves lengthways without cutting through the stalk end and spread the slices like a fan. Divide the salad among 4 plates. Garnish each with a fanned pear half and walnuts.

PREPARING BULGAR WHEAT

Bulgar wheat, a nutritious grain, is made by steaming whole wheat berries and then drying and cracking them into very small pieces. Cook like rice, either steamed plain or as a pilaf, or soak it to rehydrate. Serve as an accompaniment or use in salads.

Cooking simple bulgar pilaf
Soften 1 small finely chopped onion in 1oz (30g) butter. Add 6oz (170g) bulgar wheat, ¾pint (450ml) chicken stock and a bay leaf. Cover and steam. Season and add 2 tablespoons chopped parsley.

---

1 ▲ To steam bulgar: Use two parts liquid to one part bulgar. Put the bulgar in a saucepan with water or other liquid such as stock, add flavourings if directed and bring to the boil. Cover and simmer over low heat for 12–15 minutes or until tender.

2 ▲ To soak bulgar: Put the bulgar in a sieve and rinse under cold running water until the water runs clear. Put the bulgar in a bowl, cover with fresh cold water and soak for 1 hour or until plump. Drain, pressing out all excess moisture.

Bulgar Wheat Salad with Herbs

SERVES 6

4oz (115g) bulgar wheat, soaked and well drained

8oz (225g) tomatoes, seeded and diced

1 small red onion, chopped

3 spring onions, chopped

2oz (55g) parsley, finely chopped

4 tablespoons chopped fresh mint

4floz (120ml) olive or vegetable oil

5 tablespoons lemon juice

salt and pepper

black olives and mint leaves, to garnish

1 ▲ Combine all the ingredients in a large bowl.

2 ◄ Stir to mix the ingredients thoroughly. Taste and adjust the seasoning if necessary.

3 Serve the salad at room temperature, garnished with black olives and mint leaves, if liked.

PREPARING COUSCOUS

A staple in North-African cooking, couscous is a type of tiny pasta made from semolina (which is ground from durum wheat). Its mild taste makes it the perfect accompaniment for spicy dishes, in particular the Moroccan and Tunisian stew also called couscous. It is delicious in stuffings and baked casseroles and even as a breakfast cereal.

1 ▲ To prepare regular couscous: Put the couscous in a sieve and rinse under cold running water until the water runs clear. Put the couscous in a bowl, cover with plenty of fresh cold water and soak for 30 minutes. Drain well in a sieve.

2 ▲ Rub the couscous in your fingers to be sure there are no lumps, then put it in a muslin-lined colander. Set over a pan of boiling water (or over the pot containing the spicy stew) and steam, uncovered, for 30 minutes or until soft and heated through.

Couscous Stuffing

Prepare 6 oz (170 g) quick-cooking couscous with stock, using ¾ pint (450 ml) chicken stock, 1 oz (30 g) butter, 1 teaspoon ground cinnamon, and ½ teaspoon each ground cumin and coriander. Season with salt and pepper, then stir in 3 oz (85 g) each chopped dried apricots and sultanas. Use to stuff poussins, chicken, turkey or boned chicken pieces before roasting or pot-roasting. Makes enough to stuff 1 large chicken or 4 poussins.

3 ▲ To prepare quick-cooking couscous with stock: Put the stock in a saucepan, with 1 oz (30 g) butter if liked, and bring to the boil. Off the heat, gradually add the couscous and stir. Return to the boil, cover the pan, remove from the heat and leave for 5–10 minutes. Fluff the couscous with a fork. Serve hot as an accompaniment, adding seasoning and other flavourings as required, or use as a stuffing for vegetables or poultry.

4 ▲ To prepare quick-cooking couscous with water: Put the couscous in a bowl, cover with boiling water and soak for 20–30 minutes or until plump. Drain well. Use for salads.

Special equipment

A special pot (called a couscous-sière) is traditionally used for cooking this grain. The bottom part of the pot is filled with a spicy stew; the perforated top part holds the couscous, where it cooks in the fragrant steam.

Spicy Vegetable Stew with Couscous

SERVES 4

1½ tablespoons vegetable oil

2 large onions, cut into chunks

½ teaspoon ground cumin

½ teaspoon ground cinnamon

¼ teaspoon turmeric

12 oz (340 g) carrots, cut into chunks

12 oz (340 g) white turnips, cut into chunks

1½ pints (900 ml) chicken or vegetable stock or water

12 oz (340 g) courgettes, cut into chunks

1 red pepper, seeded and cut into large squares

1½ oz (45 g) raisins

12 oz (340 g) quick-cooking couscous

1 oz (30 g) butter

5 oz (145 g) thawed frozen peas

salt and pepper

1 Heat the oil in a large pot. Add the onions and cook until they begin to soften, stirring occasionally.

2 Stir in the spices and cook, stirring, for 1 minute.

3 ▲ Add the carrots, turnips and ¼ pint (150 ml) of the stock. Bring to the boil. Cover and cook for 5 minutes.

4 ▲ Add the courgettes, red pepper and raisins. Cover again and simmer for a further 10 minutes or until the vegetables are almost tender.

5 Meanwhile, prepare the couscous with stock, using the remaining stock and the butter.

6 ▼ Add the peas to the vegetable stew. Cover and cook for 3–5 minutes or until all the vegetables are tender. Season with salt and pepper.

7 Fluff the couscous and divide among hot bowls. Make a well in the centre of each and spoon in the vegetable stew.

COOKING CORNMEAL AND POLENTA

Cornmeal, finely ground from yellow or white sweetcorn, is used as an ingredient in many American recipes – from a breakfast 'porridge' cereal through muffins, breads and dumplings. It also serves as a coating for fried foods.

Polenta is a more coarsely ground cornmeal, much used in Italian cooking. It may be served plain or mixed with butter and cheese, to take the place of rice or potatoes, or it can be cooled until firm, sliced and then fried or toasted.

1 ▲ **For cornmeal 'porridge'**: Use four parts water to one part cornmeal. Bring the liquid just to the boil in a saucepan. Gradually add the cornmeal in a steady stream, stirring constantly. Do not add the cornmeal all at once or it will form lumps.

2 ▲ Cover the pan, reduce the heat and cook gently for about 10 minutes or until very thick. Stir occasionally. Serve hot with butter, milk or maple syrup. (This can be cooled, sliced and fried like polenta.)

Cornmeal and Cheese Topping
Combine 12 fl oz (360 ml) milk, 1 oz (30 g) butter and ½ teaspoon salt in a saucepan. Bring just to the boil, then gradually add 2 oz (55 g) cornmeal, stirring. Cook, uncovered, for 2–3 minutes or until thick, stirring constantly. Remove from the heat and stir in 2 beaten eggs and 6 oz (170 g) grated Cheddar cheese. Spread over chilli (made with or without meat) in a baking dish, covering the chilli completely. Bake in a preheated 375°F/190°C/Gas 5 oven for 35–40 minutes or until set and lightly browned. *Serves 4.*

3 ▲ **For polenta:** Add polenta gradually to boiling liquid as for cornmeal (see above). Reduce the heat to low and simmer, uncovered, for 10–20 minutes or until thick and pulling away from the sides of the pan. Stir constantly. The polenta is now ready to be served or moulded.

5 ▲ Cut the set polenta into shapes or slices, about ½ in (1.5 cm) thick.

4 ▲ If to be cooled and then later fried or toasted, pour the polenta into an oiled or buttered pan or dish and leave it to cool completely.

Polenta with Cheese
Toast polenta slices under the grill until lightly browned on both sides. Top with slices of a strong cheese such as gorgonzola. Grill briefly until the cheese starts to melt, then serve.

Polenta with Chicken Livers

SERVES 8 AS A STARTER

1¼ pints (750 ml) chicken stock or water
4½ oz (135 g) polenta
2 oz (55 g) butter
2 tablespoons olive oil
1 lb (450 g) chicken livers, trimmed and cut in half
1–2 garlic cloves, finely chopped
4 tablespoons chopped parsley, preferably flat-leaf
1 teaspoon chopped fresh oregano or ½ teaspoon dried oregano
squeeze of lemon juice
salt and pepper
12 fl oz (360 ml) tomato sauce (page 172), heated

1 Bring the stock or salted water to the boil in a large saucepan. Gradually stir in the polenta. Cook over low heat until very thick, stirring constantly.

2 ▲ Pour the polenta into a buttered 8 in (20 cm) round pan. Set aside for at least 30 minutes to firm up.

~ **VARIATION** ~

For Polenta with Mushrooms, use 1 lb (450 g) sliced mushrooms sautéed in 1½ oz (45 g) butter in place of the chicken livers and serve with tomato-wine sauce (page 172), if preferred.

3 ▼ Invert the block of polenta on to a board. Cut it into 8 wedges. Fry in 1½ oz (45 g) butter until golden brown on both sides, turning once.

4 Heat the remaining butter and the oil in a frying pan over moderately high heat. Add the livers and fry for 2–3 minutes or until they are starting to brown, turning once.

5 ▲ Add the garlic, herbs, lemon juice and seasoning. Continue cooking for a further 1–2 minutes or until the livers are lightly browned on both sides but still pink in the centre.

6 Put a wedge of polenta on each warmed plate. Spoon the tomato sauce over the polenta and arrange the chicken livers on top. Serve hot.

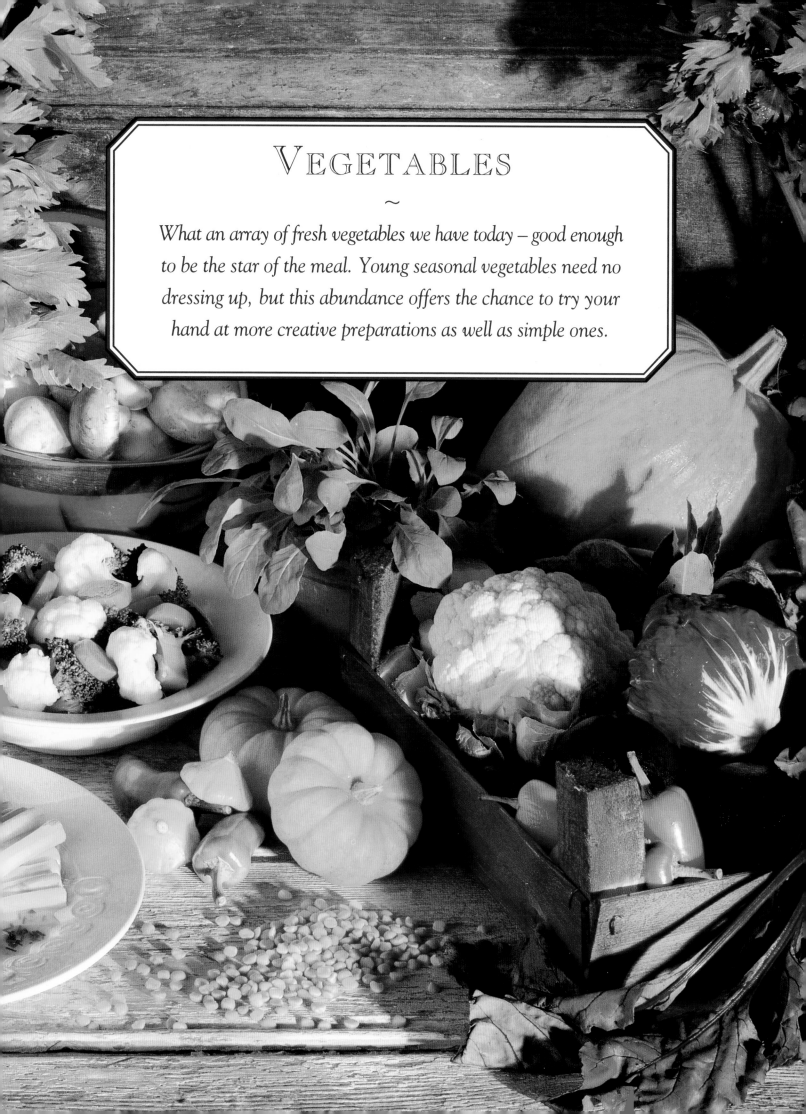

VEGETABLES

~

What an array of fresh vegetables we have today – good enough to be the star of the meal. Young seasonal vegetables need no dressing up, but this abundance offers the chance to try your hand at more creative preparations as well as simple ones.

PREPARING AND COOKING VEGETABLES

To enjoy their full flavour, fresh vegetables are often best prepared and served simply. These guidelines for vegetable preparation and cooking will help you make the most of seasonal bounty.

Serving ideas include suggested amounts of raw prepared vegetable to serve per person. Season all dishes to taste. Recipes in these sections serve 4.

ROOTS AND BULBS
Carrots
Naturally sweet, carrots are used in innumerable dishes, and are tasty hot and cold, raw and cooked.

Preparation: If they are young, there is no need to peel them; just trim the ends and scrub well. Larger carrots should be peeled. Leave whole or cut as specified. If carrots have a woody core, cut it out.

Cooking: *To boil*, drop into boiling salted water and simmer until just tender: 8–10 minutes for whole baby carrots, 10–20 minutes for larger whole carrots, 4–10 minutes for sliced or grated carrots. *To steam*, cook whole baby carrots, covered, over boiling water for about 10 minutes. *To braise*, cook whole baby carrots or thinly sliced carrots, with 3

tablespoons stock or water and 1 oz (30 g) butter per 1 lb (450 g), tightly covered, for about 5 minutes. Boil, uncovered, to evaporate excess liquid before serving.

Serving ideas (4 oz/115 g each)
● Dress hot carrots with butter and chopped fresh herbs such as parsley, chives, thyme or marjoram.
● Add a little sugar or honey and a squeeze of lemon or orange juice when braising. Or, try spices such as nutmeg, ginger or curry powder.
● Serve raw carrot sticks with a dip.

Parsnips
Their sweet, nutty flavour makes a delicious addition to soups and stews or enjoy them on their own.

Preparation: Trim the ends and peel thinly. Leave small parsnips whole; cut up larger ones. If large parsnips have a woody core, cut it out.

Cooking: *To roast*, blanch in boiling salted water, then put in a roasting tin with butter or oil and cook in a 400°F/200°C/Gas 6 oven for about 40 minutes. Baste occasionally. *To boil*, drop into boiling salted water and simmer for 5–10 minutes or until just tender. *To fry*, blanch in boiling water

for 1–2 minutes and drain. Fry in butter for 10–12 minutes or until golden brown and tender.

Serving ideas (5 oz/145 g each)
● Mix 1¼ lb (600 g) boiled parsnips, 2 oz (55 g) butter and 4 tablespoons honey; cook, covered, for 5 minutes.
● Sauté sliced parsnips with sliced carrots; sprinkle with chopped herbs.
● Bake 1¼ lb (600 g) small parsnips with ¼ pint (150 ml) orange juice and 1½ oz (45 g) butter, covered, in a 350°F/180°C/Gas 4 oven for 1 hour.
● Roast blanched parsnips in the tin around a joint of beef or pork.

Turnips
Mildly piquant, turnips go well with both sweet and savoury seasonings.

Preparation: Trim the ends and peel the turnips thinly.

Cooking: *To steam*, cook cubes, covered, over boiling water for about 15 minutes or until tender. *To boil*, drop into boiling salted water and simmer until tender: 20–30 minutes if whole, about 7 minutes if diced. *To braise*, cook thin slices, with 1 oz (30 g) butter and 5 tablespoons stock or water, in a covered pan, for 4–5 minutes.

Serving ideas (4 oz/115 g each)
- Mash boiled turnips with milk and butter; mix with an equal quantity of mashed carrots, parsnips or potatoes.
- Cover 1 lb (450 g) steamed turnips with 1 pint (600 ml) hot white sauce (page 170), sprinkle with breadcrumbs and grated cheese; brown under grill.
- Add 1 tablespoon sugar when braising turnips; uncover and boil to evaporate excess liquid and to caramelize the turnips.

Swede

The orangey-yellow flesh of this root vegetable is sweet and full of flavour.

Preparation: Peel, removing all tough skin and roots. Cut as recipe specifies.

Cooking: *To boil*, put chunks into boiling salted water and simmer for 15 minutes or until tender. Do not overcook or the vegetable will be watery and mushy. *To steam*, cook slices, covered, over boiling water for 9–12 minutes or until tender. *To braise*, cook, with 1 oz (30 g) butter and 5 tablespoons stock or water per 1 lb (450 g), covered, for 5–7 minutes. *To roast*, put chunks or sticks around roasting meat and turn to coat with the dripping. Roast at 400°F/200°C/Gas 6 for about 45 minutes.

Serving ideas (5 oz/145 g each)
- Braise 1¼ lb (600 g) grated swede seasoned with 1 tablespoon soft brown sugar and 1 teaspoon soy sauce.
- Mash 1¼ lb (600 g) boiled swede until smooth; beat in 2 eggs, 4 tablespoons cream, 2 tablespoons flour and ¼ teaspoon nutmeg until fluffy. Bake in a buttered dish in a 350°F/180°C/Gas 4 oven for about 30 minutes.

Potatoes

Boiling potatoes are moist with a waxy texture so they keep their shape when cooked. Baking potatoes are dry and starchy and their texture is more floury after cooking. In addition, there are orange- and white-fleshed sweet potatoes.

Preparation: If the potato skins will be eaten, scrub them well. Otherwise, peel potatoes.

Cooking: *To bake*, prick skins all over with a fork and bake in a 400°F/200°C/Gas 6 oven until tender: 1–1½ hours or 30–40 minutes for sweet potatoes. *To boil*, put into a pan of cold salted water, bring to the boil, and simmer until just tender: 10–20 minutes according to size. *To roast*, blanch peeled potatoes for 1–2 minutes; drain and pat dry. Put

around meat in a roasting tin and turn to coat with dripping; roast for 1–1½ hours, turning occasionally. *To sauté*, boil until partly cooked (in skin if specified), then fry slices or cubes in butter or oil until brown and crisp.

To deep-fry (chips), cut into sticks and soak in cold water for at least 30 minutes; drain and pat dry. Fry (in small batches) in oil heated to 375°F/190°C until beginning to colour: 3–7 minutes according to size. Drain on paper towels, then fry again for 3 minutes or until golden brown and crisp.

Stuffed Jacket-baked Potatoes
Cut baked potatoes in half and scoop out the centres, leaving a thin wall of flesh. Mash the scooped-out flesh with a little butter and 3 tablespoons each grated Cheddar cheese and diced cooked ham per potato. Season to taste. Fill the potato shells with the mixture, mounding it. Sprinkle the tops with grated Cheddar, then bake at 400°F/200°C/Gas 6 for 10–15 minutes.

Serving ideas (6 oz/170 g each)
● Dress boiled new potatoes with butter and chopped mixed parsley and mint or toasted pine nuts.
● Mash boiled or baked sweet potatoes with an electric mixer. Add butter to taste, orange juice to moisten and ground cinnamon. Season and beat well.

Celeriac

The coarse knobby appearance of celeriac belies its delicate and delicious flavour.

Preparation: Peel off the thick skin. Do this just before cooking because celeriac discolours when cut. If serving it raw, drop the peeled root or pieces into water acidulated with lemon juice or vinegar. Cut as instructed in recipe.

Cooking: *To steam*, cook cubes, covered, over boiling water until tender. *To boil*, drop cubes into boiling salted water, cover and simmer until just tender: 5–15 minutes according to the size of the pieces. *To braise*, cook grated celeriac, with 2 oz (55 g) butter and 2 tablespoons stock per 1 lb (450 g), covered, for 5 minutes. Uncover and boil to evaporate excess liquid.

Serving ideas (4–5 oz/115–145 g each)
● Dress matchsticks of celeriac with spicy mayonnaise (page 180) and sprinkle with shredded salami.
● Boil slices of celeriac in beef stock; drain. Sprinkle with grated Parmesan cheese and serve hot.

Onions

The onion is one of those ingredients basic to almost every savoury dish. They come in all sizes and shapes: pungent round onions and sweet mild onions, flat ones, large spherical ones (Spanish-type) and elongated Italian red ones. In addition, there are small pickling and button onions, shallots and spring onions.

Preparation: Peel off the papery skin. Then slice, chop, etc as the recipe specifies. For spring onions, trim the root end and cut off any wilted or discoloured green leaves. Cut as specified, using just the white bulbs or both white and green parts.

Cooking: *To fry*, cook chopped or sliced onions, uncovered, in butter and/or oil over moderate heat, stirring occasionally, for about 5 minutes or until soft and translucent. If directed, continue cooking until the onions are golden brown. *To slow-cook*, cook sliced or chopped onions, covered, in butter and/or oil over low heat, stirring occasionally, for about 30 minutes or until very soft and golden. *To boil* small onions, drop into boiling salted water and simmer for 15–20 minutes or until tender.

Serving ideas
● Top hamburgers or steaks with slow-cooked sliced onions.
● Combine 1 lb (450 g) boiled button onions with 1½ oz (45 g) butter and 2½ oz (70 g) soft light brown sugar; cook over low heat, stirring, for about 10 minutes or until caramelized.
● Trim all but 2 in (5 cm) of green from spring onions. Stir-fry in hot oil and sprinkle with soy sauce.
● Use thin slices of sweet red onions raw in salads.
● Bake whole onions in a 425°F/ 220°C/Gas 7 oven for 45 minutes or until tender when pierced with a fork.

Leeks

This sweet and subtle member of the onion family has myriad uses – both as a vegetable on its own and as a flavouring in soups, stews and so on.

Preparation: Trim the root end and the dark green leaves, leaving just the pale green and white. (Save the dark green leaves for the stockpot.) Unless the leeks are to be cooked whole, slit them open lengthways, to the centre. Put them in cold water and soak for about 20 minutes. Drain well, squeezing out the excess water. If leeks are to be sliced or chopped, do this before rinsing them thoroughly in a colander under cold running water.

Cooking: *To braise,* cook, with 1 oz (30 g) butter and 5 tablespoons stock or water per 1 lb (450 g), tightly covered, until just tender. *To boil,* drop into boiling salted water or stock and simmer for 10–15 minutes or until tender. *To steam,* cook in a covered steamer over boiling water, allowing 5–7 minutes for sliced or whole baby leeks.

Serving ideas (6 oz/170 g each)
● Boil whole leeks, then cool slightly. Marinate in a vinaigrette dressing (page 182); serve the leeks cool, not cold.
● Toss hot sliced leeks with butter and fresh herbs such as sage, tarragon, thyme or parsley.
● Wrap whole boiled leeks in slices of ham. Cover with cheese sauce (page 170), sprinkle with grated cheese and grill until the top is golden.

FRUITING VEGETABLES
Aubergines
The most familiar aubergines are the large ones with shiny purple skins, but there are also smaller purple ones and long, pale purple Chinese ones. All can be used interchangeably.

Preparation: Trim off the stalk end. Leave aubergines whole or cut according to recipe instructions.

Cooking: *To grill,* brush cut surfaces with oil. Grill, 3–4 in (7.5–10 cm) from the heat, for 10 minutes or until tender and well browned; turn once and brush with oil. *To fry,* coat slices or thick sticks with flour if recipe specifies, then fry in hot oil or butter for 5 minutes on each side or until golden. *To braise,* brown slices or wedges in a little hot oil, add 4 tablespoons stock or water per 1 lb (450 g), cover and cook for 12 minutes or until tender. Add more liquid if necessary. *To bake,* prick whole aubergines all over with a fork. Bake in a 400°F/200°C/Gas 6 oven for about 20 minutes or until soft.

Serving ideas (5 oz/145 g each)
● Baste grilled aubergines with garlic- and herb-flavoured olive oil.
● When braising aubergines, after browning add skinned, seeded and chopped tomatoes and basil.
● Serve fried flour-coated aubergines with garlic mayonnaise (page 180).

Courgettes
Courgettes and other thin-skinned squashes, such as pattypan, are completely edible, skin and all.

Preparation: Trim the ends from courgettes. Cut as specified.

Cooking: *To fry,* cook sliced courgettes in butter or oil for 5–10 minutes or until tender and golden brown. *To boil,* drop into boiling salted water and simmer until tender: 10–12 minutes for whole courgettes, 3–8 minutes for slices. *To steam,* cook in a covered steamer over boiling water until tender. *To braise,* cook sliced courgettes in a covered pan, with 1 oz (30 g) butter and 5 table- spoons stock or water per 1 lb (450 g), for 4–5 minutes or until tender.

Serving ideas (4–5 oz/115–145 g each)
● Sauté sliced courgettes with finely chopped garlic and chopped fresh parsley and oregano.
● Cut small courgettes in half lengthways and spread cut surfaces with wholegrain mustard. Grill about 4 in (10 cm) from the heat for about 5 minutes or until tender but still firm.

Pumpkins
Pumpkin and other squashes such as acorn and butternut, have a hard rind and central seeds and fibres that should be removed before cooking.

Preparation: Unless baking in the skin, peel pumpkin with a large, sturdy knife. Scrape away all the seeds and stringy fibres.

Cooking: *To steam,* cook in a covered steamer over boiling water until tender. *To bake,* cut into serving pieces, leaving on the rind, and score the flesh. Arrange cut side up in greased baking dish, dot with butter and bake in a 375°F/190°C/Gas 5 oven for 45 minutes or until tender. *To boil,* drop pieces into boiling salted water and simmer for 4–5 minutes or until tender. *To braise,* cook cubes of pumpkin as for courgettes.

Serving ideas (5–8 oz/145–225 g each)
● Add diced apple, a squeeze of lemon juice and 2 tablespoons soft brown sugar when braising pumpkin. If desired, spice with a little cinnamon and nutmeg or curry powder.
● Bake acorn squash halves with a knob of butter and 1 teaspoon maple syrup in each.

LEAFY, GREEN AND OTHER VEGETABLES
Spinach
Small tender leaves have a delicate flavour and can be used raw in salads. Large, strongly flavoured, darker leaves taste better cooked.

Preparation: Spinach can hide a lot of grit so needs careful rinsing. Immerse in cold water, swish round and soak

for 3–4 minutes. Then lift out the spinach and immerse in fresh cold water. Repeat, then drain in a colander. Discard any damaged or yellowed leaves. Pull off tough stalks.

Cooking: *To steam-boil,* put into a large pan (there should be sufficient water left on the leaves after rinsing so that no more is needed). Cook for 5–7 minutes or until just wilted, stirring occasionally to help evaporate the liquid. Drain well and press the spinach between two plates or squeeze it in your fist. *To braise,* cook, covered, with a large knob of butter until wilted. Uncover and boil to evaporate excess liquid. *To stir-fry,* cook small or shredded leaves in hot oil for 3–5 minutes or until wilted.

Serving ideas (5–6 oz/145–175 g each)
● Add 3–4 tablespoons double or whipping cream and a good pinch of grated nutmeg to braised spinach.
● Stir-fry chopped onion and garlic, then add spinach with halved cherry tomatoes and stir-fry for 1 minute.
● Steam-boil spinach leaves; chop finely after draining. Fry in olive oil with chopped garlic, stirring, until the garlic just starts to turn golden and the spinach is piping hot.
● Combine equal parts of chopped cooked spinach and cooked rice with butter and seasoning to taste.

Greens
Hearty greens include those from the cabbage family – kale, spring greens, turnip leaves – as well as beet greens and Swiss chard or seakale beet. Serve alone, or in soups and stews.

Preparation: Discard damaged or yellowed leaves. Trim off root ends and large or coarse stalks. Leave the leaves whole or shred, according to recipe instructions. Cut leaves from stalks of Swiss chard and cook separately (the stalks take longer).

Cooking: *To braise,* put shredded leaves (or Swiss chard stalks) in a pan, with 1 oz (30 g) butter and 3 tablespoons stock per 1 lb (450 g). Cook, covered, until just tender. Boil, uncovered, to evaporate excess liquid. *To steam-boil,* put into a large pan (there should be sufficient water left on the leaves after rinsing so that no more is needed). Cover and cook until just wilted: 5–15 minutes according to variety. *To boil,* drop shredded leaves (or Swiss chard stalks) into boiling salted water and simmer until tender.

Serving ideas (8 oz/225 g each)
● Toss hot braised greens with whipping cream or soured cream and grated nutmeg; heat gently.
● Mix boiled greens with mashed potato. Shape into cakes, coat in fine breadcrumbs and fry in butter until golden brown on both sides.
● Top boiled or braised greens with crisply fried bacon and grated Gruyère cheese; grill to melt the cheese.

Green beans

Crisp green beans are available in varying sizes, from tiny French ones ('haricots verts') to very large runner beans. French beans are stringless, whereas runner beans when mature have a stringy casing. Bobby beans are shorter and plumper than French beans. Chinese long beans are similar to runner beans, but longer.

Preparation: Top and tail using scissors or a knife. For older beans with strings, snap off the ends, pulling the strings from the sides as you do so. Cut large beans diagonally or sliver.

Cooking: *To boil*, drop into boiling salted water and simmer until just tender but still crisp and bright green: 3–15 minutes, according to size. *To steam*, cook in a covered steamer over boiling water until tender. *To braise*, cook tightly covered, with about 5 tablespoons stock or water and 1 oz (30 g) butter per 1 lb (450 g), until tender. *To stir-fry*, blanch in boiling water for 2 minutes; drain, refresh and dry. Stir-fry in hot oil for 2–3 minutes.

Serving ideas (4 oz/115 g each)
● Dress boiled or steamed beans with melted butter, chopped herbs and a squeeze of lemon juice.

● Add 6 tablespoons cream to 1 lb (450 g) braised beans. Cook, uncovered, stirring, until the liquid has reduced and the beans are glazed.
● Top hot beans with quickly fried shreds of Parma ham. Or, top with flaked almonds or pecan nuts lightly browned in butter.

Peas

Mange-touts and sugar-snap peas are completely edible, pod and all. Green peas are removed from their pods for cooking; the pods weigh as much as the peas, so you need to allow twice the weight of edible-pod peas.

Preparation: If green peas are in the pod, split it open and pop out the peas. Top and tail mange-touts and sugar-snap peas, pulling any tough strings from the sides as you do so.

Cooking: *To steam*, cook in a covered steamer over boiling water until tender. *To boil*, drop into boiling salted water and simmer until tender: 5–10 minutes for peas, 1–2 minutes for mange-touts. *To braise*, cook covered, with 1 oz (30 g) butter and 4 tablespoons stock or water per 1 lb (450 g), until tender: 5–10 minutes for green peas, 2 minutes for mange-touts and sugar-snap peas.

Serving ideas (4 oz/115 g each)
● Add sliced spring onions, shredded lettuce and a little sugar when braising green peas.
● Stir-fry mange-touts with thinly sliced onion and mushrooms.
● Add 4 tablespoons whipping cream to 1 lb (450 g) braised sugar-snap peas and cook uncovered, stirring, until almost all liquid has evaporated.

Broccoli

Serve this green vegetable hot or leave it to cool and use in salads. It is also excellent in stir-fries.

Preparation: Trim off the end of the stalk. If the rest of the stalk is to be used in the recipe, peel it. According to recipe instructions, leave the head whole or cut off the florets, or flowers, taking a little stalk with each one. Cut the remainder of the peeled stalk across into thin slices.

Cooking: *To steam*, cook in a covered steamer over boiling water until tender. *To boil*, drop into boiling salted water and simmer until just tender: 7–12 minutes for whole, 4–6 minutes for florets and stalks. *To braise*, cook covered, with 5 tablespoons stock or water and 1 oz (30 g) butter per 1 lb (450 g), until tender.

Serving ideas (5 oz/145 g each)
● Toss hot broccoli with a flavoured butter (page 174).
● Cover hot broccoli with cheese sauce (page 170), sprinkle with grated Parmesan and brown under grill.
● Blanch small broccoli florets for 1 minute; drain and refresh. Serve cold dressed with vinaigrette (page 182) and sprinkled with toasted nuts.

Cauliflower
White or ivory cauliflower is the most widely available, although there are also green and purple varieties.

Preparation: Cut away the large green leaves, leaving only the tiny ones if liked. Trim the stalk level with the the head. Cut out the core. Leave the head whole, or break into florets before or after cooking.

Cooking: *To steam*, cook florets in a covered steamer over boiling water for 12–15 minutes. *To steam-boil*, put core down in a pan with 1 in (2.5 cm) boiling salted water and a bay leaf. Cover and cook until just tender: 15–30 minutes for whole heads, 5–9 minutes for florets. Drain well. *To braise*, cook florets, covered, with 1 oz (30 g) butter and 5 tablespoons stock or water per 1 lb (450 g), for 5–7 minutes.

Serving ideas (5 oz/145 g each)
● Dress hot cauliflower with butter; sprinkle with chopped fresh chives, toasted flaked almonds or chopped pecan nuts, or paprika.
● Top hot cauliflower with Hollandaise sauce (page 178).
● Coat florets in egg and crumbs, then deep-fry and serve with garlic or spicy mayonnaise (page 180).

Cabbage
Rich in vitamins and very versatile, cabbage is good cooked or raw. The many varieties available include firm, round heads (green, white and red), looser round heads (Savoy with its crinkly leaves), and long, loose heads (pak choi and Chinese leaves or Chinese cabbage).

Preparation: Discard any wilted or discoloured outer leaves. Cut the heads into small wedges or halve long, loose heads. Cut out the coarse stalk from the wedges before cooking, if preferred. Or, quarter heads and shred them. Leave long, loose heads whole and cut across the leaves to shred.

Cooking: *To braise*, quickly blanch chopped or shredded green, Savoy or red cabbage. (There is no need to blanch Chinese leaves.) Cook, tightly covered, with about 5 tablespoons stock or water and 1 oz (30 g) butter per 1 lb (450 g), allowing 3–4 minutes for green, Savoy and Chinese leaves and 30 minutes for red cabbage (use more liquid). *To boil*, drop into boiling salted water and simmer until just tender: 6–8 minutes for wedges and 3–5 minutes for shredded green, Savoy or Chinese leaves. *To steam*, cook in a covered steamer over boiling water until tender.

Serving ideas (4 oz/115 g each)
● Add chopped fresh dill when braising green or Savoy cabbage.
● Blanch larger outer leaves of green or Savoy cabbage, then roll them up around a minced meat stuffing and simmer in a rich tomato sauce.
● Add sliced apples, cooked diced bacon and spices (cinnamon, nutmeg) when braising red cabbage.
● Use shredded Chinese leaves raw in tossed salads.

Cauliflower Cheese
Cut a large cauliflower into florets and steam until just tender. Spread in a buttered gratin dish and scatter over 3 oz (85 g) sliced, sautéed mushrooms. Pour 1 pint (600 ml) cheese sauce (page 170) evenly over the top and sprinkle with a mixture of grated Cheddar and fine bread-crumbs. Brown quickly under the grill. *Serves 4.*

Brussels sprouts

These miniature heads of cabbage are best cooked just until tender.

Preparation: Remove any discoloured leaves. Trim the stalks level with the heads. Cut an 'x' in the base of the stalk so that it will cook in the same time as the rest.

Cooking: To *braise*, put in a pan, with 5 tablespoons stock or water and 1 oz (30 g) butter per 1 lb (450 g). Cover tightly for cooking. *To boil*, drop into boiling salted water and simmer for 7–10 minutes or until just tender. *To steam*, cook in a covered steamer over boiling water for 10–12 minutes.

Serving ideas (4–5 oz/115–145 g each)
- Toss with butter and orange zest.
- Toss with toasted nuts, braised or poached chestnuts or canned water chestnuts.
- Cut the heads lengthways in half and blanch in boiling water for 2–3 minutes; drain and refresh. Stir-fry in hot oil with finely chopped ginger and garlic for 2–3 minutes or until tender and lightly browned.
- Shred and blanch for 2–3 minutes; drain and refresh. Add chopped onion and celery and toss with a lemony vinaigrette dressing (page 182).

Celery

Crisp green or white celery is a popular salad ingredient and favourite flavouring in soups, stews and stuffings.

Preparation: Separate the stalks. Scrub with a vegetable brush under cold running water. Trim off the root end, leaves and any blemishes (keep leaves for the stockpot). If the stalks have tough strings, remove these with a vegetable peeler. Cut as specified. For celery hearts, cut in half lengthways. Trim off the leaves.

Cooking: To *steam-boil*, put in a pan with 1 in (2.5 cm) of boiling salted water. Cover and cook until just tender: 5–10 minutes for pieces, 10–20 minutes for celery hearts. *To braise*, cook slices, with 2 tablespoons stock or water and 1 oz (30 g) butter per 8 oz (225 g), or hearts with ½ pint (300 ml) liquid, covered: about 3 minutes for thin slices, 10–20 minutes for hearts.

Serving ideas (4 oz/115 g each)
- Stuff finger-length sticks of raw celery with blue cheese, flavoured soft cheese or peanut butter.
- Sprinkle braised celery with chopped walnuts and chopped parsley.
- Braise celery hearts with chopped tomatoes and tarragon or thyme.

Mushrooms

Cultivated button and open mushrooms are widely available; you may also find fresh wild mushrooms such as shiitake and oyster.

Preparation: Rinse or wipe with a damp paper towel (don't immerse in water as mushrooms absorb liquid readily). Trim gritty stalks, and remove tough stalks from wild mushrooms. Small mushrooms can be left whole; larger ones are normally halved, quartered or sliced, or they may be diced or chopped. To stuff large mushrooms, pull off the stalks.

Cooking: To *fry*, cook in hot butter and/or oil for about 4 minutes or until tender, stirring frequently. The mushrooms will give up liquid; if the recipe specifies, continue frying until the liquid has evaporated and the mushrooms have browned. *To grill*, brush with melted butter or oil. Grill 4 in (10 cm) from the heat, turning and basting occasionally, for 5–8 minutes or until tender and browned.

Serving ideas (4 oz/115 g each)
- Sauté sliced mushrooms with chopped garlic and thyme.
- Top grilled mushroom caps with a pat of flavoured butter (page 174).

PREPARING ASPARAGUS

When asparagus is young and tender, you need do nothing more than trim off the ends of the stalks. However, larger spears, with stalk ends that are tough and woody, require some further preparation.

A standing alternative
Asparagus spears can be cooked loose and flat in simmering water (as described below) or they can be tied into bundles and cooked standing upright in a tall pot. With the latter method, the tips are kept above the water so they cook gently in the steam.

1 ▲ Cut off the tough, woody ends. Cut the spears so they are all about the same length.

2 ▲ If you like, remove the skin: Lay a spear flat and hold it just below the tip. With a vegetable peeler, shave off the skin, working lengthways down the spear to the end of the stalk. Roll the spear so you can remove the skin from all sides.

Asparagus with Ham

SERVES 4

1½–2 lb (700–900 g) medium-size asparagus spears, prepared for cooking

6 fl oz (180 ml) clarified butter (page 176)

2 teaspoons lemon juice

2 tablespoons chopped spring onions

1 tablespoon chopped parsley

salt and pepper

4 slices Westphalian or Parma ham

1 ▼ Half fill a frying pan with salted water. Bring to the boil. Simmer asparagus spears for 4–5 minutes or until they are just tender. (Pierce the stalk to test.) Remove and drain well.

2 Combine the butter, lemon juice, spring onions and parsley in a small saucepan. Season with salt and pepper to taste. Heat the mixture until lukewarm.

3 Divide the asparagus among 4 warm plates. Drape a slice of ham over each portion. Spoon over the herb butter and serve.

PREPARING FRESH SWEETCORN

Tender sweetcorn is a favourite, eaten on the cob or off – as kernels in soups, salad, casseroles etc. Buy the freshest sweetcorn you can find.

Cooking corn on the cob

Bring a large pot of water to the boil and add 1 teaspoon sugar. Drop freshly prepared sweetcorn into the water. Bring back to the boil and simmer for 4–7 minutes or until just tender (test by piercing a kernel with the tip of a sharp knife). Alternatively, steam the corn with a little boiling water in a covered saucepan. Drain well before serving.

1 ▲ Just before cooking, strip off the husks and pull off all the silk. (If grilling or oven-roasting in the husk, just pull back the husks and remove the silk, then reshape.) Trim the stalk so it is level with the base.

2 ▲ **To remove the kernels**: Use a sharp knife to cut them lengthways, several rows at a time, from the cob. If the recipe specifies, after removing the kernels set each cob upright on a plate and run the blunt edge of the knife down the cob, pressing firmly, to scrape off the milky liquid.

Sweetcorn with Courgettes and Bacon

SERVES 4

4 smoked streaky bacon rashers
½ oz (15 g) butter
1 onion, chopped
1 small green pepper, seeded and diced
kernels scraped from 6 fresh sweetcorn
6 oz (170 g) courgettes, diced
¼ pint (150 ml) whipping cream
salt and pepper

1 ▲ Fry the bacon rashers until they are crisp. Remove the rashers with tongs and drain on paper towels.

2 ◄ Add the butter, onion and pepper to the pan and fry until soft, stirring occasionally. Add the sweetcorn. Cover and cook gently for 10 minutes. Stir in the courgettes and cream. Season with salt and pepper. Cook, covered, for 10 minutes or until all the vegetables are tender. Chop the bacon and stir into the mixture. Adjust the seasoning and serve.

Skinning and Seeding Tomatoes

Some tomatoes have tough skins and seeds. In cooking, these can become separated from the flesh and can spoil the appearance and texture of a dish. In addition, some people find tomato skins indigestible, so it is often desirable to remove them. In these cases, unless a soup, sauce or other dish is sieved before serving, it is best to skin and seed the tomatoes before using them.

If the tomatoes have tender skins and they will be eaten raw, or only briefly cooked, removing the peel is less essential. However, many people prefer to skin tomatoes for eating raw as well.

1 ▲ **To skin tomatoes**: Cut a small cross in the skin at the base of each tomato. Immerse, 3 or 4 at a time, in boiling water. Once the cut skin begins to roll back, in about 10 seconds, lift the tomatoes out and immerse in iced water. Drain and peel.

2 ▲ **To seed tomatoes**: Cut out the core, then cut each tomato in half across (around the 'equator'). Gently squeeze each half and shake the seeds and juice into a bowl. Scrape out any remaining seeds with the tip of a spoon or table knife.

Spicy Tomato Barbecue Sauce

Serves 6

2 tablespoons vegetable oil
1 onion, finely chopped
1 garlic clove, finely chopped
½ pint (300 ml) passata
8 oz (225 g) tomatoes, skinned, seeded and chopped
4 fl oz (120 ml) cider vinegar
1 tablespoon Worcestershire sauce
2½ oz (70 g) soft light brown sugar
2 teaspoons chilli powder, or to taste
1 bay leaf
few drops of mesquite liquid smoke flavouring (optional)
salt and pepper

1 ▶ Heat the oil in a saucepan, add the onion and cook until soft, stirring occasionally. Stir in the garlic and cook for 30 seconds. Add the passata, tomatoes, vinegar, Worcestershire sauce, brown sugar, chilli powder, bay leaf and liquid smoke, if using. Season with salt and pepper to taste.

2 Bring to the boil, reduce the heat, and simmer for 15 minutes, stirring from time to time. Taste and adjust the seasoning, if needed.

3 Use as a basting sauce for grilled or barbecued hamburgers, chicken, spareribs and steak. Serve additional sauce to accompany the food.

ROASTING AND PEELING PEPPERS

There are several methods for peeling peppers, the most basic of which is shaving off the skin with a vegetable peeler. However, because peppers have awkward curves, other methods, such as roasting, are often easier. Roasting peppers also heightens the sweetness of the flesh.

Handling chillies

Do not touch eyes and lips when handling chillies, and afterwards be sure to wash your hands well. Better yet, wear rubber gloves. Remove cores and seeds from chillies as for peppers.

1 ▲ Set the peppers on a rack in a grill pan and grill close to the heat. Turn the peppers to char and blister the skin all over. Alternatively, spear each pepper on a long-handled fork and hold it over a flame – over a gas burner or charcoal fire – turning the pepper slowly so that the skin is charred and blistered on all sides.

2 ▲ Once the skin is charred, put the peppers in a plastic bag and seal it. Cool – the steam trapped inside the bag will help loosen the skin. When the peppers are cool enough to handle, peel with the help of a small knife. (Work over a bowl so you can save the juices.) Cut out the stem and core; scrape out remaining seeds.

Marinated Pepper Salad with Cheese

SERVES 6

3 small peppers of different colours

6 tablespoons olive or vegetable oil

3 tablespoons fresh lime juice

2 tablespoons fresh lemon juice

1 teaspoon Worcestershire sauce

1 small garlic clove, finely chopped (optional)

salt and pepper

8 oz (225 g) mozzarella or firm goat's cheese, sliced

2 oz (55 g) toasted walnuts, coarsely chopped, to garnish

1 Roast the peppers, then peel them, reserving the juices. Cut the roasted pepper flesh lengthways into strips.

2 Combine the oil, lime and lemon juices, Worcestershire sauce and garlic, if using, in a bowl. Season to taste with salt and pepper.

3 ◄ Add the pepper strips and juices and toss to mix thoroughly with the marinade. Cover and marinate for 1–2 hours at room temperature.

4 To serve, arrange the pepper salad and overlapping slices of cheese on individual plates. Garnish with chopped nuts.

PREPARING AND COOKING GLOBE ARTICHOKES

Artichokes can be served whole, with or without a stuffing, or just the meaty bottoms, or bases, may be used. Very small artichokes, 2½ in (6 cm) or less in diameter, are often called hearts; this can be confusing, as artichoke bottoms are also sometimes called hearts. These baby artichokes are best braised whole, or halved or quartered. Be sure to rub all cut surfaces with lemon juice as you work and use a stainless steel knife, to prevent darkening and discoloration.

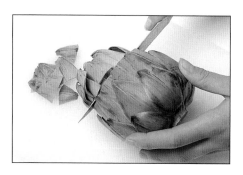

1 ▲ Whole artichokes: Break off the stalk close to the base. Cut off the pointed top about one-third of the way down. Snip off the pointed end of each large outside leaf using scissors. Open up the leaves and rinse thoroughly between them.

2 ▲ Artichoke bottoms: Break off all the coarse outer leaves down to the pale inner leaves. Scrape off the fuzzy centre, or 'choke' (or do this after cooking) and peel away all the leaves with a stainless steel knife, leaving just the edible base or bottom.

Artichokes with Herb Butter
Serve boiled artichokes hot with clarified butter (page 176) mixed with freshly chopped dill and parsley or other herbs.

3 ▲ To cook whole artichokes:
Bring a large pot of salted water to the boil. Add the juice of 1 lemon or 3–4 tablespoons vinegar. Add the prepared artichokes and put a plate on top to keep them submerged. Cover and simmer until you can pierce the stalk end easily with a fork: 15–20 minutes for small artichokes, 25–50 minutes for large artichokes.

4 ▲ Remove and drain well, upside down. Open up the leaves so you can insert a spoon into the centre and scrape out the fuzzy choke.

Ideas for artichokes
• Serve boiled artichokes hot with Hollandaise sauce (page 178).
• Serve boiled artichokes cool (not chilled) with a vinaigrette dressing (page 182) or mayonnaise (page 180).
• Serve cool artichoke bottoms filled with prawn or crab mayonnaise salad.
• Boil artichoke bottoms with flavourings such as garlic, bay leaf and black peppercorns. Drain and cool, then slice and marinate in a vinaigrette dressing with chopped onion and olives.

Eating a whole artichoke
One by one, pull off a leaf and dip the base into the sauce. Scrape the flesh from the base of the leaf with your teeth, then discard the leaf. When you have removed all the large leaves, you will have exposed the fuzzy choke. Scrape this off and discard it. Cut the meaty bottom, or base, of the artichoke for eating with a fork.

5 ▲ To cook artichoke bottoms:
Boil gently in salted water to cover for 15–20 minutes or until tender.

CHOPPING VEGETABLES

In countless recipes, vegetables and other ingredients are required to be chopped to varying degrees of fineness. For most chopping, a large chef's knife should be used (be sure it is sharp). You can also use a food processor, but take care not to over-process the vegetables to a pulp.

Cheese and Herb Dip

Combine 8 oz (225 g) each full-fat soft cheese and cottage cheese in a food processor or blender and blend until smooth. Turn into a bowl and stir in 2 tablespoons chopped fresh dill and ¾ oz (25 g) chopped chives. Season to taste with salt and pepper. If the dip is too thick, stir in a few spoonfuls of cream or milk. Cover and chill for at least 1 hour before serving, with crudités, savoury biscuits and crisps for dipping. *Makes about 1 lb (450 g).*

Peeling whole garlic

If you want to peel garlic and keep the clove whole, drop it into boiling water, count to 30, then drain and rinse with cold water. The skin will slip off easily.

1 ▲ To chop an onion: Peel it, leaving on the root end to hold the onion together. Cut it in half, straight through the root.

3 ▲ Make vertical lengthways cuts in the onion half, again not cutting the root. Then, cut across the onion to chop it, guiding the side of the knife with your knuckles. Discard the root.

5 ▲ Crush the peeled clove again with the knife to flatten it, then begin to chop it. When it is coarsely chopped, continue chopping and crushing it until it is almost a paste. Hold the tip of the knife on the board and raise and lower the knife handle with your other hand, moving the blade back and forth over the garlic.

2 ▲ Put one half flat on the work surface and hold the onion steady at the root end. With a chef's knife, make horizontal cuts in the onion half, to the root but without cutting all the way through it.

4 ▲ To chop garlic finely: Set a chef's knife flat on top of the clove and bang it gently with the side of your fist to crush the garlic slightly and loosen the peel. Remove the peel.

6 ▲ To chop fresh herbs: Hold the leaves or sprigs together in a bunch and chop coarsely, then continue chopping as for garlic (without crushing). You can also use this method of fine chopping for vegetables and fresh root ginger.

CUBING AND DICING VEGETABLES

When vegetables play a starring role in a dish, they should be cut into neat shapes such as cubes or dice. This also promotes even cooking. Cubes are generally ½ in (1.5 cm) square, and dice are ⅛–¼ in (3–6 mm) square.

Coarsely chopping vegetables
For coarsely chopped vegetables, follow the steps above, without shaving off curved sides. There is no need to cut uniform slices and strips. Alternatively, you can coarsely chop vegetables in a food processor by pulsing, but take care not to turn the vegetables into a purée (this can happen very quickly with juicy kinds like onions, leeks, celery and peppers).

1 ▲ Peel the vegetable, if instructed. If it is long, like a carrot or celery stalk, cut it across into pieces about 3 in (7.5 cm) long. This will make cubing and dicing easier. For a neat appearance, shave off curved sides so the pieces of vegetable have straight edges. Lay the vegetable flat and cut it lengthways into uniform slices of the required thickness, guiding the side of the knife with your knuckles.

2 ▲ Stack the slices and cut lengthways into uniform strips of the required thickness. Gather the strips together and cut across the strips into cubes or dice.

Sautéed Potatoes

SERVES 4

1½ lb (700 g) boiling potatoes, peeled and cut into ½ in (1.5 cm) cubes

3 tablespoons vegetable oil

1 small onion, chopped

½–1 oz (15–30 g) butter

salt and pepper

1 ▼ Put the potatoes into a saucepan and cover with cold salted water. Bring to the boil. Simmer for 1 minute, then drain well in a colander. Turn on to a tea towel and pat dry.

2 Heat the oil in a frying pan over moderately high heat. Add the potato cubes and fry for 10 minutes or until they start to turn golden. Stir and turn the potatoes frequently so they brown evenly on all sides.

3 Add the onion and cook, stirring, until the potatoes are just tender. Add the butter. Season with salt and pepper. Cook for a further 2 minutes, stirring constantly. Serve hot.

CUTTING VEGETABLE MATCHSTICKS

These decorative shapes, also called 'julienne', are simple to cut yet look very special. Many other foods can also be cut into matchsticks, for example citrus zest, fresh root ginger, cooked meats, firm cheese and firm fruits such as apple.

For matchsticks, vegetables should be peeled and cut across into pieces about 2 in (5 cm) long. If necessary, cut off curved sides so the vegetable has straight edges.

1 ▲ Lay each piece of vegetable flat and cut it lengthways into slices ⅛ in (3 mm) thick or less, guiding the side of the knife with your knuckles.

2 ▲ Stack the vegetable slices and cut them lengthways into strips about ⅛ in (3 mm) thick or less.

Stir-fried Vegetables

SERVES 4

2½ tablespoons groundnut oil

1½ tablespoons sesame seeds

2 carrots, cut into matchsticks

4 oz (115 g) French beans, blanched for 2 minutes and refreshed

6 fresh shiitake mushrooms, stalks removed and caps thinly sliced

2 thin yellow or green courgettes, cut into matchsticks

1 tablespoon soy sauce

few drops of sesame oil

1 ▲ Heat ½ tablespoon of the oil in a hot wok or frying pan. Add the sesame seeds and cook, stirring and shaking the wok, for 1 minutes or until the seeds are golden. Turn the seeds on to paper towels to drain.

2 ◀ Heat the remaining oil. Add the carrots and stir-fry for 2 minutes. Add the beans and mushrooms. Stir-fry for 1 minute. Add the courgettes and stir-fry for 2–3 minutes or until all the vegetables are just tender. Add the soy sauce and sesame oil with the sesame seeds. Toss well and serve.

SHREDDING VEGETABLE HEADS

Leaf vegetables that form compact heads, such as cabbage and lettuce, are often shredded for cooking or using in a salad. A large sharp knife is essential for good results. Alternatively, you can use the appropriate blade in a food processor.

Keep knives sharp
Vegetable preparation is easy with sharp knives. Hone the edge regularly with a sharpening steel.

1 ▲ Cut the head in half through the core. Cut each half in half. Cut out the core from each quarter. Discard any damaged outside leaves.

2 ▲ Set each quarter flat on a cutting surface and slice across into shreds of the required thickness, guiding the side of the knife with your knuckles.

Hot Coleslaw

SERVES 4–6

1 oz (30 g) butter
1 small firm white cabbage, finely shredded
1 teaspoon caraway seeds
salt and pepper
1 teaspoon sugar
1 tablespoon cider vinegar
¼ pint (150 ml) soured cream

1 ▲ Melt the butter in a large frying pan. Add the cabbage and sprinkle with the caraway seeds. Season with salt and pepper.

2 Cook over low heat, stirring and turning the cabbage, until it is just tender and beginning to turn golden. Remove from the heat.

3 ◀ In a jug, stir together the sugar, vinegar and soured cream. Add to the cabbage, toss well to mix and serve immediately.

SHREDDING VEGETABLE LEAVES

Individual leaves – cabbage, lettuce, spinach and other greens, and herbs such as basil – are cut into neat shreds with this method.

A clean cut
Leaves of very tender greens such as basil and round lettuce can turn black at the cut edge if the cut is not clean. To avoid this, be sure the knife is very sharp, and cut straight down through the roll.

1 ▲ Stack the leaves, 6–8 at a time, and roll up tightly parallel with the central rib. If the leaves are very large, roll them up individually.

2 ▲ With a sharp knife, slice across the roll into shreds of the required thickness, guiding the side of the knife with your knuckles.

Chinese-style Vegetable and Noodle Soup

SERVES 4

2 pints (1.2 litres) vegetable or chicken stock

1 garlic clove, lightly crushed with the flat side of a knife

1 in (2.5 cm) peeled cube of fresh root ginger, cut into fine matchsticks

2 tablespoons soy sauce

1 tablespoon cider vinegar

3 oz (85 g) fresh shiitake or button mushrooms, stalks removed and thinly sliced

2 large spring onions, thinly sliced on the diagonal

1½ oz (45 g) vermicelli or other fine noodles

6 oz (170 g) Chinese leaves, shredded

a few fresh coriander leaves

1 Pour the stock into a saucepan. Add the garlic, root ginger, soy sauce and vinegar. Bring to the boil, then cover the pan and reduce the heat to very low. Leave to simmer gently for 10 minutes. Remove the garlic clove and discard it.

2 ◄ Add the sliced mushrooms and spring onions and bring the soup back to the boil. Simmer for 5 minutes, uncovered, stirring occasionally. Add the noodles and shredded Chinese leaves. Simmer for 3–4 minutes or until the noodles and vegetables are just tender. Stir in the coriander leaves. Simmer for a final 1 minute. Serve the soup hot.

BLANCHING AND REFRESHING

Foods are blanched for several reasons: to loosen skins before skinning (tomatoes, peaches and nuts), to set colour and flavour (for vegetables before freezing), to reduce bitterness (in some vegetables), to firm flesh (sweetbreads), and to remove excess salt (gammon, bacon). Vegetables are often blanched as an initial cooking, when further cooking is to be done by stir-frying or a brief reheating in butter before serving, or if they are to be used in a salad. After blanching, most foods are 'refreshed' to stop them cooking any further.

1 ▲ **To blanch:** Immerse the food in a large pan of boiling water (ideally use a wire basket or sieve so the food can be lifted out easily). Bring the water back to the boil and boil for the time specified, usually 1–2 minutes. Immediately lift the food out of the water (in its basket or with a slotted spoon, or drain in a colander).

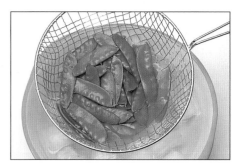

2 ▲ **To refresh:** Quickly immerse the food in iced water or hold under cold running water. If the recipe specifies, leave until it has cooled completely. Drain well.

Broccoli, Cauliflower and Carrot Salad

SERVES 4

1 small cauliflower, cut into florets and stalks trimmed
8 oz (225 g) broccoli, cut into florets and stalks trimmed
2 carrots, thickly sliced
5 tablespoons vegetable oil
3 tablespoons chopped almonds
2 tablespoons red wine vinegar
½ teaspoon ground cumin
salt and pepper

1 Blanch the cauliflower, broccoli and carrots separately in boiling salted water, allowing 10 minutes for the cauliflower and 5 minutes for the broccoli and carrots. Drain well and refresh in iced water.

2 ▶ Heat 1 tablespoon of the oil in a small frying pan. Add the almonds. Fry for about 5 minutes or until golden brown, stirring frequently. Drain on paper towels and leave to cool.

3 Combine the remaining oil with the vinegar, cumin, salt and pepper in a large bowl. Whisk well together. Add the vegetables and toss to coat with the dressing. Scatter the almonds on top. Serve at room temperature.

SWEATING

Sweating is a common preliminary step in vegetable cooking, particularly for onions and leeks. This process, which is essentially a form of steaming, draws out the juices and develops the vegetable's flavour.

A matter of weight

Be sure the pan you use for sweating has a heavy base that will conduct the heat evenly, so the vegetables don't stick and burn. It is also important that the lid be tight fitting to keep in moisture.

1 ▲ Heat fat (usually butter) in a heavy saucepan or frying pan over low heat. Add the vegetable and stir to coat with the melted fat.

2 ▲ Cover the pan tightly and cook gently until the vegetable is softened but not brown; onions will be translucent. This can take 10–15 minutes or longer. Stir occasionally during the cooking.

Pasta with Courgette and Walnut Sauce

SERVES 4

2½ oz (70 g) butter

1 large Spanish-type onion, halved and thinly sliced

1 lb (450 g) courgettes, very thinly sliced

12 oz (340 g) short pasta shapes such as penne, ziti, rotini or fusilli

2 oz (55 g) walnuts, coarsely chopped

3 tablespoons chopped fresh parsley

2 tablespoons single cream

salt and pepper

freshly grated Parmesan cheese, to serve

1 ▲ Melt the butter in a frying pan. Add the onion, cover and sweat for 5 minutes, then add the courgettes.

2 Stir well, cover again and sweat until the vegetables are very soft, stirring occasionally.

3 Meanwhile, bring a large pot of salted water to the boil. Add the pasta to the boiling water, stir and cook for 10 minutes or until it is just tender to the bite ('al dente'). Check the packet instructions for timing.

4 While the pasta is cooking, add the walnuts, parsley and cream to the courgette mixture and stir well. Season with salt and pepper.

5 Drain the pasta and return it to the pot. Add the courgette sauce and mix well together. Serve immediately, with freshly grated Parmesan to sprinkle on top of each portion.

MASHING AND PURÉEING

The smooth texture of a mashed or puréed vegetable is very appealing, perhaps because it reminds us of nursery food. Vegetables to be finished this way may be first boiled, steamed, sweated or baked.

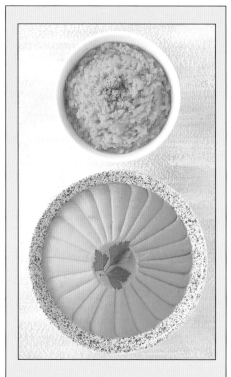

Carrot Purée

Thinly slice 1½ lb (700 g) carrots. Put them in a saucepan, cover with water and add a pinch of salt. Bring to the boil and simmer for 10–15 minutes or until tender. Drain well, then purée in a food processor. Add 1 oz (30 g) butter, 4 tablespoons each milk and orange juice, and ½ teaspoon ground cardamom or a pinch of grated nutmeg. Season with salt and pepper. Reheat, stirring frequently. *Serves 4.*

Sweet Potato Purée

Mash 1½ lb (700 g) boiled or baked sweet potatoes with an electric mixer. Beat in butter, 4 tablespoons orange juice and ¼ teaspoon ground cinnamon.

1 ▲ To mash potatoes and sweet potatoes: Mash warm, freshly cooked potatoes with a potato masher or put them through a potato ricer. With a wooden spoon, beat in butter and milk or cream, and season to taste.

3 ▲ To purée other root vegetables or pumpkin: Put the freshly cooked vegetable in a food processor and process until smooth, scraping down the sides of the container as necessary. Season to taste.

2 ▲ Alternatively, beat the potatoes with an electric mixer. Do not use a food processor for puréeing starchy vegetables such as potatoes because it will make them gluey.

4 ▲ To purée vegetables with fibres or skins (such as asparagus or pulses): Use a vegetable mill, unless you are prepared to push the food-processor purée through a sieve.

5 ◄ To purée greens: Remove the stalks of leaves such as spinach or chard before cooking. Purée in a food processor. Be sure to squeeze out as much water as possible, both before and after puréeing, especially if adding cream.

Mashed Potatoes with Celeriac

SERVES 4

2 lb (900 g) baking potatoes, peeled
12 oz (340 g) celeriac
1½ oz (45 g) butter
¼ pint (150 ml) soured cream
good pinch of grated nutmeg
salt and pepper

1 Cut the potatoes, if large. Bring to the boil in salted water, then simmer for 20 minutes or until very tender.

2 ▲ Meanwhile, peel the celeriac, chop it coarsely and drop immediately into a pan of salted water. (If exposed to the air too long, celeriac will turn brown.) Bring to the boil, then simmer for 15–20 minutes or until very tender.

3 ▲ Drain the potatoes and return them to the saucepan. Return to very low heat for 1–2 minutes to evaporate excess moisture, shaking the pan to turn the potatoes.

4 Mash the potatoes or press through a potato ricer into a warmed bowl. Drain the celeriac and purée in a food processor. Add to the bowl.

> ~ **VARIATION** ~
>
> Substitute 1 medium-size swede for the celeriac. The swede can be mashed at the same time as the potatoes.

5 ▼ Add the butter, soured cream and nutmeg. Season to taste with salt and pepper. Beat well with a wooden spoon or, for a fluffier result, with an electric mixer. Serve hot.

MAKING VEGETABLE STOCK

Vary the ingredients for this fresh-flavoured stock according to what you have to hand. Refrigerate, covered, for up to 5 days; freeze up to 1 month.

MAKES ABOUT 4 PINTS (2.5 LITRES)

2 large onions, coarsely chopped

2 leeks, sliced

3 garlic cloves, crushed with the flat side of a knife

3 carrots, coarsely chopped

4 celery stalks, coarsely chopped

a large strip of lemon zest

a handful of parsley stalks (about 12)

a few fresh thyme sprigs

2 bay leaves

4 pints (2.5 litres) water

1 ▲ Put the vegetables, lemon zest, herbs and water in a stockpot and bring to the boil. Skim off the foam that rises to the surface, frequently at first and then from time to time.

2 ▲ Reduce the heat and simmer, uncovered, for 30 minutes. Strain the stock and leave it to cool.

Vegetable and Herb Chowder

SERVES 4

1 oz (30 g) butter

1 onion, finely chopped

1 leek, thinly sliced

1 celery stalk, diced

1 pepper, yellow or green, seeded and diced

2 tablespoons chopped fresh parsley

1 tablespoon plain flour

2 pints (1.2 litres) vegetable stock

12 oz (340 g) boiling potatoes, peeled and diced

a few fresh thyme sprigs or ½ teaspoon dried thyme

1 bay leaf

4 oz (115 g) young runner beans, thinly sliced on the diagonal

4 fl oz (120 ml) milk

salt and pepper

1 ▲ Melt the butter in a heavy saucepan or flameproof casserole and add the onion, leek, celery, pepper and parsley. Cover and cook over low heat until the vegetables are soft.

2 Add the flour and stir until well blended. Add the stock slowly, stirring to combine. Bring to the boil, stirring frequently.

3 ▼ Add the potatoes, thyme and bay leaf. Simmer, uncovered, for about 10 minutes.

4 Add the beans and simmer for a further 10–15 minutes or until all the vegetables are tender.

5 Stir in the milk. Season with salt and pepper. Heat through. Before serving, discard the thyme stalks and bay leaf. Serve hot.

PREPARING SALAD GREENS

Crisp, fresh green and variegated leaves are very appetizing. Use them as the background for a vegetable, fish, meat or fruit salad or make the leaves the focus.

Lettuce

The four main types are: crisphead, with solid heads of tightly packed, crisp leaves (iceberg); butterhead, with looser heads of soft-textured leaves (round, 'quattro stagioni'); Cos and romaine, with elongated heads of crisp leaves; and looseleaf, with leaves that do not form a compact head ('feuilles de chêne', 'lollo rosso').

Preparation: Discard wilted or damaged leaves. Twist or cut out the central core. Rinse the leaves thoroughly in cold water and soak briefly to draw out any grit trapped in the folds. Drain and blot or spin dry. If the leaves are large, tear into pieces.

Other salad ingredients

To provide contrast in texture and flavour, add brightly coloured and crunchy leaves, such as red cabbage, with plain salad leaves – just a little goes a long way. Cucumber, spring onions and carrot are also appealing in a mixed salad, as are raw or lightly cooked French beans or mange-touts. Nuts or dried fruit are other tasty additions.

Chicory and Endive

These have an appealing bitterness. Paler leaves are more delicate and sweet. 'Frisée' or curly endive has fine, frilly green leaves with a coarse texture. Escarole has broader, fleshier leaves with jagged edges and a firm texture. The slim leaves of chicory are white with greenish tips. Radicchio is red Italian chicory.

Preparation: Core the base of chicory. Discard wilted or damaged leaves. Rinse thoroughly and dry the leaves. If large, cut into pieces.

Lamb's Lettuce

Also known as corn salad or 'mâche', this salad green has a pleasantly firm, chewy texture and mild, slightly nutty flavour. The leaves are small and may be spoon-shaped or round.

Preparation: Remove any wilted or damaged leaves. Trim roots. Rinse well as the leaves can be sandy.

Rocket

In a salad of mixed greens, the pungent peppery, nutty taste of rocket is unmistakable and welcome. This member of the mustard family, also called 'roquette' and 'arugula', has deep green leaves with curved edges and a texture somewhat like spinach.

Preparation: Discard any wilted or damaged leaves. Pull off roots. Rinse thoroughly and dry on paper towels – it's best not to use a salad spinner, which could bruise the tender leaves.

Watercress

Another member of the mustard family, the round dark green leaves have a wonderful peppery flavour that enlivens any salad, and the fresh attractive appearance of watercress makes it a popular garnish.

Preparation: Discard wilted or damaged leaves and snap off thick stalks. Rinse well and spin dry.

Wilted Spinach and Bacon Salad

SERVES 6

1 lb (450 g) fresh young spinach leaves
8 oz (225 g) streaky bacon rashers
1½ tablespoons vegetable oil
4 tablespoons red wine vinegar
4 tablespoons water
4 teaspoons caster sugar
1 teaspoon dry mustard
salt and pepper
8 spring onions, thinly sliced
6 radishes, thinly sliced
2 hard-boiled eggs, coarsely grated

1 ▲ Pull any coarse stalks from the spinach leaves and rinse well. Put the leaves in a large salad bowl.

2 ▲ Fry the bacon rashers in the oil until crisp and brown. Remove with tongs and drain on paper towels. Chop the bacon and set aside.

3 ▲ Combine the vinegar, water, sugar, mustard, salt and pepper in a bowl and stir until smoothly blended. Add to the fat in the frying pan. Bring the dressing to the boil, stirring.

4 ▼ Pour the hot dressing over the spinach leaves. Sprinkle on the bacon, spring onions, radishes and eggs and toss. Serve immediately.

RINSING AND CRISPING SALAD GREENS

It is vital that all salad leaves be thoroughly rinsed with cold water to remove any grit or insects, as well as residues of sprays. Just as important is to dry the salad leaves well so that the dressing will not be diluted.

Lettuce with Blue Cheese Dressing
For each serving, use 1 small head round lettuce or Little Gem lettuce, washed and spun or blotted dry. Top with 3–4 tablespoons blue cheese dressing (page 180). Garnish with cherry tomatoes and chives, if wished.

Salad success
• Dress salad greens just before serving, otherwise the leaves will wilt and become unpleasantly soggy.
• Match the dressing to the greens: sharp leaves need hearty flavours, but the same dressing used on delicate greens would overpower them.
• Be imaginative with salad additions. A few blanched French beans, for instance, can lift a plain salad, especially with a sprinkling of fresh herbs.

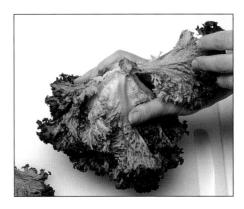

1 ▲ Discard any wilted, discoloured or damaged leaves. For spinach and similar greens, pull off the stalks. Pull off roots from lamb's lettuce.

3 ▲ Put the leaves in a sink or large basin of cold water and swirl them round to wash off any dirt or insects. Leave to settle for 1–2 minutes.

5 ▲ Alternatively, put the washed leaves in a salad spinner to spin off the water. (Do not use a salad spinner for leaves that bruise easily.)

2 ▲ For leaves in compact or loose heads, pull them individually from the core or stalk.

4 ▲ Lift the leaves out of the water on to a tea towel and pat dry gently with paper towels or another tea towel.

6 ▲ Wrap the leaves loosely in a clean tea towel or paper towels and put in a large plastic bag. Refrigerate for about 1 hour. When assembling the salad, tear any large leaves into smaller pieces.

Green Salad with Oranges and Avocado

SERVES 4

1 round lettuce
1 small bunch of watercress
a few leaves of frisée
1 small bunch of rocket
1 red onion, thinly sliced into rings
2 seedless oranges, peeled and segmented (page 189)
1 ripe avocado, peeled, stoned and cubed
2 oz (55 g) walnut pieces, toasted

FOR THE DRESSING

6 tablespoons olive oil
1 tablespoon walnut oil
3 tablespoons lemon juice
2 tablespoons orange juice
1 teaspoon grated orange zest
1 teaspoon Dijon mustard
pinch of caster sugar
salt and pepper

1 ▲ Combine all the dressing ingredients in a bowl or screwtop jar. Whisk or shake well together.

~ **VARIATION** ~

For Green Salad with Tuna and Peppers, omit oranges and walnuts. Add 1 × 7 oz (200 g) can drained, flaked tuna and 1 roasted red pepper, peeled and sliced.

2 ▼ Put the rinsed and crisped salad greens in a bowl and add the onion, orange segments and avocado.

3 ▲ Add the dressing and toss the salad to combine well.

4 Scatter the walnuts on top and serve immediately.

PREPARING PULSES

Pulses – dried beans, peas and lentils – are a high-protein food. They keep well, making them a useful storecupboard staple. Most pulses require the same initial preparation.

> **An extra safeguard**
> To remove potentially harmful toxins, boil most pulses uncovered for 10 minutes before reducing the heat to a simmer for the rest of the cooking time.

1 ▲ First rinse the pulses and pick out any small stones.

2 ▲ **To soak dried beans and peas**: Put them in a bowl, cover with plenty of cold water and soak for at least 4 hours. (Lentils do not need soaking.)

3 ▲ A quick alternative method is to put the dried beans or peas in a large pan of water, bring to the boil and boil for 2 minutes, then leave them to soak for 1 hour.

4 ▲ In either case, drain the pulses and rinse them well. They are now ready for cooking according to the recipe.

5 ▲ **To cook**: Put the soaked and drained beans or peas or the lentils in a pan of fresh cold water (3 parts water to 1 part pulses) and bring to the boil. Then cover the pan, reduce the heat and simmer until tender.

A LOOK AT PULSES

Dried beans, peas and lentils range widely in colour, shape and size. Some of the most commonly available include: **haricot beans**, large to medium-sized, kidney-shaped, white; **kidney beans**, medium-sized, kidney-shaped, smooth, shiny, may be reddish-brown, black or white (when normally called cannellini beans); **flageolet**, small, oval, pale green; **black beans** (also called turtle beans), small, oval, smooth, shiny, jet-black; **borlotti beans**, medium-sized, kidney-shaped, creamy brown with red streaks; **pinto beans**, small, oval,

smooth, beige with brown specks; **black-eye beans**, small, oval, smooth, creamy colour, with small cream-centred black dot on one side; **butter beans**, large, oval/round, flattish, off-white; **chickpeas**, medium-sized, round, not smooth, beige-tan in colour; **peas**, small, round or split in half, may be grey-green or yellow; **lentils**, tiny, disc-shaped, smooth, may be brownish-green, reddish-orange or yellow.

Pulses are easy to prepare, and they can be used in many ways – in casseroles, soups, stews and salads.

The minimum soaking time for most dried pulses is 4 hours, but they can be soaked overnight if that is more convenient. Lentils do not need soaking, and it is not essential for split peas, although they may be soaked to speed cooking.

Most pulses require about 1½–2 hours' cooking time. This includes white haricot beans, borlotti beans, pinto beans, butter beans, kidney beans and chickpeas. Black-eye beans, split peas and flageolet beans require less time, about 1–1¼ hours. Lentils cook in less than 30 minutes.

Split Pea Soup

SERVES 4–6

1 oz (30 g) butter
1 large onion, chopped
1 large celery stalk with leaves, chopped
2 carrots, chopped
1 smoked gammon knuckle, 1 lb (450 g)
3½ pints (2 litres) water
12 oz (340 g) split peas
2 tablespoons chopped fresh parsley, plus more to garnish
½ teaspoon dried thyme
1 bay leaf
about 2 tablespoons lemon juice
salt and pepper

1 ▲ Melt the butter in a large heavy-based saucepan. Add the onion, celery and carrots and cook until soft, stirring occasionally.

2 ▲ Add the remaining ingredients. Bring to the boil, cover and simmer gently for 2 hours or until the peas are very tender.

3 ▼ Remove the gammon knuckle. Leave it to cool slightly, then remove the skin and cut the meat from the bones. Discard skin and bones; cut the meat into chunks.

4 ▲ Return the chunks of gammon to the soup. Discard the bay leaf. Taste and adjust the seasoning with more lemon juice, salt and pepper.

5 Serve hot, sprinkled with parsley.

Tuna and Black-eye Bean Salad

SERVES 4

5 oz (145 g) dried black-eye beans

¼ pint (150 ml) garlic vinaigrette (page 182)

1 small red onion, chopped

3 tablespoons chopped fresh parsley

1 × 7 oz (200 g) can tuna, drained

cherry tomatoes, to garnish

2 ▲ Pour the vinaigrette dressing over the beans and mix well.

4 ▲ Add the tuna and stir gently into the salad.

5 Garnish with halved cherry tomatoes and serve at cool room temperature.

1 ▲ Soak the black-eye beans for at least 4 hours. Drain, then cook in fresh water until tender. Drain well and cool slightly.

3 ▲ Add the onion and parsley and stir to combine.

~ **VARIATION** ~

For Italian Bean Salad, use cannellini beans (canned, if liked, for quicker preparation) instead of black-eye beans.

Mexican Chickpea Dip

SERVES 6–8

14 oz (400 g) dried chickpeas, soaked overnight, cooked and drained

4 tablespoons fromage frais

3 tablespoons lemon juice

2 tablespoons olive oil

1–2 garlic cloves, finely chopped

1–2 tablespoons tequila (optional)

4–5 tablespoons seeded and chopped green chillies (fresh or canned)

salt

¾ oz (25 g) pine nuts, to garnish

hot tortilla or corn chips, to serve

1 Combine the chickpeas, fromage frais, lemon juice, oil, garlic and tequila in a blender or food processor. Blend until smooth.

2 ▲ Turn into a bowl and stir in the chillies. Season with salt. Cover and chill for at least 1 hour.

3 ▲ Toast the pine nuts in a dry frying pan over moderate heat. Serve the dip at room temperature, with the pine nuts sprinkled over the surface or stirred in, with warmed tortilla or corn chips.

Mexican Chickpea Dip (left), Tuna and Black-eye Bean Salad

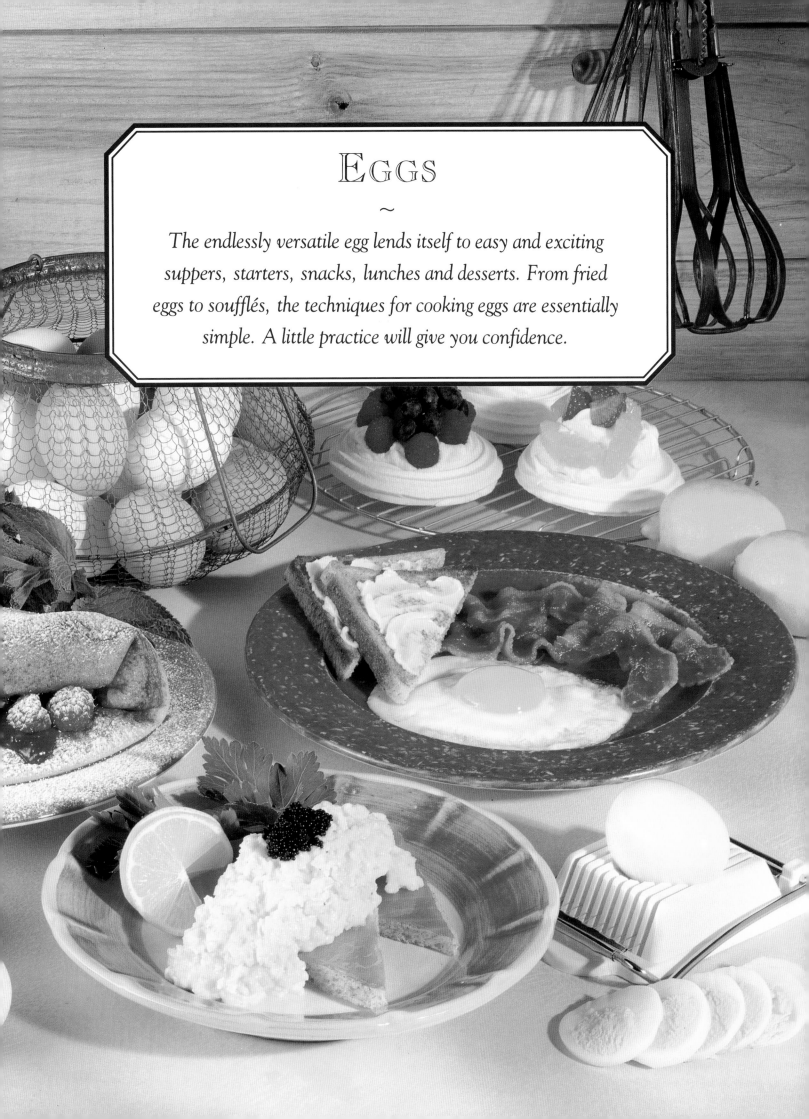

EGGS

~

The endlessly versatile egg lends itself to easy and exciting suppers, starters, snacks, lunches and desserts. From fried eggs to soufflés, the techniques for cooking eggs are essentially simple. A little practice will give you confidence.

BOILING EGGS

The derisive expression, 'can't boil an egg', indicates the importance of this basic cooking skill, although, to be accurate, eggs are simmered rather than boiled.

For many people, a boiled egg with toast is an everyday breakfast. But the soft-boiled egg and its cousin the coddled egg have many delicious applications. If they are to be peeled for serving, cook them for the longest time suggested below. The salt in the cooking water aids in peeling.

Hard-boiled eggs make classic salads and sandwich fillings, as well as cold first course and buffet dishes and hot main dishes.

1 ▲ **To hard-boil eggs**: Bring a pan of well-salted water to the boil. Using a slotted spoon, lower each egg into the water. Reduce the heat so the water is just simmering. Cook for 10 minutes. Immediately plunge the eggs into a bowl of iced water to cool.

2 ▲ When the eggs are cool enough to handle, peel them. If they are not to be used immediately, keep the peeled eggs in a bowl of cold salted water. Or store the eggs, still in the shell, in the refrigerator; they will keep for up to 1 week.

Egg, Potato and Bean Salad
Bring a pot of salted water to the boil. Add 1 lb (450 g) small un-peeled new potatoes. Bring back to the boil and simmer for 10 minutes. Add 8 oz (225 g) French beans and simmer for 4–5 minutes or until the potatoes and beans are just tender. Drain well in a colander and refresh under cold running water. Turn the vegetables into a large bowl. Sprinkle 4 tablespoons olive oil and 2 tablespoons balsamic vinegar over them. Season with salt and pepper and toss well. Scatter 2 grated hard-boiled eggs and 3 tablespoons coarsely shredded mixed fresh mint and basil over the top. Serve warm or at room temperature. *Serves 4–6.*

3 ▲ **To coddle eggs**: Lower them into a pan of boiling salted water. Cover the pan and remove it from the heat. Leave for 6–8 minutes or until the eggs are done to your taste. Lift out each egg, place in an egg cup and cut off the top of the shell for serving. Or, to peel, plunge the eggs into a bowl of cold water. When they are cool enough to handle, peel carefully. To reheat for serving, immerse in a bowl of hot water for 1–2 minutes.

Hard-boiled egg tips
● Always cool hard-boiled eggs in iced water. The abrupt temperature change helps prevent a grey layer from forming round the yolk.
● To peel hard-boiled eggs, tap them gently on a hard surface to crack the shell. Carefully peel under cold running water.

4 ▲ **To soft-boil eggs**: Bring a pan of well-salted water to the boil. Using a slotted spoon, lower each egg into the water. Reduce the heat so the water just simmers. Cook for 3–5 minutes or until the eggs are done to your taste (depending on how firm you like the white; the yolk will be runny).

Ideas for soft-boiled and coddled eggs
● For *Caviar-crowned Eggs*: Cut the top ¾ in (2 cm) from each egg, in its shell. Put a spoonful of soured cream and caviar on top.
● For *Smoked Salmon Eggs*: Prepare as above and top each with a spoonful each of soured cream and diced smoked salmon.
● Put a hot peeled egg in the centre of a bowl of cream of spinach or watercress soup.

Caesar Salad

6 fl oz (180 ml) salad oil, preferably olive oil

3 oz (85 g) French or Italian bread, cut into 1 in (2.5 cm) cubes

1 large garlic clove, crushed with the flat side of a knife

2 small heads of Cos lettuce, separated into leaves, rinsed and crisped

salt and pepper

2 eggs, soft-boiled for 1 minute

5 tablespoons lemon juice

2½ oz (75 g) Parmesan cheese, freshly grated

6 anchovy fillets, drained and finely chopped (optional)

Ideas for hard-boiled eggs

• For *Devilled Eggs*: Halve the eggs lengthways and scoop out the yolks. Mash the yolks with a fork and mix with enough mayonnaise to make a creamy consistency. Season with Dijon mustard, salt and pepper. Spoon or pipe the yolk mixture into the hollows in the egg white halves and sprinkle the tops with a little paprika or cayenne pepper.

• For *Herb-stuffed Eggs*: Add chopped fresh herbs such as parsley, tarragon and chives to the egg yolk and mayonnaise mixture; omit the mustard.

• For *Egg Mayonnaise*: Chop eggs. Mix with chopped spring onions or red onion to taste and a little chopped parsley. Bind with mayonnaise. Season with mustard.

• For *Eggs in Aspic*: Put cooled peeled eggs in individual ramekins and surround with chopped herbs in aspic. Refrigerate to set.

• For *Eggs in Cream Sauce*: Add quartered eggs to hot mushroom or mustard sauce (page 170). Add 6 oz (170 g) slow-cooked onions (page 114) and heat through.

1 ▼ Heat 4 tablespoons of the oil in a large frying pan. Add the bread cubes and garlic. Fry, stirring and turning constantly, until the cubes are golden brown all over. Drain on paper towels. Discard the garlic.

2 Tear large lettuce leaves into smaller pieces. Put all the lettuce into a large salad bowl.

3 ▲ Add the remaining oil and season with salt and pepper. Toss the leaves to coat well.

4 Break the eggs on top. Sprinkle with the lemon juice. Toss well again.

5 Add the cheese and anchovies, if using. Toss gently to mix.

6 Scatter the fried bread cubes on top and serve immediately.

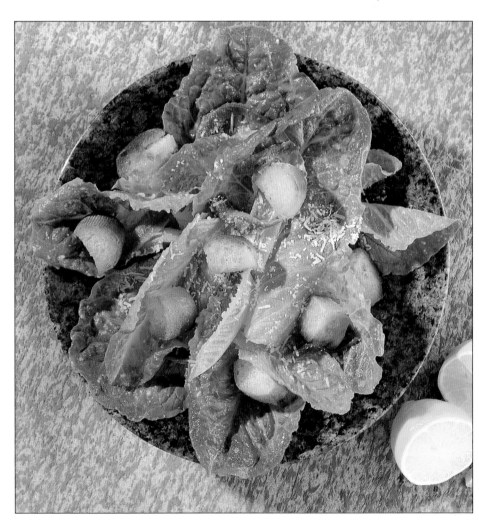

SCRAMBLING EGGS

Tender, creamy scrambled eggs are perfect for breakfast or brunch, but you can also add flavourings for a more unusual snack or supper dish.

Ideas for scrambled eggs
- Add chopped fresh herbs (chives, tarragon) to the eggs.
- Cook diced vegetables (onions, mushrooms, peppers) or ham in butter before adding the eggs.
- Stir in a little grated cheese or bits of full-fat soft cheese just before the eggs are ready.
- Fold peeled cooked prawns into scrambled eggs.

1 ▲ Put the eggs in a bowl and add a little salt and pepper. Beat the eggs with a fork until they are well blended. Melt butter in a frying pan over moderately low heat (it should cover the bottom of the pan generously). Pour in the beaten eggs.

2 ▲ Cook, scraping up and turning the eggs over, for 3–5 minutes or until they are softly set and still moist. The eggs will continue to cook after being removed from the heat, so undercook them slightly even if you prefer a firmer end result.

Scrambled Eggs with Smoked Salmon

SERVES 4 AS A SNACK

6 eggs
salt and pepper
2 oz (55 g) butter
2 tablespoons whipping cream
4 tablespoons mayonnaise
4 slices of pumpernickel or wholemeal bread, crusts trimmed
4 oz (115 g) thinly sliced smoked salmon
lumpfish or salmon caviar, to garnish

1 ▲ Season the eggs with salt and pepper. Scramble them using half of the butter. Mix in the cream just before they have finished cooking.

2 Remove from the heat and mix in the mayonnaise. Leave to cool.

3 Spread the slices of bread with the remaining butter. Cover with smoked salmon, trimming it to fit. Cut in half.

4 Divide the scrambled eggs among the plates, spreading it neatly on the smoked salmon. Top each serving with a heaped tablespoon of caviar.

FRYING EGGS

Fried eggs are a natural partner for bacon, sausages, fried tomatoes and mushrooms, and even black pudding in that great British institution – the 'cooked breakfast'.

1 Heat butter, bacon fat or oil (to generously cover the bottom) in a frying pan over moderate heat. When the fat is sizzling, break each egg and slip it into the pan.

2 ◀ Fry for 1–1½ minutes or until the egg white is just set and opaque or more firm, according to your taste. The yolk will still be runny and the base of the egg will be golden brown and crisp. The egg is ready to serve now, 'sunny side up'. Or gently turn the fried egg over with a fish slice, taking care not to break the yolk. Cook for a further 10–15 seconds or until the other side is just browned.

Fried Eggs and Sausage on Tortillas

SERVES 4

8 oz (225 g) minced pork

½ small onion, finely chopped

1 teaspoon chilli powder (or to taste)

½ teaspoon ground cumin

½ teaspoon dried oregano

1 tablespoon vinegar

1 garlic clove, finely chopped

salt and pepper

oil, for frying

4 large fresh or canned corn tortillas

4 eggs

2 oz (55 g) butter or bacon fat

Mexican hot sauce or salsa, to serve

1 ▲ Put the pork in a bowl and add the onion, spices, oregano, vinegar, garlic, salt and pepper. Mix well, cover and refrigerate overnight.

2 ▼ Cook the pork mixture in a large frying pan until it is browned and crumbly, stirring occasionally.

3 Meanwhile, heat 1 in (2.5 cm) oil in a wide pan to 365°F (180°C). Fry the tortillas until they are crisp and golden brown, keeping them flat. Drain on paper towels and put on a baking sheet. Keep warm in the oven.

4 Fry the eggs in the butter or bacon fat (or use oil for frying if you prefer).

5 Put a tortilla on each plate. Using a slotted spoon, divide the pork mixture among the tortillas. Top each serving with a fried egg. Serve with hot sauce or salsa.

POACHING EGGS

The perfect poached egg has a neat oval shape, a tender white and a soft yolk. It is unbeatable on a slice of hot buttered toast, or it can be partnered with vegetables (artichoke hearts, asparagus), seafood (crab, smoked salmon) or meat (ham, bacon, steak) and dressed with a rich sauce. Use the freshest eggs possible because they will be the easiest to poach.

1 First, bring a large deep pan of water to the boil.

2 ▲ Break each egg and slip it gently into the water. Reduce the heat to low so the water just simmers. Poach for 3–4 minutes or until the eggs are done.

3 ▲ With a slotted spoon, lift out each egg and press it gently; the white should feel just firm but the yolk should still be soft.

4 ◀ If there are any strings of cooked egg white, trim them off with a knife or kitchen scissors. Drain briefly on paper towels. Serve immediately, if wished. Or warm the eggs in a bowl of hot water for serving. If the eggs will be served cold, immerse them in a bowl of iced water until ready to serve. Drain and blot dry gently before serving.

> **The clotting factor**
> If your eggs are not really fresh, adding white wine vinegar to the poaching water will help the egg white to coagulate, although it will slightly flavour the egg. Use 2 tablespoons vinegar to 2 pints (1 litre) of water.

Poached Eggs Florentine

SERVES 4

1½ lb (700 g) spinach leaves, shredded
1 oz (30 g) butter
3–4 tablespoons whipping cream
good pinch of grated nutmeg
salt and pepper
4 eggs
½ pint (300 ml) cheese sauce made with Gruyère cheese (page 170)
1 oz (30 g) Gruyère cheese, grated

1 Preheat the grill.

2 Put the spinach in a large pan with the butter. Cover and cook until the leaves are wilted. Uncover and boil to evaporate the excess liquid.

3 ▲ Mix in the cream, nutmeg and seasoning. Poach the eggs.

4 Divide the spinach among 4 individual shallow gratin dishes or a large gratin dish. Spread it evenly and make hollows for the eggs. Set a poached egg in each hollow.

5 ▼ Spoon over cheese sauce to coat the eggs lightly. Sprinkle the grated cheese evenly over the top. Grill for 2–3 minutes or until the cheese has melted and is lightly browned. Serve immediately.

BAKING EGGS

Baking is one of the simplest ways to cook eggs, yet it produces elegant results. The eggs can be baked individually, in buttered pots such as ramekins or small shallow dishes, or several can be baked in a large dish, on a bed of vegetables, sauce, etc.

Ideas for baked eggs

- Coat buttered ramekins with freshly grated Parmesan cheese. Dot eggs with butter and sprinkle each egg very lightly with Parmesan before baking.
- Put a little diced cooked ham, or a few sautéed sliced mushrooms or crisp garlic-flavoured croutons in the bottom of each buttered ramekin before breaking in the egg.
- Bake eggs on a bed of creamed spinach, mashed potato or other root vegetables, puréed broccoli or peas.
- Bake eggs on tomato sauce and roasted vegetables (page 173).
- Bake eggs in hollows made in a cooked stuffing, such as sausage stuffing for chicken (page 13) or smoked ham and almond stuffing for turkey (page 27).
- Bake potatoes, then cut off a lengthways slice from one side. Scoop out the flesh, leaving a shell ⅛–¼ in (3–5 mm) thick. Mash the potato with butter, milk, salt and pepper. Spoon it back into the potato shells and press down firmly. Make a hollow in the top of the mashed potato in each shell and break in an egg. Dribble a little melted butter over the egg. Bake at 400°F/200°C/ Gas 6 for 5–7 minutes to set the egg white.

1 ▲ To bake in individual ramekins: Butter the dishes and sprinkle them with salt and pepper. Break an egg into each, taking care not to pierce the yolk.

3 ▲ Set the dishes in a baking tin. Add enough water to come halfway up the sides of the dishes. Bring to a simmer on top of the stove. Transfer to a 400°F/200°C/Gas 6 oven. Bake for 5–7 minutes or until the whites are just set and the yolks still soft.

2 ▲ Dot the top of each egg with a few small pieces of butter, or add 1 tablespoon of whipping cream to each ramekin.

4 ▲ To bake on a bed: Spread a hot savoury mixture in a buttered shallow baking dish or in individual ramekins or gratin dishes. Make hollows in the mixture with the back of a spoon. Break an egg into each hollow.

5 ◄ According to recipe instructions, dot the eggs with butter, sprinkle with cheese, drizzle with cream, etc. These toppings help to prevent the eggs from drying out during cooking. Bake until the whites are just set and the yolks are still soft.

Eggs Baked in Ham and Potato Hash

SERVES 6

2 oz (55 g) butter

1 large onion, chopped

12 oz (340 g) cooked ham, diced

1 lb (450 g) cooked potatoes, diced

4 oz (115 g) Cheddar cheese, grated

2 tablespoons tomato ketchup

1–2 tablespoons Worcestershire sauce

salt and pepper

6 eggs

few drops of Tabasco sauce

chopped fresh parsley, to garnish

1 Preheat a 325°F/170°C/Gas 3 oven.

2 Melt half of the butter in a frying pan. Cook the onion until soft, stirring occasionally.

3 ▲ Turn the onion into a bowl. Add the ham, potatoes, cheese, ketchup and Worcestershire sauce. Season with salt and pepper. Stir the mixture to combine.

4 ▲ Spread the hash in a buttered baking dish in a layer about 1 in (2.5 cm) deep. Bake for 10 minutes.

5 ▼ Make 6 hollows in the hash. Slip an egg into each.

6 Melt the remaining butter in a small pan. Season with Tabasco sauce to taste.

7 ▲ Dribble the seasoned butter over the eggs and hash.

8 Bake for 15–20 minutes or until the eggs are set and cooked to your taste. Serve immediately, in the dish, garnished with parsley.

MAKING A ROLLED OMELETTE

The versatile rolled or folded omelette can be served plain or filled. There are also flat omelettes and soufflé omelettes. At its simplest, an omelette is made with 2 or 3 eggs, 1–2 teaspoons water, salt and pepper.

1 ▲ Break the eggs into a bowl and add the water and some salt and pepper. Beat with a fork until just blended but not frothy.

2 ▲ In an 8 in (20 cm) omelette pan, melt a knob of butter over moderately high heat. Tilt and rotate the pan so the bottom and sides are thoroughly coated with butter.

Ideas for omelettes
* Add 1 tablespoon chopped fresh herbs (a mixture of parsley, chives and tarragon, for example) to the beaten eggs.
* Scatter 2–3 tablespoons grated cheese (Gruyère, Cheddar) over the omelette before folding it.
* Sauté skinned, seeded and chopped tomatoes in butter for 1–2 minutes. Season with salt and pepper and stir in a little chopped fresh basil. Use to fill the omelette.
* Fill the omelette with strips of cooked ham or with Parma ham, roasted vegetables (page 173), sautéed sliced mushrooms, sautéed potatoes (page 126), buttered asparagus tips or slow-cooked onions (page 114).
* Warm left-over pasta (buttered or in sauce); if the shape is long, such as spaghetti, cut it into short pieces. If using buttered pasta, add strips of canned pimiento, sliced black olives, capers etc. Use to fill the omelette, fold and sprinkle with grated Parmesan.

3 ▲ When the butter is foaming and just beginning to turn golden, pour in the egg mixture. Tilt and rotate the pan to spread the eggs in an even layer over the bottom.

4 ▲ Cook for 5–10 seconds or until the omelette starts to set on the base. With a palette knife, lift the cooked base and tilt the pan so the uncooked egg mixture runs underneath on to the hot pan. Continue cooking in this way until most of the omelette is set but the top is still moist and creamy.

The right pan
Although you can use a frying pan, a special omelette pan, with its curved edge, will make folding and turning out the omelette so much easier.

5 ▲ With the palette knife, loosen the edge of the omelette on one side and tilt the pan so that a third of the omelette folds over on to itself.

6 ▲ Continue loosening the omelette from its folded edge, holding the pan over a warmed plate. As the omelette slides out on to the plate, tilt the pan so the omelette folds over again on itself into thirds, using the edge of the pan to guide it.

Omelette Foo Yung

1 tablespoon groundnut or vegetable oil

2–3 spring onions, chopped

1 celery stalk, diced

2 teaspoons finely chopped fresh ginger

1 garlic clove, finely chopped

4 oz (115 g) peeled cooked prawns

2 oz (55 g) white crabmeat

1 oz (30 g) cooked ham, diced

1½ tablespoons chopped fresh coriander

1–2 tablespoons soy sauce, plus more to serve

8 or 12 eggs

salt and pepper

2–3 oz (55–85 g) butter

1 Heat the oil in a frying pan over moderate heat. Add the spring onions, celery, ginger and garlic and cook for 1 minute, stirring frequently.

2 ▼ Add the prawns, crabmeat and ham. Sprinkle with the coriander and soy sauce. Reduce the heat to low and leave the mixture to heat through, stirring occasionally.

3 ▲ Meanwhile, make 4 omelettes, using 2 or 3 eggs for each. Before folding each omelette, spoon one-quarter of the prawn and crab filling over the centre. Serve hot, with more soy sauce for sprinkling.

MAKING A FLAT OMELETTE

Called a 'frittata' in Italy and a 'tortilla' in Spain, a flat omelette is thicker than a folded omelette. It is usually cut into wedges for serving hot, warm or cold. Use a pan with a heatproof handle, or wrap the handle well in foil.

Fillings used for folded omelettes can be used in flat ones too. The quantities here will make a flat omelette to serve 4 people.

1 ▲ Break 8 eggs into a bowl and season with salt and pepper. Beat lightly with a fork. Meanwhile, preheat the grill.

2 ▲ In a 9–10 in (23–25 cm) frying pan with a heatproof handle, melt ½ oz (15 g) butter with 1 tablespoon oil over moderate heat. Tilt and rotate the pan to coat the bottom and sides.

Flat omelette fillings

• Prepare ½ quantity sautéed potatoes (page 126). Spread out the cooked potatoes in the frying pan. Pour the egg mixture over the potatoes. Continue cooking the flat omelette as described.

• Prepare roasted vegetables (page 173). Transfer to the frying pan and spread them out before pouring in the egg mixture. Cook the flat omelette as described.

• Roast and peel 2 peppers (page 123) and cut into thin strips. Cook in oil and butter in a frying pan over moderate heat with 1 chopped onion until very soft. Stir in some thawed frozen peas. Spread out the vegetables in the pan. Pour in the egg mixture and continue cooking as described.

---

3 ▲ When the fat is sizzling and just beginning to turn golden, pour in the egg mixture. Tilt and rotate the pan to spread the eggs in an even layer over the bottom. Reduce the heat to low. (If the omelette has other ingredients add them now, or spread in the pan before pouring in the egg mixture.)

4 ▲ Cook for 5–10 seconds or until the omelette starts to set on the base. With a palette knife, lift the cooked base and tilt the pan so the uncooked egg mixture runs underneath on to the hot pan. Continue cooking in this way until most of the omelette is set but the top is still moist and creamy.

Flat Omelette with Ham and Cheese
For each 8-egg omelette, scatter 4 oz (115 g) strips of cooked ham, or 2 oz (55 g) Parma ham, and 3–4 tablespoons finely chopped spring onion or red onion in the pan after pouring in the beaten egg mixture. Before transferring the omelette to the grill, sprinkle 3–4 tablespoons of freshly grated Parmesan cheese or 1½–2 oz (45–55 g) grated Cheddar or Gruyère cheese evenly over the top. Serve hot or warm. *Serves 4.*

5 ▲ Transfer the pan to the grill, setting it about 4 in (10 cm) from the heat. Cook for 3–4 minutes or until the top is lightly browned and just set.

MAKING A SOUFFLÉ OMELETTE

This cross between a flat omelette and a soufflé starts cooking on top of the stove and finishes in the oven. Fillings are normally sweet.

Soufflé omelette fillings
- Mix lightly crushed berries (raspberries, strawberries, blackberries etc) with a dash of Cognac, orange liqueur or kirsch. Use to fill the omelette. Drizzle warmed honey over the top and serve with sweetened whipped cream (page 160).
- Add 2 tablespoons orange liqueur or brandy to the egg yolks with the sugar. Fill the omelette with sweet orange segments. Sprinkle the folded omelette with icing sugar and pour on 3 tablespoons warmed orange liqueur or brandy. Set alight, and serve the omelette flaming.

Soufflé Omelette with Peaches
For each 4-egg omelette, spread 2 tablespoons warmed apricot, raspberry or strawberry jam over the cooked omelette and top with a peeled and thinly sliced ripe peach. After folding, sprinkle with icing sugar. Decorate with berries, if liked. *Serves 2.*

1 ▲ Separate 4 eggs. To the yolks, add 6 tablespoons caster sugar and beat until thick and pale. Preheat a 350°F/180°C/Gas 4 oven.

3 ▲ With a rubber spatula, fold the egg whites into the yolk mixture as lightly as possible, cutting down to the bottom of the bowl and turning the mixture over, while rotating the bowl at the same time.

5 ▲ Cook, without stirring, for 5 minutes or until the omelette is puffy and set round the edges but still soft in the centre. Transfer the pan to the oven. Bake for 3–5 minutes or until the top is set and lightly browned.

2 ▲ Whisk the egg whites until they hold stiff peaks. (Add a pinch of cream of tartar if not using a copper bowl.)

4 ▲ Heat a 9–10 in (23–25 cm) frying pan with an ovenproof handle over moderately high heat. Melt enough butter in the pan to cover the bottom generously. Tilt the pan to coat the bottom and sides. Pour in the egg mixture. Reduce the heat to low.

6 ▲ Spread a filling over the centre. Fold the omelette in half. Turn it on to a warmed plate and finish according to the recipe. Serve immediately.

MAKING A SOUFFLÉ

Despite their reputation as tricky, soufflés are not difficult to make. The base for a soufflé is simply a thick sauce (sweet or savoury) or a purée. Into this, stiffly whisked egg whites are folded, and the whole is baked until it has risen and is lightly set.

Proper preparation of the dish, enabling the soufflé to 'climb' up the sides, encourages rising. Generously butter or oil the dish, including the top edge. If the recipe specifies, coat the bottom and sides with a thin layer of fine crumbs, caster sugar, etc.

1 ▲ Separate the eggs, taking care that there is no trace of egg yolk in the whites. (It is best to separate 1 egg at a time and check each white before adding to the rest.)

2 ▲ For a savoury soufflé, make a thick white sauce. Beat in the yolks and the soufflé flavouring. For a sweet soufflé, make a thick custard using the yolks; mix in the flavouring.

3 ▲ In a large, scrupulously clean bowl, whisk the egg whites until they hold stiff peaks. (Any grease on the bowl or beaters will prevent maximum volume.) If not using a copper bowl, add a pinch of cream of tartar once the whites are frothy. For a sweet soufflé, add sugar once the whites hold soft peaks (the tips flop over), then continue whisking.

4 ▲ Add one-quarter of the egg whites to the sauce base. Using a large metal spoon or a rubber spatula, stir the whites in to lighten the base. Add the remaining whites and fold them in as lightly as possible by cutting down with the spatula to the bottom of the bowl and then turning the mixture over on itself.

5 ▲ Spoon the mixture into the prepared dish. Bake in a preheated oven until the soufflé has risen about 2 in (5 cm) above the rim of the dish and is lightly browned. Serve the soufflé immediately because it will only hold its puff out of the oven for a few minutes before it begins to deflate.

Separating eggs

It is easier to separate the yolks and whites if eggs are cold, so take the eggs straight from the refrigerator. Tap the egg once or twice against the rim of a small bowl to crack the shell. Break open the shell and hold half in each hand. Carefully transfer the un-broken yolk from one half shell to the other several times, letting the egg white dribble into the bowl. Put the yolk in a second bowl.

Cheese Soufflé

Butter a 2½ pint (1.5 litre) soufflé dish and coat it with fine bread-crumbs. Make ½ pint (300 ml) thick white sauce (page 170). Add 4 egg yolks and 4 oz (115 g) grated cheese (Gruyère, Cheddar, blue, or a mixture of Parmesan and Gruyère). If you like, season with 2 teaspoons Dijon mustard. Whisk 6 egg whites until stiff; fold into the sauce base. Bake in a 400°F/200°C/ Gas 6 oven for 20–25 minutes. *Serves 4.*

Amaretto Soufflé

SERVES 6

6 amaretti biscuits, coarsely crushed

6 tablespoons Amaretto liqueur

4 eggs, separated, plus 1 egg white

7 tablespoons caster sugar

2 tablespoons plain flour

8 fl oz (240 ml) milk

pinch of cream of tartar (if needed)

icing sugar, for decorating

1 Preheat a 400°F/200°C/Gas 6 oven. Butter a 2½ pint (1.5 litre) soufflé dish and sprinkle it with caster sugar.

2 Put the biscuits in a bowl. Sprinkle them with 2 tablespoons of the Amaretto liqueur and set aside.

3 ▲ Mix together the 4 egg yolks, 2 tablespoons of the sugar and flour.

4 ▲ Heat the milk just to the boil in a heavy saucepan. Gradually add the hot milk to the egg mixture, stirring.

5 Pour the mixture back into the pan. Set over moderately low heat and simmer gently for 3–4 minutes or until thickened, stirring constantly.

6 ▲ Add the remaining Amaretto liqueur. Remove from the heat.

7 In a scrupulously clean, grease-free bowl, whisk the 5 egg whites until they will hold soft peaks. (If not using a copper bowl, add the cream of tartar as soon as the whites are frothy.) Add the remaining sugar and continue whisking until stiff.

8 Add about one-quarter of the whites to the liqueur mixture and stir in with a rubber spatula. Add the remaining whites and fold in gently.

9 Spoon half of the mixture into the prepared soufflé dish. Cover with a layer of the moistened amaretti biscuits, then spoon the remaining soufflé mixture on top.

10 Bake for 20 minutes or until the soufflé is risen and lightly browned. Sprinkle with sifted icing sugar and serve immediately.

~ COOK'S TIP ~

Some people like soufflés to be completely cooked. Others prefer a soft, creamy centre. The choice is up to you. To check how cooked the middle is, insert a thin skewer into the centre: it will come out almost clean or with moist particles clinging to it.

MAKING SIMPLE MERINGUE

There are two types of this egg white and sugar foam: a soft meringue used as an insulating topping for pies and baked Alaska and a firm meringue that can be shaped into containers for luscious fillings.

Take care when separating the egg whites and yolks because even the smallest trace of yolk will prevent the whites from being whisked to their maximum volume. All equipment must be scrupulously clean and free of grease.

1 ▲ Put the egg whites in a large, scrupulously clean and grease-free bowl. With a whisk or electric mixer, whisk the whites until they are foamy. If not using a copper bowl, add a pinch of cream of tartar.

2 ▲ Continue whisking until the whites hold soft peaks when you lift the whisk or beaters (the tips of the peaks will flop over).

3 ▲ **For a soft meringue:** Sprinkle the sugar over the whites, whisking constantly. Continue whisking for about 1 minute or until the meringue is glossy and holds stiff peaks when you lift the whisk or beaters. The meringue is now ready to be spread on a pie filling or used for baked Alaska.

4 ▲ **For a firm meringue:** Add a little of the sugar (about 1½ teaspoons for each egg white). Continue whisking until the meringue is glossy and will hold stiff peaks.

5 ▲ Add the remaining sugar to the bowl, with any flavouring the recipe specifies. With a rubber spatula, fold the sugar into the meringue as lightly as possible by cutting down with the spatula to the bottom of the bowl and then turning the mixture over. The meringue is now ready to be shaped into containers or gâteau layers.

Meringue Nests
Make a firm meringue using 2 egg whites and 4 oz (115 g) caster sugar. Scoop large spoonfuls of meringue on to a baking sheet lined with baking parchment. Slightly hollow out the centre of each with the back of the spoon, to make a nest shape. Alternatively, put the meringue into a piping bag fitted with a ½ in (1.5 cm) plain nozzle and pipe the nest shapes. Sprinkle lightly with a little extra sugar. Dry in a 200°F/ 100°C/Gas low oven for 3–4 hours or until crisp and firm but not brown. Leave to cool. To serve, fill with sweetened whipped cream and fresh fruit. *Makes 4–6.*

Sweetened whipped cream
This is used as a topping and filling for many hot and cold desserts. Whip ½ pint (300 ml) chilled whipping or double cream until it starts to thicken. Add 2 tablespoons sifted icing sugar and continue whipping until the cream holds a soft peak on the beaters. If liked, the cream may be flavoured with ½ teaspoon vanilla or almond essence or 2 teaspoons brandy or liqueur, added with the sugar.

Lemon Meringue Pie

SERVES 6–8

9 in (23 cm) pastry case, made from shortcrust pastry (page 222) or French flan pastry (page 230), baked blind (page 232)
10 oz (300 g) caster sugar
1 oz (30 g) cornflour
pinch of salt
2 teaspoons finely grated lemon zest
4 fl oz (120 ml) fresh lemon juice
8 fl oz (240 ml) water
3 eggs, separated
1½ oz (45 g) butter
pinch of cream of tartar (if needed)

1 ▼ Combine 7 oz (200 g) sugar, the cornflour, salt and lemon zest in a saucepan. Stir in the lemon juice and water until smoothly blended.

2 Bring to the boil over moderately high heat, stirring constantly. Simmer for 1 minute or until thickened.

3 Blend in the egg yolks. Cook over low heat for a further 2 minutes, stirring constantly.

4 Remove from the heat. Add the butter and mix well.

5 ▲ Pour the lemon filling into the pastry case. Spread it evenly and level the surface. Leave to cool completely.

6 Preheat a 350°F/180°C/Gas 4 oven.

7 In a scrupulously clean, grease-free bowl, whisk the egg whites until they will hold soft peaks. (If not using a copper bowl, add the cream of tartar as soon as the whites are frothy.) Add the remaining sugar and continue whisking until stiff and glossy.

8 ▲ Spread the meringue evenly over the filling. Take care to seal it to the edges of the pastry case all round.

9 Bake for 10–15 minutes or until the meringue is just set and lightly golden brown on the surface. Leave to cool before serving.

~ COOK'S TIP ~

Egg whites can be whisked to their greatest volume if they are at room temperature rather than cold. A copper bowl and wire balloon whisk are the best tools to use, although a stainless steel bowl and electric mixer produce very good results. Take care not to over-whisk whites (they will start to look grainy and then will separate into lumps and liquid). Using a copper bowl helps produce a stable foam that is hard to over-whisk; adding a pinch of cream of tartar has the same effect.

MAKING A BATTER

Batters consist mainly of flour, eggs and liquid. They may be thick – for making fritters or coating food to be fried – or thin and pourable, for Yorkshire pudding, or other batter puddings, and pancakes. For a very light result, the eggs can be separated and the whites whisked and folded in.

Pork and Apple Batter Puddings
Make the batter with 4oz (115g) plain flour, a pinch of salt, 1 egg and ½ pint (300ml) mixed milk and water. Mix together 1lb (450g) pork sausagemeat, 4oz (115g) finely chopped or coarsely grated cooking apple, 1 small grated onion, 1 tablespoon chopped fresh parsley, salt and pepper. Form into 16 small balls. Oil 4 individual 1 pint (600ml) baking dishes and heat in a 425°F/220°C/Gas 7 oven. Divide the balls among the dishes and bake for 10 minutes. Pour the batter over the balls and bake for 35–40 minutes or until risen and golden brown. Serve hot. *Serves 4.*

A speedy tip
Most batters can be made quickly in a blender or food processor. But take care not to overmix.

---

1 ▲ Sift the flour into a bowl along with other dry ingredients such as sugar, baking powder or bicarbonate of soda, salt, ground spices etc.

3 ▲ With a wooden spoon, beat together the eggs and liquid in the well just to mix them.

5 ▲ When the mixture is smooth, stir in the remaining liquid. Stir just until the ingredients are combined – the trick is not to overmix.

---

2 ▲ Make a well in the centre of the dry ingredients and put in the eggs or egg yolks and some of the liquid.

4 ▲ Gradually draw in some of the flour from the sides, stirring vigorously.

6 ▲ If the recipe specifies, whisk egg whites to a soft peak and fold them into the batter (made with yolks). Do this just before using the batter.

MAKING PANCAKES

Thin, lacy pancakes, or crêpes, are wonderfully versatile. They can be served very simply with just lemon juice and sugar, or turned into more elaborate dishes: folded and warmed in a sauce, rolled round a savoury or sweet filling, or stacked in layers with a filling.

MAKES ABOUT 12

6 oz (170 g) plain flour

2 teaspoons caster sugar (for sweet pancakes)

2 eggs

¾ pint (450 ml) milk

about 1 oz (30 g) melted butter

Ricotta and Peach Pancakes
Combine 1 lb (450 g) ricotta cheese, 1 oz (30 g) icing sugar, 1 teaspoon vanilla essence and 2 tablespoons brandy in a bowl. Mix well. Add 4 large ripe peaches, peeled and diced, and fold in gently. Divide the ricotta and peach mixture among 12 pancakes and spread it evenly over them. Fold each pancake in half and then in half again, into quarters. Arrange the pancakes in a buttered large oval baking dish, slightly overlapping them. Brush with 1 oz (30 g) melted butter and sprinkle generously with icing sugar. Bake in a 375°F/190°C/Gas 5 oven for 10 minutes. Serve hot, with a berry sauce (page 194) if you wish. *Serves 6.*

1 ▲ Make the pancake batter and leave to stand for 20 minutes. Heat an 8 in (20 cm) pancake pan over moderate heat. The pan is ready when a few drops of water sprinkled on the surface jump and sizzle immediately. Grease the pan lightly with a little melted butter. Pour 3–4 tablespoons batter into the pan. Quickly tilt and rotate the pan so the batter spreads out to cover the bottom thinly and evenly; pour out any excess batter.

3 ▲ **To fill pancakes**: For folded pancakes, spread 3–4 tablespoons of filling evenly over each pancake. Fold in half then in half again, into quarters. For rolled pancakes, put 3–4 tablespoons of filling near one edge of each pancake and roll up tightly from that side. For pancake parcels, spoon 3–4 tablespoons of filling in the centre of each pancake. Fold in two opposite sides, over the filling, then fold in the other two sides. Turn the parcel over for serving. Filled pancakes are usually baked before serving, to reheat them.

2 ▲ Cook for 30–45 seconds or until the pancake is set and small holes have appeared. If the cooking seems to be taking too long, increase the heat slightly. Lift the edge of the pancake with a palette knife; the base of the pancake should be lightly brown. Shake the pan vigorously back and forth to loosen the pancake completely, then turn or flip it over. Cook the other side for about 30 seconds. Serve or leave to cool.

Pancake-making tips
- Pancake batter should be the consistency of whipping cream. If the batter is at all lumpy, strain it. If it doesn't flow smoothly to make a thin pancake, add a little more liquid.
- Like most batters, pancake batter can be made in a blender or food processor. It must have time to stand before using, as more air is incorporated by this method.
- Your first pancake may well be unsuccessful because it will test the consistency of the batter and the temperature of the pan, both of which may need adjusting.
- If more convenient, pancakes can be made ahead of time. Cool, then stack them, interleaved with greaseproof, and wrap in foil. They can be refrigerated for up to 3 days or frozen for 1 month.
- A pancake pan has a flat bottom and sides that rise straight out of it without curving; these give the pancake a well-defined edge.

MAKING CUSTARD

A home-made custard is a luscious sauce for many hot and cold puddings. It is also the basis for a very rich ice cream, which is essentially a frozen custard enriched with cream.

The secret for success is patience. Don't try to hurry the cooking of the custard by raising the heat.

MAKES ABOUT ¾ PINT (450 ML)

¾ pint (450 ml) milk

1 vanilla pod, split in half

4 egg yolks

3–4 tablespoons caster sugar, to sprinkle

Custard variations

- Use 1 teaspoon vanilla essence instead of the vanilla pod. Omit steps 1 and 2, and add the essence after straining the custard.
- For *Chocolate Custard*: Add 2 oz (55 g) plain chocolate, grated, to the hot milk and sugar mixture. Stir until smooth before adding to the egg yolks.
- For *Mocha Custard*: Add 2 oz (55 g) plain chocolate, grated, and 2 teaspoons instant coffee powder or granules.
- For *Orange Custard*: Omit the vanilla pod and instead infuse the milk with the finely pared zest of 1 orange.
- For *Liqueur Custard*: Add 2–3 tablespoons brandy, kirsch or other liqueur to the custard.

Damage repair

If the custard gets too hot and starts to curdle, remove it from the heat immediately and pour it into a bowl. Whisk vigorously for 2–3 seconds or until smooth. Then pour it back into the pan and continue cooking.

1 ▲ Put the milk in a heavy-based saucepan. Hold the vanilla pod over the pan and scrape out the tiny black seeds into the milk. Add the split pod to the milk.

2 ▲ Heat the milk until bubbles appear round the edge. Remove from the heat, cover and set aside to infuse for 10 minutes. Remove the split vanilla pod.

3 ▲ In a bowl, lightly beat the egg yolks with the sugar until smoothly blended and creamy. Gradually add the hot milk to the egg yolks, stirring constantly.

4 ▲ Pour the mixture into the top of a double saucepan (or a bowl). Set over the bottom pan containing hot water. Put on a moderately low heat, so the water stays below the boil.

5 ▲ Cook, stirring constantly, for 10–12 minutes or until the custard thickens to a creamy consistency that coats the spoon. Immediately remove the pan of custard from over the pan of hot water.

6 ▲ Strain the custard into a bowl. If using cold, sprinkle a little caster sugar over the surface of the custard to help prevent a skin from forming. Set the bowl in a container of iced water and leave to cool.

Sherry Trifle

SERVES 6 OR MORE

6 oz (170 g) trifle sponges, or 1 in (2.5 cm) cubes of plain Victoria sponge or coarsely crumbled sponge fingers

4 tablespoons medium sherry

4 oz (115 g) raspberry jam

10 oz (300 g) raspberries

¾ pint (450 ml) custard, flavoured with 2 tablespoons medium or sweet sherry

½ pint (300 ml) sweetened whipped cream (page 160)

toasted flaked almonds and mint leaves, to decorate

1 Spread half of the sponges, cake cubes or sponge fingers over the bottom of a large serving bowl. (A glass bowl is best for presentation.)

2 ▲ Sprinkle half of the sherry over the cake to moisten it. Spoon over half of the jam, dotting it evenly over the cake cubes.

3 ▲ Reserve a few raspberries for decoration. Make a layer of half of the remaining raspberries on top.

4 ▼ Pour over half of the custard, covering the fruit and cake. Repeat the layers. Cover and chill for at least 2 hours.

~ **VARIATIONS** ~

Use other ripe fruit in the trifle, with jam and liqueur to suit: apricots, peaches, nectarines, strawberries, etc.

5 ▲ Before serving, spoon the sweetened whipped cream evenly over the top. To decorate, sprinkle with toasted flaked almonds and arrange the reserved raspberries and the mint leaves on the top.

COOKING IN A BAIN-MARIE

Setting a dish in a pan of water for cooking ensures that delicate mixtures such as baked egg custards do not overheat and curdle. The pan of water, called a 'bain-marie', can be used on top of the stove or in the oven.

A double saucepan is a type of bain-marie, where the mixture for cooking is set over hot water rather than in it.

Sometimes a pan of iced water is used to protect fragile foods during cooking, such as with crème brûlée.

1 ◀ Set the dish or dishes in a roasting tin or in a wide shallow saucepan. Pour enough water into the tin to come halfway up the sides of the dish or dishes. Set the tin over moderately high heat and bring the water almost to the boil. Reduce the heat so the water is just simmering, or not moving at all, according to recipe instructions. Or transfer the dish or dishes, in the bain-marie, to the oven to finish cooking.

Crème Brûlée Pralinée

SERVES 6

¾ pint (450 ml) double cream

4 egg yolks

4 oz (115 g) caster sugar

1 teaspoon vanilla essence

1 oz (30 g) pecan nuts or walnuts, finely chopped

1 Preheat a 300°F/150°C/Gas 2 oven.

2 Heat the cream in a saucepan until bubbles form round the edge.

3 Meanwhile, whisk the egg yolks with half of the sugar until the mixture is pale and creamy. Gradually stir the hot cream into the egg yolk mixture. Stir in the vanilla.

4 Strain the mixture into a jug. Pour it into 6 ramekins. Set the ramekins in a bain-marie and bring the water to the boil on top of the stove.

5 Transfer to the oven and bake for 20–25 minutes or until the custards are just set. Remove from the bain-marie and cool. Cover and chill.

6 Preheat the grill.

7 Mix together the remaining sugar and the nuts. Sprinkle over the tops of the custards in an even layer.

8 ▲ Set the ramekins in a baking tin containing iced water. Grill, about 5 in (12.5 cm) from the heat, until the sugar has melted and caramelized. Turn the ramekins for even browning. Leave to cool and set before serving.

Making Ice Cream

At its most basic, home-made ice cream is just frozen cream, sweetened and flavoured. More often it has a custard base enriched with cream. Flavourings range from ever-popular vanilla and chocolate to fresh fruit and liqueur.

An electric ice cream machine makes light work of the arduous task of churning and freezing ice cream. Models and capacities vary, so follow manufacturer's instructions.

1 Make an egg custard, using cream or a mixture of milk and cream. For ice cream, the custard should be quite sweet. Strain and leave to cool.

2 ▶ Pour into an ice cream machine and freeze following the manufacturer's instructions. Serve as soon as possible after making. If the ice cream is left in the freezer and becomes very hard, let it soften for 20 minutes at room temperature before serving.

Old-fashioned Chocolate Ice Cream

Makes about 1⅔ pints (1 litre)

| 1¼ pints (750 ml) whipping cream |
| 8 fl oz (250 ml) milk |
| 1 vanilla pod, split in half |
| 5 oz (145 g) caster sugar, plus ½ teaspoon to sprinkle |
| 4 oz (115 g) plain chocolate, grated |
| 4 egg yolks |

1 Put 8 fl oz (240 ml) cream and the milk in a heavy-based saucepan with the vanilla pod. Heat until bubbles appear round the edge.

2 ▲ Add 5 oz (145 g) of the sugar and the chocolate. Heat almost to boiling point, stirring until the chocolate is melted and smooth.

3 In a bowl, lightly beat the egg yolks until smooth. Add the hot mixture to the egg yolks, stirring constantly.

4 Pour into the top of a double saucepan set over hot water. Cook, stirring, until the custard thickens enough to coat the spoon. Strain into a bowl. Stir in the remaining cream and sprinkle with the remaining sugar. Cool to room temperature.

5 Transfer to an ice cream machine and freeze.

Ice cream variations
- For *Vanilla Ice Cream*: Omit the chocolate.
- For *Strawberry Ice Cream*: Omit the chocolate. Mash 1 lb 2 oz (500 g) strawberries with a little lemon juice and 1 oz (30 g) sugar. Add to custard before freezing.
- For *Peach Ice Cream*: Omit the chocolate. Mash 6 large ripe peaches, peeled and stoned. Add to custard before freezing.

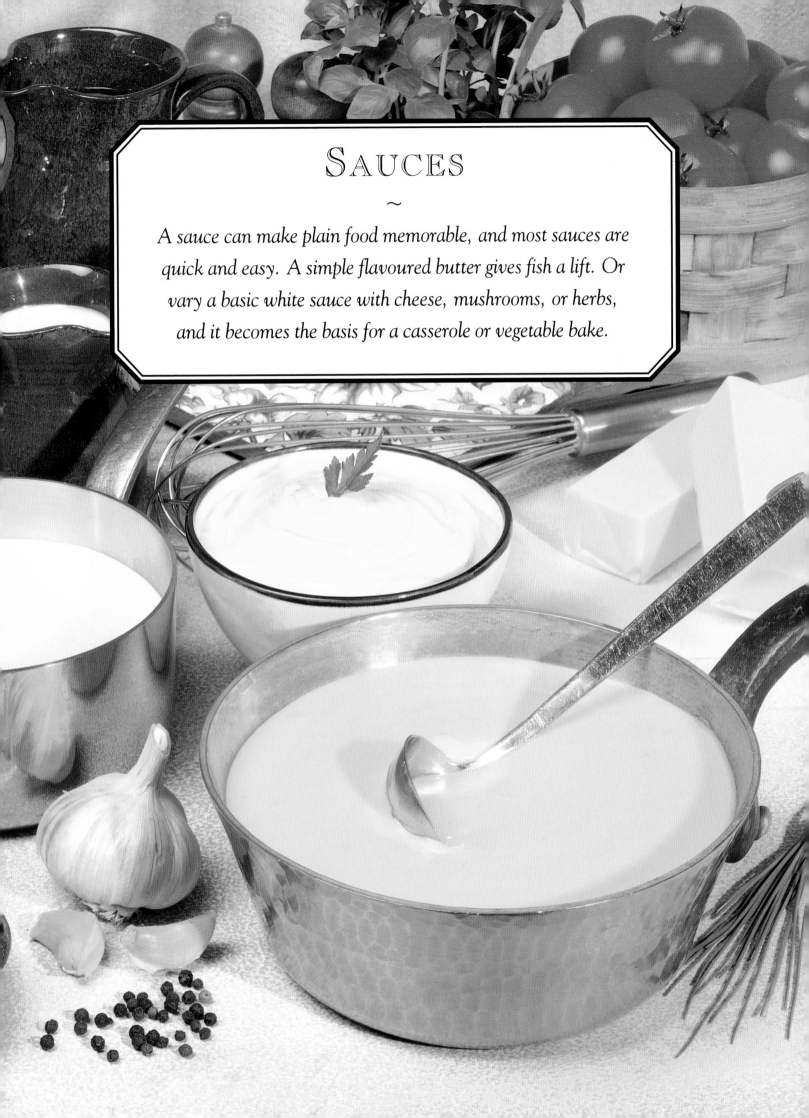

SAUCES

~

A sauce can make plain food memorable, and most sauces are quick and easy. A simple flavoured butter gives fish a lift. Or vary a basic white sauce with cheese, mushrooms, or herbs, and it becomes the basis for a casserole or vegetable bake.

MAKING WHITE SAUCE

Some modern chefs consider flour-thickened sauces old-fashioned and replace them with butter sauces, vegetable purées or reduced cream. But a basic white sauce is an essential ingredient in many dishes, and lends itself to an endless variety of flavourings. This recipe makes a medium-thick sauce to coat food.

MAKES ABOUT 1 PINT (600 ML)

1½ oz (45 g) butter
1½ oz (45 g) plain flour
1 pint (600 ml) milk
good pinch of grated nutmeg
salt and pepper

1 ▲ Melt the butter in a heavy saucepan over low heat. Remove the pan from the heat and stir in the flour to make a smooth, soft paste (called a 'roux' in French).

2 ▲ Add about one-quarter of the milk and mix it in well with a whisk. When it is smooth, mix in the remaining milk.

3 ▲ Set the pan over moderately high heat and bring to the boil, whisking constantly.

4 ▲ When the sauce bubbles and starts to thicken, reduce the heat to very low and simmer the sauce gently for 5–10 minutes, whisking well from time to time. Add the grated nutmeg and season the sauce to taste with salt and pepper. Serve the sauce hot.

Sauce-making tips
● A whisk will blend the mixture more thoroughly than a spoon and will help avoid lumps. In the event of a lumpy sauce, push it through a fine-mesh sieve into a clean pan and then reheat it, whisking constantly.
● White sauces can be made ahead of time. Pour the sauce into a bowl or other container, dab the surface with butter and cool. Cover and refrigerate for up to 2 days. Before serving, whisk over moderate heat until boiling.

White sauce variations
● For *Thin White Sauce* to serve with meat or to use as a base for cream soups: Use 1 oz (30 g) each butter and flour.
● For *Thick White Sauce* to use as a soufflé base or to bind croquettes: Use 2 oz (55 g) each butter and flour.
● For *Blond Sauce*: Add the flour to the melted butter and cook, stirring constantly, for 1–2 minutes or until the roux is a pale beige colour. Heat the liquid and add it, off the heat. Bring to the boil, whisking, and simmer for 3–5 minutes.
● For *Velouté Sauce*: Cook the roux as for a blond sauce for 3 minutes or until it is lightly browned and smells nutty. Use hot chicken or fish stock, or a mixture of stock and wine, instead of milk.
● For *Béchamel Sauce*: Heat the milk with a slice of onion, 1 bay leaf and a few black peppercorns. Remove from the heat, cover and infuse for 20 minutes. Strain before adding to the roux, made as for a blond sauce.
● For *Cream Sauce*: Substitute cream for some of the milk.
● For *Cheese Sauce*: Stir 4–8 oz (115–225 g) grated cheese and 1–2 teaspoons spicy brown mustard into white, blond or béchamel sauce; add a pinch of cayenne pepper instead of nutmeg. Use a flavourful cheese that melts easily.
● For *Mustard Sauce*: Stir 1 tablespoon Dijon mustard and ½ teaspoon sugar into white, blond or béchamel sauce.
● For *Mushroom Sauce*: Cook 8 oz (225 g) sliced mushrooms in ½–1 oz (15–30 g) butter until soft; continue cooking until excess liquid has evaporated. Add to white, blond, béchamel, velouté or cream sauce.

Moussaka

SERVES 4–6

2 aubergines, weighing about 1½ lb (700 g), trimmed and sliced across
about ¼ pint (150 ml) olive oil
1 large onion, chopped
1–2 garlic cloves, finely chopped
1½ lb (700 g) minced lean lamb
8 oz (225 g) tomatoes, skinned, seeded and chopped or canned chopped tomatoes
2 tablespoons chopped fresh parsley
1 tablespoon chopped fresh marjoram or 1 teaspoon dried oregano
½ teaspoon ground cinnamon
2 tablespoons tomato purée
salt and pepper
1 pint (600 ml) hot white or blond sauce
1 egg yolk

1 Preheat the grill.

2 ▲ Spread out the aubergine slices on a large baking sheet and brush them with a little oil. Grill until lightly browned and beginning to soften. Turn the aubergine slices over and brush the other side with oil. Grill until lightly browned and soft.

> ~ **VARIATION** ~
>
> Use left-over roast lamb or beef, finely chopped, instead of fresh minced lamb.

3 Meanwhile, heat 2 tablespoons oil in a frying pan and cook the onion, stirring occasionally, until soft.

4 ▲ Add the garlic and lamb and cook until the meat is browned and crumbly, stirring frequently. Stir in the tomatoes. Bring the mixture to the boil and simmer until the excess liquid has evaporated.

5 Add the herbs, cinnamon and tomato purée. Season to taste with salt and pepper.

6 Preheat a 375°F/190°C/Gas 5 oven.

7 Layer the lamb mixture and aubergine slices in a baking dish, starting with meat and ending with aubergine.

8 ▼ Mix together the sauce and egg yolk. Pour over the top layer of aubergine slices in an even layer.

9 Bake for 30 minutes or until the sauce is golden and the moussaka is bubbling. Serve hot, in the baking dish.

MAKING TOMATO SAUCE

Tomato sauce is a useful standby to have on hand in the refrigerator or freezer. When tomatoes are in season make a large batch. At other times of the year, use canned whole Italian plum tomatoes (drain, cut in half, scrape out seeds and chop).

MAKES ABOUT 1 PINT (600 ML)

1 oz (30 g) butter

2 lb (900 g) tomatoes, skinned, seeded and finely chopped

¼–½ teaspoon sugar

salt and pepper

1 ▲ Melt the butter in a heavy-based saucepan over low heat. Add the tomatoes and stir to mix with the butter. Cover and cook for 5 minutes.

2 ▲ Uncover and stir in the sugar. Partly cover the pan and simmer gently, stirring occasionally, for 30 minutes or until the tomatoes have softened and the sauce is thick.

3 ▲ Season the sauce to taste with salt and pepper. Use immediately, or cool and then refrigerate or freeze.

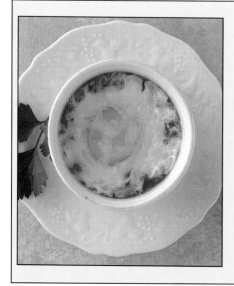

Eggs Baked in Tomato Sauce
For each serving, put 1½ tablespoons of tomato sauce in a lightly buttered ramekin. Break an egg into the ramekin and sprinkle with pepper to taste and 1 tablespoon of freshly grated Parmesan or Cheddar cheese. Put the ramekins in a roasting tin and add cold water to come halfway up the sides of the ramekins. Bring to the boil on top of the stove, then transfer to a 400°F/200°C/Gas 6 oven and bake for 5–7 minutes or until the eggs are set. Serve immediately.

Tomato sauce variations
● For *Rich Tomato Sauce*: Stir another ½–1 oz (15–30 g) butter into the sauce before serving.
● For *Smooth Tomato Sauce*: Purée in a blender or food processor.
● For *Tomato-garlic Sauce*: Use 1 tablespoon olive oil instead of butter. In a separate small pan, cook 1–2 finely chopped garlic cloves in 1 tablespoon olive oil for 1 minute. Add the garlic to the tomato sauce for the last 5 minutes of cooking.
● For *Tomato-herb Sauce*: Stir in ½–1 oz (15–30 g) chopped fresh herbs (parsley, basil, chives, thyme, oregano, marjoram – singly or a mixture of 2 or 3 at most) before serving.
● For *Italian Tomato Sauce*: Finely chop 1 onion, 1 small carrot and 1 celery stalk. Cook in 2 tablespoons olive oil until soft. Add 1–2 finely chopped garlic cloves and cook for a further 1 minute. Add the tomatoes with 1 bay leaf and 1 large sprig of fresh rosemary or ½ teaspoon crumbled dried rosemary. Continue cooking as for tomato sauce. Discard the herbs before serving.
● For *Tomato-wine Sauce*: Finely chop 3 shallots or ½ onion and cook in 1 oz (30 g) butter or 2 tablespoons olive oil until soft. Add 1 finely chopped garlic clove and cook for a further 1 minute. Stir in 4 fl oz (120 ml) dry white wine, bring to the boil and boil until almost completely evaporated. Add the tomatoes and continue cooking as for tomato sauce. For a smooth sauce, purée in a blender or food processor.
● For *Tomato-mushroom Sauce*: Fry 8 oz (225 g) sliced mushrooms in the butter until lightly browned. Add the tomatoes and cook as for tomato sauce.

Pasta with Tomato Sauce and Roasted Vegetables

SERVES 4

1 aubergine

2 courgettes

1 large onion

2 peppers, preferably red or yellow, seeded

1 lb (450 g) tomatoes, preferably plum-type

2–3 garlic cloves, coarsely chopped

4 tablespoons olive oil

salt and pepper

½ pint (300 ml) smooth tomato sauce

2 oz (55 g) black olives, stoned and halved

¾–1 lb (340–450 g) dried pasta shapes such as rigatoni or penne

½ oz (15 g) fresh basil, shredded

1 Preheat a 475°F/240°C/Gas 9 oven.

2 ▲ Cut the aubergine, courgettes, onion, peppers and tomatoes into 1–1½ in (2.5–4 cm) chunks. Discard the tomato seeds.

3 ▲ Spread out the vegetables in a large roasting tin. Sprinkle the garlic and oil over the vegetables and stir and turn to mix evenly. Season with salt and pepper.

4 Roast the vegetables for 30 minutes or until they are soft and browned (don't worry if the edges are charred black). Stir halfway through.

5 ▼ Scrape the vegetable mixture into a saucepan. Add the tomato sauce and olives.

6 Bring a large pot of water to the boil. Add the pasta and cook until it is just tender to the bite ('al dente').

7 Meanwhile, heat the tomato and roasted vegetable sauce. Taste and adjust the seasoning.

8 Drain the pasta and return it to the pot. Add the tomato and roasted vegetable sauce and stir to mix well. Serve hot, sprinkled with the basil. If liked, serve with freshly grated Parmesan or pecorino cheese.

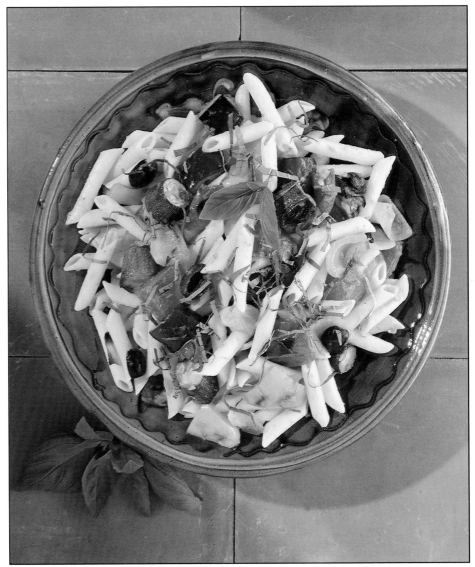

MAKING FLAVOURED BUTTERS

A pat of flavoured butter melting over hot, freshly cooked vegetables, meat or seafood is an impressive finishing touch. Yet flavoured butters are so easy to make. They can be used as a spread for sandwiches or canapés, too. In addition to savoury flavoured butters, you can make sweet ones to serve with warm breads and rolls, teacakes and waffles.

MAKES ABOUT 4 OZ (115 G)

4 oz (115 g) butter, preferably unsalted, at room temperature

chosen flavouring (see Butter flavourings)

salt and pepper (for savoury butters)

Butter flavourings
- For *Herb Butter*: Use 2–4 tablespoons chopped fresh herbs (parsley, chives, tarragon, mint and so on) and a squeeze of lemon juice.
- For *Mustard Butter*: Use 1 tablespoon Dijon mustard or spicy brown mustard.
- For *Citrus Butter*: Use 2 teaspoons orange or lime juice or 1 teaspoon lemon juice and the grated zest of 1 orange, lime or lemon.
- For *Coriander-lime Butter*: Finely chop 1 oz (30 g) fresh coriander leaves. Mix into the soft butter with the grated zest and juice of 1 lime.
- For *Parsley and Lemon Butter* ('beurre maître d'hôtel'): Use 2 tablespoons chopped parsley and 1 tablespoon lemon juice.
- For *Tomato Butter*: Use 1 tablespoon tomato purée.
- For *Garlic Butter*: Use 1–2 chopped and crushed garlic cloves.
- For *Sweet Orange Butter*: Use 1–2 tablespoons icing sugar, 2 teaspoons orange juice, and the grated zest of 1 orange.
- For *Honey Butter*: Use 3 oz (85 g) honey; beat in gradually.
- For *Maple Butter*: Use 4 tablespoons maple syrup; beat in gradually.
- For *Cinnamon Butter*: Use 1–2 tablespoons icing sugar and ½ teaspoon ground cinnamon.
- For *Almond Butter*: Use 4 tablespoons finely ground almonds.

1 ▲ **For a savoury butter:** Put the butter in a mixing bowl and beat with a wooden spoon or electric mixer until soft. Add the flavouring. Season savoury butter to taste with salt and pepper. Blend well.

2 ▲ Transfer the butter to a piece of greaseproof paper and shape it into a neat roll, handling it as little as possible because the heat of your hands can melt it. Wrap and refrigerate until firm. Cut into discs.

3 ▲ Alternatively, flatten with the back of a spoon or knife until it is about ¼ in (5 mm) thick. Refrigerate until firm, and stamp out small rounds or other shapes using a pastry cutter.

4 ▲ **For a sweet butter:** Put the butter in a mixing bowl and beat with an electric mixer or wooden spoon until fluffy. Add the flavouring and blend well. Spoon into a serving bowl, cover and refrigerate until firm.

Freezing flavoured butters
Flavoured butters can be frozen and then used straight from the freezer. Overwrap the paper-wrapped roll in foil for storage.

Fish Steaks with Coriander-lime Butter

SERVES 4

1½ lb (700 g) swordfish or tuna steak,
    1 in (2.5 cm) thick, cut into 4 pieces

4 tablespoons vegetable oil

2 tablespoons lemon juice

1 tablespoon lime juice

salt and pepper

2 oz (55 g) coriander-lime butter

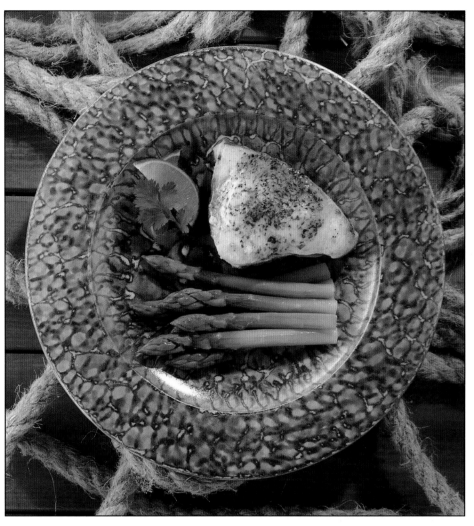

1 ▲ Lay the fish steaks side by side in a shallow dish. Combine the oil, juices, salt and pepper and pour over the fish. Cover and refrigerate for 1–2 hours, turning the fish once or twice.

2 Preheat the grill or prepare a charcoal fire in a barbecue.

~ **VARIATIONS** ~

For Salmon Steaks with Citrus Butter, lightly brush 4 salmon steaks, 1 in (2.5 cm) thick, with oil and season. Grill for 4–5 minutes on each side. Serve topped with pats of citrus butter. For Mackerel with Mustard Butter, brush 4 unskinned mackerel fillets, about 8 oz (225 g) each, with oil and season. Grill for 3–4 minutes on each side. Serve topped with pats of mustard butter.

3 ▼ Drain the fish and arrange on the rack in the grill pan, or set over the hot charcoal about 5 in (12.5 cm) from the coals. Grill for 3–4 minutes or until just firm to the touch but still moist in the centre, turning the steaks over once.

4 ▲ Transfer to warmed plates and top each fish steak with a pat of coriander-lime butter. Serve the fish immediately.

MAKING CLARIFIED BUTTER

This is butter from which the milk solids have been removed. The result is a clear yellow fat that can be heated to a higher temperature than ordinary butter without burning. Thus clarified butter is an excellent fat for pan-frying. It is also used as a dip for seafood such as lobster and crab and for globe artichokes. Indian ghee is a type of clarified butter.

MAKES ABOUT 6 OZ (170 G)

8 oz (225 g) butter

Keeping butter longer

Since clarification removes impurities, clarified butter keeps well – several weeks in the refrigerator, longer in the freezer.

1 ▲ Put the butter in a heavy saucepan over low heat. Melt gently. Skim off all the froth from the surface. You will then see a clear yellow layer on top of a milky layer.

2 Carefully pour the clear fat into a bowl or jug, leaving the milky residue in the pan. Discard the milky residue, or add it to soups.

Langoustines with Clarified Butter

To cook the langoustines (3–8 per serving), plunge them into boiling salted water, bring back to the boil and simmer for 8–10 minutes; drain. Serve hot or warm, peeling and dipping the tail meat in clarified butter.

Chicken Liver Pâté

SERVES 6 OR MORE

2 oz (55 g) butter
1 onion, finely chopped
12 oz (340 g) chicken livers, trimmed of all dark or greenish parts
4 tablespoons medium sherry
1 oz (30 g) full-fat soft cheese
1–2 tablespoons lemon juice
2 hard-boiled eggs, chopped
salt and pepper
2–3 oz (55–85 g) clarified butter

1 Melt the butter in a frying pan. Add the onion and livers and cook until the onion is soft and the livers are lightly browned and no longer pink in the centre.

2 Add the sherry and boil until reduced by half. Cool slightly.

3 ▲ Turn the mixture into a food processor or blender and add the soft cheese and 1 tablespoon lemon juice. Blend until smooth.

4 Add the hard-boiled eggs and blend briefly. Season with salt and pepper. Taste and add more lemon juice if liked.

5 ▼ Pack the liver pâté into a mould or into individual ramekins. Smooth the surface.

6 Spoon a layer of clarified butter over the surface of the pâté. Refrigerate until firm. Serve at room temperature, with hot toast or savoury biscuits.

MAKING SIMPLE HOLLANDAISE SAUCE

This classic of French cuisine has a reputation for being difficult to make. It does require care: if the sauce becomes too hot, it will separate. However, a method proposed by Harold McGee of putting all the ingredients in the pan at once – rather than the traditional method of cooking the egg yolks to thicken them and then slowly beating in melted butter – lowers the chance of failure. Just take it slow and steady, and whisk constantly.

MAKES ABOUT ½ PINT (300 ML)

3 egg yolks

1 tablespoon lemon juice, plus more if needed

pinch of cayenne pepper

salt and pepper

8 oz (225 g) butter, preferably unsalted, cut into ½ oz (15 g) chunks

1 ▲ Combine the egg yolks, lemon juice, cayenne, salt and pepper in a heavy saucepan. Whisk together until thoroughly blended.

2 ▲ Add the butter and set the pan over moderate heat. Whisk constantly so that as the butter melts it is blended into the egg yolks. Regulate the heat so it melts gradually.

3 ▲ When all the butter has melted and has been blended into the egg yolk base, continue whisking until the sauce just thickens to a creamy consistency. Taste the sauce and add more lemon juice, salt and pepper if needed.

Sauce-making tips
● If your sauce does separate into soft curds and clear butterfat, don't despair. As long as the egg yolks haven't scrambled, you can rescue the sauce. Remove the pan from the heat, add 1–2 teaspoons of water and whisk vigorously. If the sauce doesn't re-form and become creamy, put 1–2 teaspoons of water in a bowl and whisk in the separated sauce, drop by drop at first and then in a thin stream.
● Hollandaise and Béarnaise sauces can be kept warm for up to 30 minutes before serving. Set the saucepan in a bain-marie of hot water (page 166), or on a warming tray, and whisk the sauce occasionally. Alternatively, the sauce can be made 2–3 hours ahead and transferred to a wide-mouth vacuum flask to keep warm until serving time.

The Hollandaise family
● For *Mousseline Sauce*: let the sauce cool slightly, then whisk in 4 fl oz (120 ml) whipped cream.
● For *Béarnaise Sauce*: mix 5 tablespoons white wine vinegar, 2 chopped shallots, 1 tablespoon chopped fresh tarragon or 1 teaspoon dried tarragon and a little pepper in a small saucepan. Boil to reduce to about 1 tablespoon. Cool. Continue as for Hollandaise sauce, using the strained vinegar reduction in place of the lemon juice. Before serving, stir in another ½–1 tablespoon chopped fresh tarragon, if liked.

Asparagus with Hollandaise Sauce Prepare 1½ lb (700 g) asparagus (page 120). Arrange the spears on a rack in a steamer over simmering water, cover and steam for 8–12 minutes, or simmer in a large frying pan with water just to cover for 4–5 minutes, until just tender when pierced with the tip of a knife. Transfer to warmed plates and spoon over the Hollandaise sauce. *Serves 4.*

Eggs Benedict

SERVES 6

2–3 slices of ham

6 eggs

3 muffins, split in half

½ pint (300 ml) warm Hollandaise sauce

1 Preheat the grill.

2 ▲ Cut rounds from the ham about the same diameter as the muffin halves to fit neatly.

3 ▲ Arrange the ham slices on the rack in the grill pan. Grill until they are hot and golden brown.

4 Meanwhile, poach the eggs in barely simmering water for 3–4 minutes until done: the white just firm but the yolk still soft. Remove, drain and trim them if necessary. Toast the muffin halves.

5 ▼ Put a muffin half, cut side up, on each warmed plate. Arrange a slice of ham on the muffin and top with a poached egg.

6 Spoon the Hollandaise sauce over the egg and serve immediately.

~ VARIATIONS ~

If preferred, fry the ham in butter rather than grilling it. Use rashers of back bacon (1–2 per serving) instead of ham. Replace the ham with hot asparagus spears or sliced mushrooms sautéed in butter. If liked, use toasted rounds of brioche or wholemeal bread instead of muffins.

MAKING MAYONNAISE

This cold emulsified sauce of oil and egg yolks has thousands of uses – as part of a dish or as an accompaniment, in sandwiches and in salad dressings. It can be varied by using different oils, vinegars and flavourings.

MAKES ABOUT 12 FL OZ (360 ML)

2 egg yolks

salt and pepper

12 fl oz (360 ml) oil (vegetable, corn or olive)

1–2 tablespoons lemon juice or white wine vinegar

1–2 teaspoons Dijon mustard

Mayonnaise variations

● For *Garlic Mayonnaise*: Crush 3–6 garlic cloves. Beat with the egg yolks and salt. Beat in oil (vegetable and/or olive) as above.

● For *Spicy Mayonnaise*: Increase mustard to 1 tablespoon and add ½–1 teaspoon Worcestershire sauce and a dash Tabasco sauce.

● For *Green Mayonnaise*: Combine 1 oz (30 g) each parsley sprigs and watercress sprigs in a blender or food processor. Add 3–4 chopped spring onions and 1 garlic clove. Blend until finely chopped. Add 4 fl oz (120 ml) mayonnaise and blend until smooth. Season.

● For *Blue Cheese Dressing*: Mix 8 oz (225 g) crumbled Danish blue cheese into the mayonnaise.

Raw egg alert

Eggs can harbour salmonella bacteria, so there is some risk of food poisoning if you eat raw eggs (as in home-made mayonnaise) or undercooked eggs (as in Hollandaise sauce). The elderly, infants, pregnant women and those who are ill are the most susceptible.

1 ▲ Put the egg yolks in a bowl and add a pinch of salt. Beat together well.

2 ▲ Add the oil, 1–2 teaspoons at a time, beating constantly with a whisk or electric mixer.

3 ▲ After one-quarter of the oil has been added very slowly and absorbed, beat in 1–2 teaspoons of the lemon juice or vinegar.

4 ▲ Continue beating in the oil, in a thin, steady stream now. As the mayonnaise thickens, add another teaspoon of lemon juice or vinegar.

5 ◄ When all the oil has been beaten in, add the mustard. Taste the mayonnaise and add more lemon juice or vinegar. Season with salt and pepper. If the mayonnaise is too thick, beat in a spoonful or two of water. Home-made mayonnaise will keep, covered in the refrigerator, for up to 1 week.

Seafood Salad with Garlic Mayonnaise

Make a bed of salad greens (green and red leaf lettuces, rocket, watercress, etc) on 4 individual plates or in large stemmed goblets. Arrange 6 oz (175 g) coarsely flaked white crabmeat and 8 oz (225 g) cooked peeled prawns on top. Spoon garlic mayonnaise over the seafood and sprinkle with a little paprika. *Serves 4.*

Salmon Cakes with Spicy Mayonnaise

SERVES 4

2 boiling potatoes, about 12 oz (340 g), unpeeled

12 oz (340 g) salmon fillet, skinned and finely chopped

2–3 tablespoons chopped fresh dill

1 tablespoon lemon juice

salt and pepper

flour for coating

3 tablespoons vegetable oil

spicy mayonnaise, to serve

1 Put the potatoes in a saucepan of boiling salted water and parboil them for 15 minutes.

2 ▲ Meanwhile, combine the salmon, dill, lemon juice, salt and pepper in a large bowl.

3 Drain the potatoes and leave them to cool. When they are cool enough to handle, peel them.

4 Shred the potatoes into strips on the coarse side of a grater.

~ COOK'S TIP ~

The potatoes will be sticky – it is their starch that helps hold the cakes together. If necessary, you can dampen your hands a little when shaping the cakes, but do not get the cakes too wet.

---

5 Add to the salmon mixture. Mix gently together with your fingers, breaking up the strips of potato as little as possible.

6 ▼ Divide the salmon and potato mixture into 8 portions. Shape each into a compact cake, pressing well together. Flatten the cakes to about ⅜ in (1 cm) thickness.

7 ▲ Coat the salmon cakes lightly with flour, shaking off excess.

8 Heat the oil in a large frying pan. Add the salmon cakes and fry for 5 minutes or until crisp and golden brown on both sides.

9 Drain the salmon cakes on paper towels, and serve with the spicy mayonnaise.

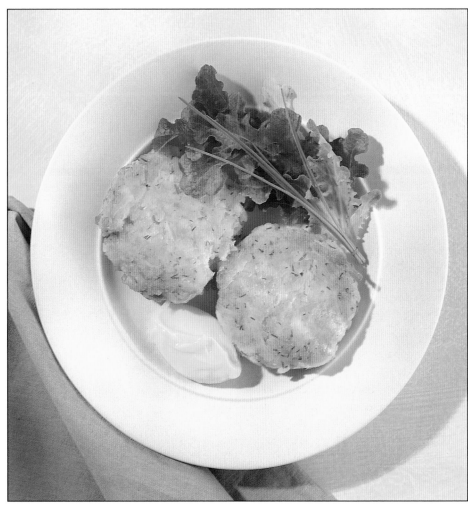

MAKING VINAIGRETTE DRESSING

A good vinaigrette can do more than dress a salad. It can also be used to baste meat, poultry, seafood or vegetables during cooking; and it can be used as a flavouring and tenderizing marinade. The basic mixture of oil, vinegar and seasoning lends itself to many variations.

The basic vinaigrette dressing will keep in the refrigerator, in a tightly closed container, for several weeks. Add flavourings, particularly fresh herbs, just before using.

A handy holder

If more convenient, you can make vinaigrette dressing in a screwtop jar. Combine all the ingredients in the jar, cover and shake well to mix and emulsify.

MAKES JUST OVER 6 FL OZ (170 ML)

3 tablespoons wine vinegar

salt and pepper

¼ pint (150 ml) vegetable oil

1 ▲ Put the vinegar, salt and pepper in a bowl and whisk to dissolve the salt. Gradually add the oil, stirring with the whisk. Taste and adjust seasoning.

Ideas for vinaigrette

- Use red or white wine vinegar. Or use a herb-flavoured vinegar.
- Use lemon juice instead of vinegar.
- Replace 1 tablespoon of the vinegar with wine.
- Use olive oil, or a mixture of vegetable and olive oils.
- Use 4 fl oz (120 ml) olive oil and 2 tablespoons walnut or hazelnut oil.
- Add 1–2 tablespoons Dijon mustard to the vinegar before whisking in the oil.
- Add 1 crushed garlic clove before whisking in the oil.
- Add 1–2 tablespoons chopped fresh herbs (parsley, basil, chives, thyme, etc) to the vinaigrette.

Orange Chicken Salad

SERVES 4

3 large seedless oranges

6 oz (170 g) long-grain rice

16 fl oz (500 ml) water

salt and pepper

6 fl oz (170 ml) vinaigrette dressing, made with red wine vinegar and a mixture of olive and vegetable oils

2 teaspoons Dijon mustard

½ teaspoon caster sugar

1 lb (450 g) cooked chicken, diced

3 tablespoons scissor-snipped chives

2½ oz (75 g) toasted cashew nuts

cucumber slices, to garnish

1 Thinly peel 1 orange, taking only the coloured part of the zest and leaving the white pith.

2 Combine the orange zest, rice and water in a saucepan. Add a pinch of salt. Bring to the boil, then cover and steam over very low heat for 15–18 minutes or until the rice is tender and all the water has been absorbed.

3 ▼ Peel all the oranges and cut out the segments, reserving the juice. Add the orange juice to the vinaigrette dressing. Add the mustard and sugar and whisk to combine well. Taste and add more salt and pepper if needed.

4 When the rice is cooked, remove it from the heat and cool slightly, uncovered. Discard the orange zest.

5 Turn the rice into a bowl and add half of the dressing. Toss well and cool completely.

6 ▲ Add the chicken, chives, cashew nuts and orange segments to the rice with the remaining dressing. Toss gently. Serve at room temperature, garnished with cucumber.

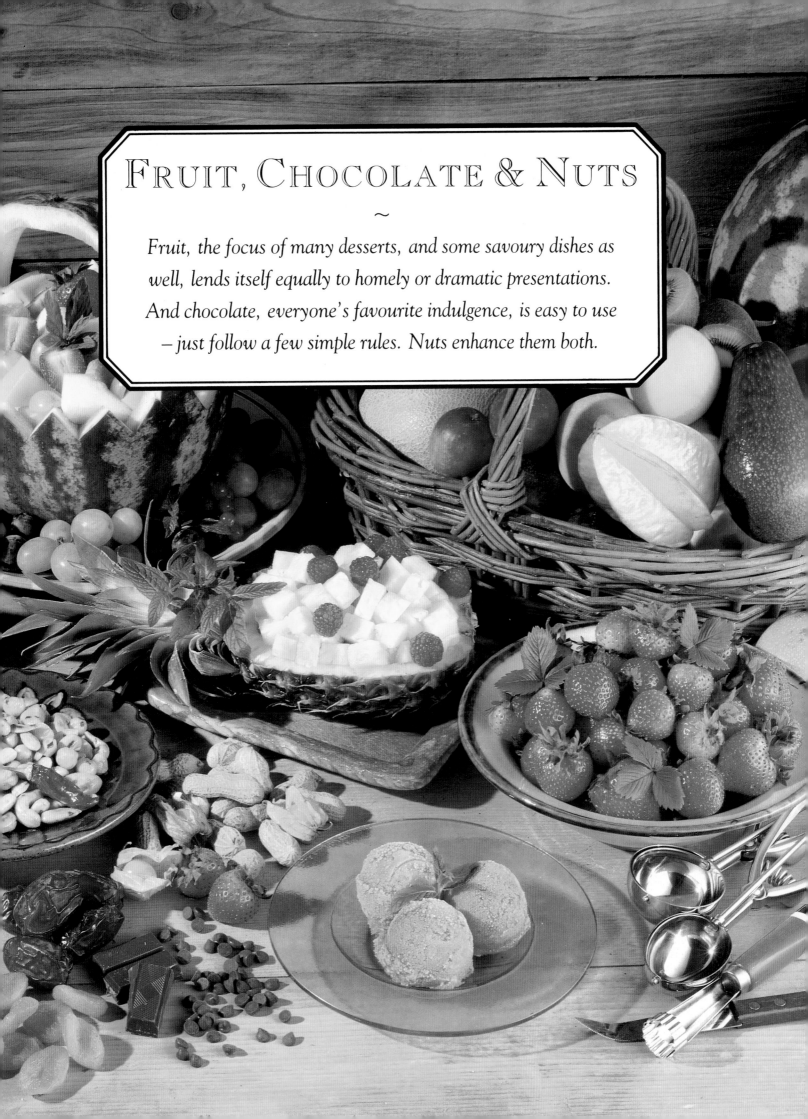

Fruit, Chocolate & Nuts

~

Fruit, the focus of many desserts, and some savoury dishes as well, lends itself equally to homely or dramatic presentations. And chocolate, everyone's favourite indulgence, is easy to use – just follow a few simple rules. Nuts enhance them both.

Preparing Fresh Fruit

PEELING AND TRIMMING FRUIT

Citrus fruit

To peel completely, cut a slice from the top and from the base. Set the fruit base down on a work surface. Using a small sharp knife, cut off the peel lengthways in thick strips. Take the coloured zest and all the white pith (which has a bitter taste). Cut following the curve of the fruit.

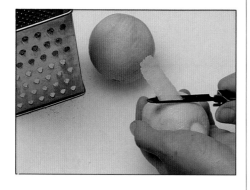

To remove zest, use a vegetable peeler to shave off the zest in wide strips, taking none of the white pith. Use these strips whole or cut them into fine shreds with a sharp knife, according to recipe directions. Or rub the fruit against the fine holes of a metal grater, turning the fruit so you take just the coloured zest and not the white pith. Or use a special tool, called a citrus zester, to take fine threads of zest. (Finely chop the threads as an alternative to grating.)

Kiwi fruit

Follow citrus fruit technique, taking off the peel in thin lengthways strips.

Apples, pears, quinces, mangoes, papayas

Use a small sharp knife or a vegetable peeler. Take off the peel in long strips, as thinly as possible.

Peaches, apricots

Cut a cross in the base. Immerse the fruit in boiling water. Leave for 10–30 seconds (according to ripeness), then drain and immerse in iced water. The skin should slip off easily.

Pineapple

Cut off the leafy crown. Cut a slice from the base and set the pineapple upright. With a sharp knife, cut off the peel lengthways, cutting thickly to remove the brown 'eyes' with it.

Bananas, lychees, avocado

Make a small cut and remove the peel with your fingers.

Passion fruit, pomegranates

Cut in half, or cut a slice off the top. With a spoon, scoop the flesh and seeds into a bowl.

Star fruit (carambola)

Trim off the tough, darkened edges of the five segments.

Rhubarb

Cut off the leaves and discard them (they are poisonous). Peel off any tough skin.

Fresh currants (red, black, white)
Pull through the prongs of a fork to remove the currants from the stalks.

For halves, use a melon baller to scoop out the core. Cut out the stalk and base with a small sharp knife.
For quarters, cut out the stalk and core with a serrated knife.

Fresh dates
Cut the fruit lengthways in half and lift out the stone. Or, if the fruit is to be used whole, cut in from the stalk end with a thin-bladed knife to loosen the stone, then remove it.

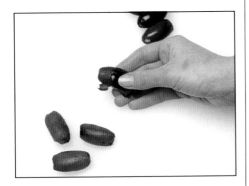

Citrus fruit
With the tip of a pointed knife, nick out pips from slices or segments.

Fresh dates
Squeeze gently at the stalk end to remove the rather tough skin.

CORING AND STONING OR SEEDING FRUIT

Cherries
Use a cherry stoner for the neatest results.

Mangoes
Cut lengthways on either side of the large flat stone in the centre. Curve the cut slightly to follow the shape of the stone. Also cut the flesh from the two thin ends of the stone.

Apples, pears, quinces
For whole fruit, use an apple corer to stamp out the whole core from stalk end to base. Alternatively, working up from the base, use a melon baller to cut out the core. Leave the stalk end intact.

Peaches, apricots, nectarines, plums
Cut the fruit in half, cutting round the indentation. Twist the halves apart. Lift out the stone, or lever it out with the tip of a sharp knife.

Papayas, melons
Cut the fruit in half. Scoop out the seeds from the central hollow, then scrape away any fibres.

Pineapple

For spears and wedges, cut out the core neatly with a sharp knife.
For rings, cut out the core with a small pastry cutter.

Grapes

Cut the fruit lengthways in half. Use a small knife to nick out the pips. Alternatively, use the curved end of a sterilized hair grip.

Gooseberries

Use scissors to trim off the stalk and flower ends.

Star fruit (carambola), watermelon

With the tip of a pointed knife, nick out pips from slices.

Strawberries

Use a special huller to remove leafy green top and central core. Or cut these out with a small sharp knife.

Avocado

Cut the fruit in half lengthways. Stick the tip of a sharp knife into the stone and lever it out without damaging the surrounding flesh.

CUTTING FRUIT

Apples, quinces

For rings, remove the core and seeds with an apple corer. Set the fruit on its side and cut across into thick or thin rings, as required.

For slices, cut the fruit in half and remove core and seeds with a melon baller. Set one half cut side down and

cut it across into neat slices, thick or thin according to recipe directions. Or cut the fruit into quarters and remove core and seeds with a knife. Cut lengthways into neat slices.

Pears

For 'fans', cut the fruit in half and remove core and seeds with a melon baller. Set one half cut side down and cut lengthways into thin slices, not cutting all the way through at the stalk end. Gently fan out the slices so they are overlapping each other evenly. Transfer the pear fan to plate or pastry case using a palette knife.
For slices, follow apple technique.

Keeping fresh colour

If exposed to the air for long, the cut flesh of some fruits and vegetables starts to turn brown. Those with a tendency to brown include apples, bananas, peaches and avocado. So if prepared fruit has to wait before being served or cooked, sprinkle the cut surfaces with lemon juice. Or you can immerse hard fruits in water and lemon juice, but do not soak or the fruit may become soggy.

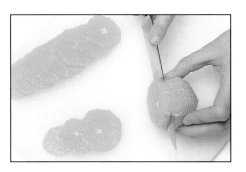

Citrus fruit

For slices, using a serrated knife, cut the fruit across into neat slices.

For segments, hold the peeled fruit in your cupped palm, over a bowl to catch the juice. Working from the side of the fruit to the centre, slide the knife down one side of a separating membrane to free the flesh from it. Then slide the knife down the other side of that segment to free it from the membrane there. Drop the segment into the bowl. Continue cutting out the segments, folding back the membrane like the pages of a book as you work. When all the segments have been cut out, squeeze all the juice from the membrane.

Peaches, nectarines, apricots, plums

For slices, follow apple technique.

Papayas, avocado

For slices, follow apple technique. Or cut the unpeeled fruit into wedges, removing the central seeds or stone. Set each wedge peel side down and slide the knife down the length to cut the flesh away from the peel.
For fans, follow pear technique.

Melon

For slices, follow papaya technique.
For balls, use a melon baller.

Mangoes

Cut the peeled flesh into slices or cubes, according to recipe directions.

Bananas Baked with Rum

Quarter 4 bananas and put in a small baking dish. Sprinkle with a mixture of 2 oz (55 g) melted butter, 3 tablespoons soft light brown sugar, 1–2 tablespoons lemon juice and 6 tablespoons light rum or orange juice. Turn to coat. Bake at 400°F/200°C/Gas 6 for 20 minutes, basting occasionally. Serve with cream. *Serves 4.*

Pineapple

For spears, cut the peeled fruit lengthways in half and then into quarters. Cut each quarter into spears and cut out the core.
For chunks, cut the peeled fruit into spears. Remove the core. Cut across each spear into chunks.
For rings, cut the peeled fruit across into slices. Stamp out the central core from each slice using a pastry cutter.

Kiwi fruit, star fruit (carambola)

Cut the fruit across into neat slices; discard the ends.

Banana

Cut the fruit across into neat slices. Or cut in half and then lengthways into quarters.

PREPARING FRESH PINEAPPLE

Pineapple can be prepared in many decorative ways, apart from rings, spears and cubes.

Tipsy Pineapple Boat
Cut 2 small to medium-sized pineapples in half and scoop out the flesh. Cut the pineapple flesh into neat, small pieces. Put them back in the pineapple halves. Sprinkle each half with 1–2 tablespoons rum, kirsch, apricot brandy or Grand Marnier. If liked, sprinkle with a little sugar to taste. Toss the fruit to mix the liquor and sugar evenly. Cover tightly and chill for 20–30 minutes before serving. *Serves 4.*

1 ▲ For a pineapple boat: Trim off any browned ends from the green leaves of the crown. Trim the stalk end if necessary. With a long sharp knife, cut the pineapple lengthways in half, through the crown.

3 ▲ With a small sharp knife, cut straight across the top and bottom of the central core in each half. Then cut lengthways at a slant on either side of the core. This will cut out the core in a V-shape.

2 ▲ Cut a thin slice from the base of each half so it has a flat surface and will not rock.

4 ▲ With a curved serrated grapefruit knife, cut out the flesh from each half. The boats are now ready for filling with a salad, a dessert, or with ice cream, fruit ice or sorbet.

5 ▲ For pineapple wedges: Trim the crown and base as above. Cut the fruit lengthways in half, through the crown, and then into quarters.

6 ▲ Cut the central core from each quarter. Slide the knife under the flesh to loosen it from the peel, but leave it in place.

7 ▲ Cut across the flesh on each wedge. Pull out the slices slightly in alternate directions. If desired, sprinkle the fruit lightly with sugar before serving.

Peanut-chicken Salad in Pineapple Boats

SERVES 4

2 small ripe pineapples

8 oz (225 g) cooked chicken breast, cut into bite-size pieces

2 celery stalks, diced

2 oz (55 g) spring onions, white and green parts, chopped

8 oz (225 g) seedless green grapes

1½ oz (45 g) salted peanuts, coarsely chopped

FOR THE DRESSING

3 oz (85 g) smooth peanut butter

4 fl oz (120 ml) mayonnaise

2 tablespoons cream or milk

1 garlic clove, finely chopped

1 teaspoon mild curry powder

1 tablespoon apricot jam

salt and pepper

1 Make 4 pineapple boats from the pineapples. Cut the flesh removed from the boats into bite-size pieces.

2 ▲ Combine the pineapple flesh, chicken, celery, spring onions and grapes in a bowl.

3 ▼ Put all the dressing ingredients in another bowl and mix with a wooden spoon or whisk until evenly blended. Season with salt and pepper. (The dressing will be thick, but will be thinned by the juices from the pineapple.)

4 ▲ Add the dressing to the pineapple and chicken mixture. Fold together gently but thoroughly.

5 Divide the chicken salad among the pineapple boats. Sprinkle the peanuts over the top before serving.

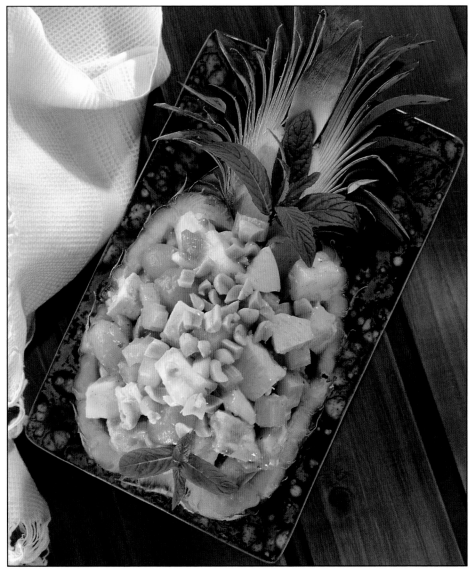

~ **VARIATION** ~

For Mango-turkey Salad in Pineapple Boats, use cooked turkey breast meat instead of chicken and cubed mango flesh in place of grapes. Omit the peanuts.

PREPARING MELON

Melons make attractive containers for salads, both sweet and savoury. Small melons can be used for individual servings, while large watermelons will hold salads to serve a crowd and provide a festive centrepiece at the same time!

Special tools, such as melon cutters with V- or U-shaped blades and melon ball scoops, make decorative preparation easier.

1 ◄ For a plain edge: Cut the melon in half and scoop out the central seeds. Remove the flesh with a melon baller. Or cut it out with a grapefruit knife or scoop it out with a large spoon. Reserve the flesh for the salad. Continue scraping out the flesh, to leave only a thin layer.

2 ▲ For a zig-zag edge: First cut a line around the circumference of the melon to ensure that your finished edge will be level. Using a sharp knife, insert it on the cut line at an angle. Continue making an angled cut about ½–2 in (1.5–5 cm) long, according to the size of the melon. Cut all the way into the centre of the melon. Remove the knife.

3 ▲ Insert the knife at the top of the angled cut and cut back down to the line at a right angle to the first cut, forming a V. Continue cutting V-shapes in this way all round the melon. If available, a special melon cutter with a V-shaped blade will make the job easier.

4 ▲ Lift the melon halves apart. Remove the seeds and scoop out the flesh as above.

Citrus garnishes
The technique for preparing melons can also be used for lemons and oranges. These make attractive containers for cold and iced desserts. Another idea: cut a lemon in half with a zig-zag edge, but don't hollow out the halves. Instead, trim the base of each so it will sit flat, then dip the points of the edge in chopped parsley. Serve this instead of plain lemon wedges with fish.

5 ▲ For a scalloped edge: You can do this freehand following the technique for cutting a zig-zag edge, but instead cutting curves. However, it is much easier, and the results are better, if you use a special melon cutter with a U-shaped blade.

Watermelon Basket
Cut a watermelon basket as directed above. Scoop out the flesh with a melon baller and nick out as many of the black pips as you can. Mix the melon balls with balls of charentais and honeydew melon, blueberries and strawberries. Pile the fruit in the watermelon basket for serving.

6 ▲ **For a melon basket**: Cut a plain, zig-zag or scalloped edge, starting just off centre. Cut round the melon to a point opposite where you started.

7 ▲ Cut up over the top of the melon and down to the point you began. Lift off the freed wedge of melon. Repeat on the other end.

8 ▲ Cut out the flesh from under the 'handle'. Cut the flesh from the 'basket' as shown.

Melon Salad with Herbs

SERVES 4

2 charentais melons
½ honeydew melon
½ cucumber
6 oz (170 g) small cherry tomatoes
1½ tablespoons chopped fresh parsley
1 tablespoon snipped fresh chives
1 tablespoon chopped fresh mint
FOR THE DRESSING
6 tablespoons vegetable oil
2 tablespoons red wine vinegar
1 teaspoon caster sugar
salt and pepper

1 Cut the charentais in half, with a plain, zig-zag or scalloped edge. Scoop out the seeds and central fibres. Using a melon baller, take small balls of flesh and put them in a bowl. Scrape most of the remaining flesh from the melon halves. Set the melon shells aside.

2 Remove seeds and fibres from the honeydew melon. Scoop out the flesh in small balls and add to the charentais balls.

3 ▲ Use the melon baller to make balls of cucumber, or cut into cubes.

4 Add the cucumber to the melon balls with the cherry tomatoes.

5 For the dressing, combine the ingredients in a screwtop jar and shake well. Add the dressing to the bowl and toss together. Cover and refrigerate the salad for 2–3 hours.

6 Just before serving, stir in the herbs. Divide the salad among the melon shells, with all the juice.

MAKING A BERRY SAUCE

A smooth, uncooked berry sauce, called a 'coulis' in French, has a refreshing flavour and beautiful colour. According to how much sugar you add, a berry sauce can be a sweet complement or tart contrast to a cake, pastry, ice cream or fruit dessert.

You can use fresh or frozen berries for the sauce. If using frozen berries, partially thaw them and drain on paper towels before puréeing.

MAKES ABOUT 8 FL OZ (240 ML)

1 lb (450 g) berries (raspberries, strawberries, blackberries, etc)

1–2 oz (30–55 g) icing sugar, sifted

squeeze of lemon juice (optional)

1–2 tablespoons kirsch or fruit liqueur (optional)

1 ▲ Hull the berries if necessary. Put them in a bowl of cold water and swirl them round briefly. Scoop out and spread on paper towels. Pat dry. Purée the berries in a blender or food processor. Turn the machine on and off a few times and scrape down the bowl to be sure all the berries are evenly puréed.

2 ▲ For raspberries, blackberries and other berries with small seeds, press the purée through a fine-mesh nylon sieve. Add icing sugar to taste, plus a little lemon juice and/or liqueur, if using (for example, raspberry liqueur – framboise – for a raspberry sauce). Stir well to dissolve the sugar completely.

Iced Macaroon Cream with Raspberry Sauce

SERVES 6–8

1¼ pints (750 ml) whipping cream

4 tablespoons brandy or orange juice

2 tablespoons caster sugar

12 crisp almond macaroons (about 4 oz/ 115 g), coarsely crushed

raspberries, to decorate

8 fl oz (240 ml) raspberry sauce, to serve

2 Add the brandy or juice and sugar. Continue whipping until the cream will hold stiff peaks.

3 ▼ Add the macaroons and fold evenly into the cream.

~ **VARIATION** ~

Use coarsely broken meringue nests (page 160) instead of macaroons. Use almond liqueur instead of brandy or juice.

4 Spoon into 6–8 ramekins, or a 2 pint (1.5 litre) smooth-sided mould. Press in evenly to be sure there are no air pockets. Smooth the surface. Cover and freeze until firm. (Do not freeze longer than 1 day.)

5 ▼ To serve, dip the moulds in hot water for 5–10 seconds, then invert on to a serving plate. Lift off the moulds. Refrigerate the desserts for 15–20 minutes to soften slightly.

1 ▲ Put the cream in a large bowl, preferably chilled, and whip until it starts to thicken.

6 Decorate with raspberries and serve with the sauce.

MAKING SORBETS AND FRUIT ICES

Sorbets and fruit ices are most refreshing desserts. A fruit ice is made by freezing a sweetened fruit purée, whereas a sorbet is made from fruit juice or purée mixed with a sugar syrup. In addition, there are sorbets based on wine or liqueur. The Italian 'granita' uses the same mixture as a sorbet, but it is stirred during freezing to give it its characteristic coarse texture. A sherbet normally contains milk or cream.

Strawberry Ice

Purée 1 lb 2 oz (500 g) strawberries with 3½ oz (100 g) caster sugar and 4 fl oz (120 ml) orange juice. Be sure the sugar has dissolved completely. Add 1 tablespoon lemon juice. Taste the mixture and add more sugar or orange or lemon juice if required. (The mixture should be highly flavoured.) Chill well, then transfer to an ice cream machine and freeze until firm. *Makes about 1 pint (600 ml).*

Variations

• Use raspberries or blackberries instead of strawberries.
• Use 1½ lb (700 g) peeled and sliced peaches or nectarines instead of strawberries.
• Add 1–2 tablespoons of fruit liqueur (to match the fruit used).

1 ▲ For a fruit ice: Prepare the fruit, removing peel, stones, hulls, stalks, etc. Purée the fruit with sugar and liquid in a blender or food processor until very smooth. Be sure that the sugar has dissolved completely.

3 ▲ For a sorbet: If using citrus fruit, peel off strips of zest. Squeeze the juice from the fruit. Alternatively, purée fruit in a blender or food processor (first cooking if necessary).

5 ▲ Stir in the fruit juice or purée. Strain the mixture into a bowl, if necessary, and chill well. Then transfer the mixture to an ice cream machine and freeze following the manufacturer's instructions.

2 ▲ Add additional flavourings as directed in the recipe (alcohol, herbs, for example). If using berries with seeds (raspberries, blackberries, etc), press the purée through a fine-mesh nylon sieve. Chill the purée well. Then transfer to an ice cream machine and freeze following the manufacturer's instructions.

4 ▲ Put the strips of zest (or other flavouring items such as vanilla pod, spices) in a saucepan with sugar and water and bring to the boil, stirring to dissolve the sugar. Leave to cool.

Still-freezing fruit ice

If you don't have an ice cream machine, you can 'still-freeze' the fruit ice or sorbet in the freezer. Pour it into a metal tin or tray, cover and freeze until set round the edge. Turn it into a bowl and break it into small pieces. Beat with an electric mixer or in a food processor until slushy. Return to the metal tin and freeze again until set round the edge. Repeat the beating once or twice more, then freeze until firm.

Mango Sorbet

SERVES 6

5 oz (145 g) sugar

6 fl oz (170 ml) water

a large strip of orange zest

1 large mango, peeled, stoned, and cubed

4 tablespoons orange juice

1 Combine the sugar, water and orange zest in a saucepan. Bring to the boil, stirring to dissolve the sugar. Leave the sugar syrup to cool.

2 ▼ Purée the mango with the orange juice in a blender or food processor. There should be about 16 fl oz (500 ml) of purée.

3 ▲ Add the purée to the cooled sugar syrup and mix well. Strain. Taste the mixture (it should be well flavoured). Chill. Transfer to an ice cream machine and freeze until firm.

Sorbet variations

● For *Banana Sorbet*: Peel and cube 4–5 large bananas. Purée with 2 tablespoons lemon juice to make 16 fl oz (500 ml). If liked, replace the orange zest in the sugar syrup with 2–3 whole cloves, or omit the zest.

● For *Papaya Sorbet*: Peel, seed and cube 1½ lb (700 g) papaya. Purée with 3 tablespoons lime juice to make 16 fl oz (500 ml). Replace the orange zest with lime zest.

● For *Passion Fruit Sorbet*: Halve 16 or more passion fruit and scoop out the seeds and pulp (there should be about 16 fl oz/500 ml). Work in a blender or food processor until the seeds are like coarse pepper. Omit the orange juice and zest. Add the passion fruit to the sugar syrup, then press through a wire sieve before freezing.

● For *Lemon Sorbet*: Make the sugar syrup with 14 oz (400 g) sugar, 16 fl oz (500 ml) water and 2 tablespoons finely grated lemon zest. Add 6 fl oz (170 ml) fresh lemon juice. Do not strain out the zest before freezing.

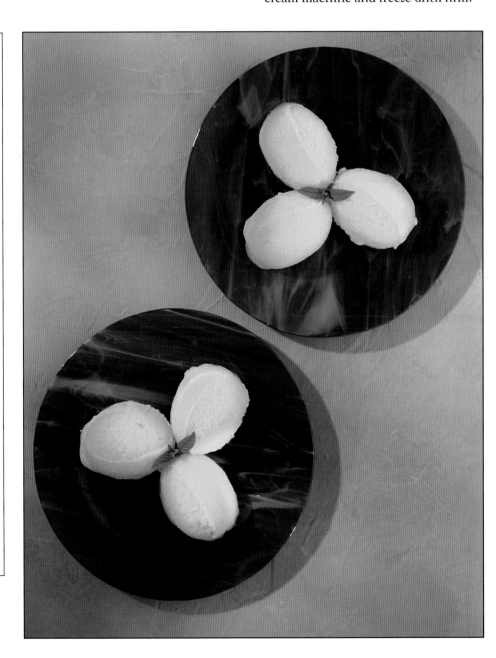

MAKING FRUIT CRUMBLE

This well-loved dessert is simple and satisfying. It consists of fruit baked with a sweet, crumbly topping. Almost any fruit can be used, and the topping mixture can be varied in many ways, according to your preferences and what you have to hand in the store-cupboard.

Pear Crumble
Make the crumble mixture with 4 oz (115 g) plain flour, 5 oz (145 g) soft light brown sugar, 1 teaspoon ground ginger and 4 oz (115 g) butter. Add 2 oz (55 g) chopped walnuts and mix lightly. Toss 1¾ lb (800 g) sliced firm pears with 2 oz (55 g) caster sugar and 1–2 tablespoons flour. Assemble the crumble and bake in a 375°F/190°C/Gas 5 oven for 30–35 minutes. *Serves 4–6.*

Variation
● Use apples instead of pears, and cinnamon instead of ginger.

A freezer standby
Fruit crumbles freeze very well and are very handy to have for an impromptu pudding. Freeze, un-cooked, in a foil container, and bake from frozen, uncovered, in a 350°F/180°C/Gas 4 oven for about 45 minutes.

1 ▲ For the topping, combine the dry ingredients (flour and sugar plus oats or other cereal, coconut, nuts, spices, etc) in a bowl. Add the fat (butter or margarine).

2 ▲ Cut or rub the fat into the dry ingredients as if making pastry dough. Do not overmix the topping: the finished texture should be like coarse crumbs.

3 ▲ Prepare the fruit as directed in the recipe, by peeling, stoning or coring, slicing or cubing.

4 ▲ If the recipe specifies, toss the fruit with sugar or a sweet syrup and spices. Add flour or cornflour for thickening the fruit juices, if required. Spread the fruit in a baking dish.

5 ▲ Scatter the crumble mixture on top to cover the fruit in an even layer.

6 ▲ Bake until the fruit is tender and the topping is golden brown and crisp. Serve warm, with whipped cream, soured cream, yogurt or ice cream.

Spiced Peach Crumble

SERVES 6

3 lb (1.35 kg) ripe but firm peaches, peeled, stoned and sliced

4 tablespoons caster sugar

½ teaspoon ground cinnamon

1 teaspoon lemon juice

whipped cream or vanilla ice cream, for serving (optional)

FOR THE TOPPING

4 oz (115 g) plain flour

¼ teaspoon ground cinnamon

¼ teaspoon ground allspice

3 oz (85 g) rolled oats

6 oz (170 g) soft light brown sugar

4 oz (115 g) butter

1 Preheat a 375°F/190°C/Gas 5 oven.

2 ▼ For the topping, sift the flour and spices into a bowl. Add the oats and sugar and stir to combine. Cut or rub in the butter until the mixture resembles coarse crumbs.

3 Toss the peaches with the sugar, cinnamon and lemon juice. Put the fruit in an 8–9 in (20–23 cm) diameter baking dish.

4 ▲ Scatter the topping over the fruit in an even layer. Bake for 30–35 minutes. Serve warm, with whipped cream or ice cream, if liked.

~ **VARIATION** ~

Use apricots or nectarines instead of peaches. Substitute nutmeg for the cinnamon.

MAKING A STEAMED PUDDING

Steamed puddings, many with fruit, range from light and delicate sponges to rich suet puddings, and the variety of flavourings is infinite, both sweet and savoury. Puddings may be steamed on top of the stove or in the oven. A pressure cooker can also be used. Some puddings, such as roly poly, are wrapped in greased foil rather than being cooked in a basin or mould.

First prepare the steamer. For cooking on top of the stove, you can use either a large saucepan with tight-fitting lid or a proper steamer. For oven steaming, use a deep casserole or roasting tin.

1 If using a saucepan, it is necessary to have something to help you put the pudding into the pan and then lift it out after cooking. Unless you are wrapping the pudding in a cloth (the knot at the top makes a convenient handle), use a wire steaming basket with handles or make a sling of foil. Put enough water into the saucepan or steamer to one-quarter fill it, and bring to the boil. Boil water in the kettle too.

2 ▲ Generously butter the pudding basin or mould(s). Put a disc of buttered greaseproof paper in the bottom. Make the pudding mixture. Turn it into the basin or mould(s), which should be about two-thirds full.

3 ▲ Cover the basin or mould(s). This must be done carefully so that the steam from the boiling water does not fall on to the pudding, thus making it soggy. First lay a disc of buttered greaseproof paper on top.

4 ▲ To cover with foil, lay a piece of foil on another sheet of paper. Holding the paper and foil together, fold a 1 in (2.5 cm) pleat across the centre (the pleat will allow for the pudding rising above the basin rim).

5 ▲ Smooth the paper and foil down over the edge. Wrap a piece of string twice around the basin, just below the rim, and tie firmly. Trim off the corners with scissors.

6 ▲ To cover with a cloth, use a square of cotton that is about three times larger than the top of the basin or mould(s). Lay it over the buttered paper, pleat and tie with string as above. Bring the corners of the cloth up over the top and tie opposite ones together into knots.

7 ▲ Lower the basin or mould(s) into the boiling water in the saucepan or steamer, or arrange in the roasting tin. Pour enough boiling water into the pan or tin to come halfway up the sides of the basin or mould(s).

8 Cover tightly with a lid or foil. Set over a moderately low heat on top of the stove or put into a preheated 350°F/180°C/Gas 4 oven. The water in the steamer should simmer but not boil up over the top of the pudding. Steam for the required time, topping up with more boiling water as needed. (With oven steaming you will need to replenish the water less often as there is much less evaporation.) When cooked, remove the basin or mould(s) from the water and cool for a few minutes. Remove the covering, set a serving plate, inverted, on top of the basin or mould(s) and, holding them firmly together, turn them over. Lift off the mould and serve.

Apple and Kumquat Sponge Puddings

SERVES 8

5 oz (145 g) butter, at room temperature

6 oz (170 g) cooking apples, peeled and thinly sliced

3 oz (85 g) kumquats, thinly sliced

5 oz (145 g) golden caster sugar

2 eggs

4 oz (115 g) self-raising flour

FOR THE SAUCE

3 oz (85 g) kumquats, thinly sliced

3 oz (85 g) caster sugar

8 fl oz (240 ml) water

¼ pint (150 ml) crème fraîche

1 teaspoon cornflour mixed with 2 teaspoons water

lemon juice to taste

1 Prepare the steamer. Butter eight ¼ pint (150 ml) dariole moulds or ramekins and put a disc of buttered greaseproof paper on the bottom of each one.

2 ▲ Melt 1 oz (30 g) butter in a frying pan. Add the apples, kumquats and 1 oz (30 g) sugar and cook over moderate heat for 5–8 minutes or until the apples start to soften and the sugar begins to caramelize. Remove from the heat and leave to cool.

3 Meanwhile, cream the remaining butter with the remaining sugar until the mixture is pale and fluffy. Add the eggs, one at a time, beating well after each addition. Fold in the flour.

4 ▼ Divide the apple and kumquat mixture among the prepared moulds. Top with the sponge mixture.

5 Cover the moulds and put into the steamer. Steam on top of the stove for 45 minutes. If oven-steaming, cook for 30 minutes.

6 For the sauce, put the kumquats, sugar and water in a frying pan and bring to the boil, stirring to dissolve the sugar. Simmer for 5 minutes.

7 ▲ Stir in the crème fraîche and bring back to the boil, stirring.

8 Remove from the heat and whisk in the cornflour mixture. Return the pan to the heat and simmer gently for 2 minutes, stirring. Add lemon juice to taste.

9 Turn out the puddings and serve hot, with the sauce.

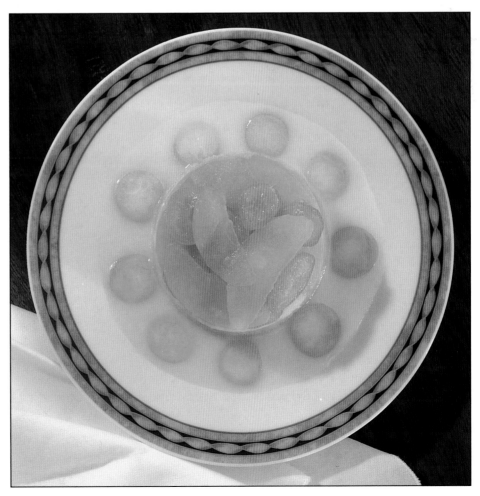

MELTING CHOCOLATE

If chocolate is overheated, it can burn or develop a grainy texture, so care must be taken when melting it. If the chocolate is being melted with butter or a large quantity of liquid, this can be done in a heavy-based pan over moderately low heat. When melting chocolate alone, use a bain-marie or microwave oven as described here.

For the richest, most intense chocolate flavour in cakes, biscuits and confectionery, use a chocolate that contains a lot of cocoa solids (the pure chocolate essence) and cocoa butter (a natural vegetable fat) rather than vegetable oil. Check the labels, and choose chocolate with at least 50 per cent cocoa solids. The more bitter it is – with less sugar content – the more chocolatey it will taste.

You can find good-quality 'luxury' chocolate in many large supermarkets now, or buy French or Belgian chocolate from a delicatessen.

Spiced Mocha Drink
Melt 6 oz (170 g) milk chocolate with 4 fl oz (120 ml) single cream. Add 1¼ pints (750 ml) hot black coffee and ¼ teaspoon ground cinnamon. Whisk until foamy. Serve hot with a dollop of whipped cream, or cool and chill, then serve over ice. *Serves 4.*

1 ▲ **In a bain-marie**: First, cut the chocolate into small pieces with a sharp knife to enable it to melt quickly and evenly.

3 ▲ According to the recipe instructions, add liquid such as milk, cream, coffee or water, or a fat such as butter.

5 ▲ **In a microwave oven**: Arrange the chocolate in a glass container and melt it in a microwave oven (consult manufacturer's handbook for timings).

2 ▲ Put the chocolate in a double saucepan or a bowl set over a saucepan of almost simmering water. The base of the bowl should not touch the water.

4 ▲ Heat gently until the chocolate is melted and smooth, stirring occasionally. Remove from the heat.

Moisture problems
If any steam from boiling water gets into the chocolate while melting, it can turn into a solid mass. If this happens, stir in a little fat, about 1 teaspoon to each 1 oz (30 g) of chocolate.

Bittersweet Chocolate Sauce

MAKES ABOUT 12 FL OZ (340 ML)

3 tablespoons sugar

4 fl oz (120 ml) water

6 oz (170 g) dark Continental chocolate, chopped into small pieces

1 oz (30 g) unsalted butter, diced

4–6 tablespoons single cream

½ teaspoon vanilla essence

~ **VARIATION** ~

If preferred, use 1–2 tablespoons orange liqueur instead of vanilla.

1 Combine the sugar and water in a heavy-based saucepan. Bring to the boil, stirring to dissolve the sugar.

2 ▲ Add the chocolate and butter and remove the pan from the heat.

3 ▲ Stir until the mixture is smooth, then stir in the cream and vanilla essence. Serve the sauce warm, over ice cream, profiteroles, etc.

Chocolate Truffles

MAKES ABOUT 24

8 oz (225 g) bittersweet or good plain chocolate, chopped into small pieces

6 tablespoons double cream

cocoa powder

1 ▲ Put the chocolate in a bowl set over a pan of hot water or in the top of a double saucepan. Heat until melted and smooth, stirring occasionally.

2 ▼ Remove from the pan of hot water. Add the cream and stir well. Leave to cool.

3 Cover and refrigerate for 35 minutes or until the mixture is just firm enough to hold its shape.

4 Sift a layer of cocoa powder on to a plate or shallow dish.

5 ▲ Take a heaped teaspoonful of the chocolate mixture and shape it into a ball.

6 ▲ Roll in the cocoa to coat all over in an even layer. Shake off excess cocoa. Set the truffle on a tray.

7 Continue shaping and coating the remaining truffles, setting them on the tray in a single layer, not touching each other.

8 Cover and refrigerate. Remove from the refrigerator 15 minutes before serving.

~ **VARIATIONS** ~

For Liqueur-flavoured Truffles, add 2 tablespoons cherry or apricot brandy or orange liqueur. For Coated Truffles, roll the truffles in finely chopped toasted hazelnuts or other nuts, or in finely grated chocolate instead of cocoa powder.

Chocolate Nut Cake

SERVES 6–8

6 oz (170 g) good plain chocolate, chopped into small pieces
4 oz (115 g) butter, preferably unsalted
7 oz (200 g) caster sugar
4 eggs, separated
4 oz (115 g) unsalted macadamia nuts or almonds, freshly ground
1 oz (30 g) plain flour
pinch of cream of tartar (if needed)
cocoa powder, to dust
sweetened whipped cream (page 160)

1 Preheat a 325°F/170°C/Gas 3 oven. Grease a 9 in (23 cm) round cake tin and line the bottom with greased paper. Dust the cake tin with cocoa powder and shake out excess.

2 Combine the chocolate and butter in a heavy-based saucepan. Set over moderately low heat and stir until melted and smooth. Leave to cool.

3 ▲ Whisk together the sugar and egg yolks until pale and thick.

4 ▲ Add the chocolate mixture, nuts and flour and beat in gently.

5 In another large bowl, scrupulously clean and grease-free, and using clean beaters, whisk the egg whites until they will hold stiff peaks. (If not using a copper bowl, add the cream of tartar when the whites are frothy.)

6 ▲ Lighten the chocolate mixture by gently mixing in about one-quarter of the whites. It is not necessary to blend thoroughly.

7 ▲ Add the remaining whites and fold them in gently but thoroughly using a rubber spatula.

8 Pour the mixture into the prepared tin. Bake for 1–1¼ hours or until a skewer inserted into the centre of the cake comes out clean. Cool in the tin for 10 minutes, then turn out on to a wire rack to cool completely.

9 Dust the cake with cocoa powder. Serve with sweetened whipped cream.

PREPARING NUTS

Nuts are enjoyed as a snack or with drinks, as well as being an important ingredient or garnish in many dishes, from breakfast cereals and breads to salads, main dishes, vegetable and grain accompaniments, and desserts.

Some nuts may be bought complete with their brown, papery skins. The skin often has a bitter taste and so should be removed before the nuts are used. The flavour of all nuts is improved by toasting; this makes them appealingly crisp too.

1 ▲ To skin almonds and pistachios: Put the nuts in a bowl and cover with boiling water. Leave for 2 minutes. (This is known as blanching.) Drain the nuts and cool slightly, then squeeze or rub each nut with your fingers to remove the skins.

2 ▲ To skin hazelnuts and brazils: Spread the nuts on a baking sheet. Toast in a 350°F/180°C/Gas 4 oven for 10–15 minutes to dry the skins. Wrap the nuts in a rough tea towel and rub to remove the skin. Pick off any bits of skin still adhering to the nuts.

Spicy Cocktail Nuts

Combine 3 tablespoons corn oil, 2 halved garlic cloves and 1 teaspoon dried hot red pepper flakes in a saucepan. Heat for 1 minute, stirring. Discard the garlic. Add 8 oz (225 g) mixed nuts, such as blanched almonds, walnuts, skinned peanuts, blanched hazelnuts, and stir well. Add salt to taste. Pour the mixture on to a baking sheet and bake in a 300°F/150°C/Gas 2 oven for about 20 minutes, stirring occasionally. Drain the nuts on paper towels and leave to cool before serving.

3 ▲ To oven-toast or grill nuts: Spread the nuts on a baking sheet. Toast in a 350°F/180°C/Gas 4 oven or under a moderate grill, until golden brown and smelling nutty. Stir the nuts occasionally.

4 ▲ To fry-toast nuts: Put the nuts in a frying pan, with no fat. Toast over moderate heat until golden brown. Stir constantly and watch carefully because nuts scorch easily.

5 ▲ To grind nuts: Using a nut mill or a clean coffee grinder, grind a small batch of nuts at a time so that you can be sure of getting an even texture. As soon as the nuts have a fine texture, stop grinding: if overworked, they will turn to a paste.

6 ▲ You can also grind nuts in a food processor, but it is not as easy to get an even texture, and thus there is more risk of overworking the nuts to a paste. To prevent this, grind the nuts with some of the sugar or flour called for in the recipe.

Bread Pudding with Pecan Nuts

SERVES 6

14 fl oz (400 ml) milk
14 fl oz (400 ml) single or whipping cream
5 oz (145 g) caster sugar
3 eggs, beaten to mix
2 teaspoons grated orange zest
1 teaspoon vanilla essence
24 slices of day-old French bread, ½ in (1.5 cm) thick
3 oz (85 g) toasted pecan nuts, chopped
icing sugar, for sprinkling
whipped cream or soured cream and maple syrup, to serve

1 ▲ Put 12 fl oz (360 ml) each of the milk and cream in a saucepan. Add the sugar. Warm over low heat, stirring to dissolve the sugar. Remove from the heat and cool. Add the eggs, orange zest and vanilla and mix well.

2 ▲ Arrange half of the bread slices in a buttered 9–10 in (23–25 cm) baking dish. Scatter two-thirds of the pecans over the bread. Arrange the remaining bread slices on top and scatter on the rest of the pecans.

3 ▼ Pour the egg mixture evenly over the bread slices. Soak for 30 minutes. Press the top layer of bread down into the liquid once or twice.

4 Preheat a 350°F/180°C/Gas 4 oven.

5 If the top layer of bread slices looks dry and all the liquid has been absorbed, moisten with the remaining milk and cream.

6 ▲ Set the baking dish in a roasting tin. Add enough water to the tin to come halfway up the sides of the dish. Bring the water to the boil.

7 Transfer to the oven. Bake for 40 minutes or until the pudding is set and golden brown on top. Sprinkle the top of the pudding with sifted icing sugar and serve warm, with whipped cream or soured cream and maple syrup, if you like.

BREADS

~

The enticing aroma of fresh bread baking is enough to lure anyone to the kitchen, and the enjoyment of teabreads, home-made loaves and bread rolls is even better than the anticipation. You can make your own pizza dough, too.

MAKING TEABREADS AND MUFFINS

These sorts of bread are very quick and easy to make. The raising agent reacts quickly with moisture and heat to make the breads and muffins rise, without the need for a rising (or proving) period before baking.

The raising agent is usually bicarbonate of soda or baking powder, which is a mixture of bicarbonate of soda and an acid salt such as cream of tartar. Many recipes use self-raising flour which conveniently includes a raising agent. Remember that the raising agent will start to work as soon as it comes into contact with liquid, so don't mix the dry and liquid ingredients until just before you are ready to fill the tin or tins and bake.

1 ▲ For muffins: Combine the dry ingredients in a bowl. It is a good idea to sift the flour with the raising agent, salt and any spices to mix them evenly. Add the liquid ingredients and stir just until the dry ingredients are moistened; the mixture will not be smooth. Do not overmix attempting to remove all the lumps. If you do, the muffins will be tough and will have air holes in them.

2 ▲ Divide the mixture evenly among the greased muffin tins or deep bun tins lined with paper cases, filling them about two-thirds full. Bake until golden brown and a wooden skewer inserted in the centre comes out clean. To prevent soggy bottoms, remove the muffins immediately from the tins to a wire rack. Cool, and serve warm or at room temperature.

Crunchy Muesli Muffins
Make the mixture from 5 oz (145 g) plain flour, 2½ teaspoons baking powder, 2 tablespoons caster sugar, 8 fl oz (240 ml) milk, 2 oz (55 g) melted butter or corn oil, and 1 egg, adding 7 oz (200 g) toasted oat cereal with raisins to the dry ingredients. Pour into muffin tins or deep bun tins. Bake in a 200°C/400°F/Gas 6 oven for 20 minutes or until golden brown. *Makes 10.*

3 ▲ For fruit and/or nut teabreads: Method 1: Stir together all the liquid ingredients. Add the dry ingredients and beat just until smoothly blended. Method 2: Beat the butter with the sugar until the mixture is light and fluffy. Beat in the eggs followed by the other liquid ingredients. Stir in the dry ingredients. Pour the mixture into a prepared tin (typically a loaf tin). Bake until a wooden skewer inserted in the centre comes out clean. If the bread is browning too quickly, cover the top with foil.

4 ▲ Cool in the tin for 5 minutes, then turn out on to a wire rack to cool completely. A lengthways crack on the surface is characteristic of teabreads. For easier slicing, wrap the bread in greaseproof paper and overwrap in foil, then store overnight at room temperature.

Banana Bread

MAKES 1 LOAF

7 oz (200 g) plain flour
2¼ teaspoons baking powder
½ teaspoon salt
¾ teaspoon ground cinnamon (optional)
4 tablespoons wheat germ
2½ oz (75 g) butter or margarine, at room temperature
4 oz (115 g) caster sugar
¾ teaspoon grated lemon zest
3 ripe bananas, mashed
2 eggs, beaten to mix

1 Preheat a 350°F/180°C/Gas 4 oven. Grease and flour an 8½ × 4½ in (21 × 11 cm) loaf tin.

2 ▲ Sift the flour, baking powder, salt and cinnamon, if using, into a bowl. Stir in the wheat germ.

3 ▲ In another bowl, combine the butter or margarine with the sugar and lemon zest. Beat until the mixture is light and fluffy.

4 ▲ Add the mashed bananas and eggs and mix well.

5 Add the dry ingredients and blend quickly and evenly.

~ **VARIATION** ~

For Banana Walnut Bread, add 2–3 oz (55–85 g) finely chopped walnuts with the dry ingredients.

6 ▼ Spoon into the prepared loaf tin. Bake for 50–60 minutes or until a wooden skewer inserted in the centre comes out clean.

7 Cool in the pan for about 5 minutes, then turn out on to a wire rack to cool completely.

MAKING SCONES

Scone dough may be rolled out and cut into shapes for baking in the oven or cooking on a griddle. To ensure light, well risen scones, do not handle the dough too much and do not roll it out too thinly.

Drop scones are made from a batter that has the consistency of thick cream. The batter is dropped in spoonfuls on to a hot griddle or frying pan.

1 Sift the dry ingredients into a bowl (flour, baking powder with or without bicarbonate of soda, salt, sugar, ground spices, etc).

2 ▲ Add the fat (butter, margarine, vegetable fat, etc). With a pastry blender or two knives used scissor-fashion, cut the fat into the dry ingredients until the mixture resembles fine crumbs, or rub in the fat with your fingertips.

3 ▲ Add the liquid ingredients (milk, cream, buttermilk, eggs). Stir with a fork until the dry ingredients are thoroughly moistened and will come together in a ball of fairly soft dough in the centre of the bowl.

Date Oven Scones
Sift 8 oz (225 g) self-raising flour with a pinch of salt and rub in 2 oz (55 g) butter. Add 2 oz (55 g) chopped dates. Mix to a soft dough with ¼ pint (150 ml) milk. Roll out and cut 2 in (5 cm) rounds. Glaze with egg or milk. Bake at 450°F/230°C/Gas 8 for 8–10 minutes or until risen and golden brown. *Makes about 12.*

4 ▲ Turn the dough on to a lightly floured surface. Knead it very lightly, folding and pressing, to mix evenly – about 30 seconds. Roll or pat out the dough to ¾ in (2 cm) thickness.

6 ▲ **For griddle scones:** If using a well-seasoned cast iron griddle, there is no need to grease it. Heat it slowly and evenly. Put scone triangles or rounds on the hot griddle and cook for 4–5 minutes on each side or until golden brown and cooked through.

5 ▲ **For oven-baked scones:** With a floured, sharp-edged cutter, cut out rounds or other shapes. Or cut diamond shapes or triangles with a floured knife. Arrange on an ungreased baking sheet, not touching. Brush the tops with beaten egg, milk or cream if the recipe specifies. Bake until risen and golden brown.

Cutting tips
● Be sure the cutter or knife is sharp so that the edges of the scone shapes are not compressed; this would inhibit rising.
● Cut the shapes close together so that you won't have to reroll the dough more than once.
● If necessary, a short, sturdy drinking glass can be pressed into service as a cutter. Flour the rim well and do not press too hard.

American Berry Shortcake

SERVES 8

½ pint (300 ml) whipping cream

1 oz (30 g) icing sugar, sifted

1½ lb (700 g) strawberries or mixed berries, halved or sliced if large

2 oz (55 g) caster sugar, or to taste

FOR THE SHORTCAKE

10 oz (300 g) plain flour

2 teaspoons baking powder

2½ oz (75 g) caster sugar

4 oz (115 g) butter

5 tablespoons milk

1 size-1 egg

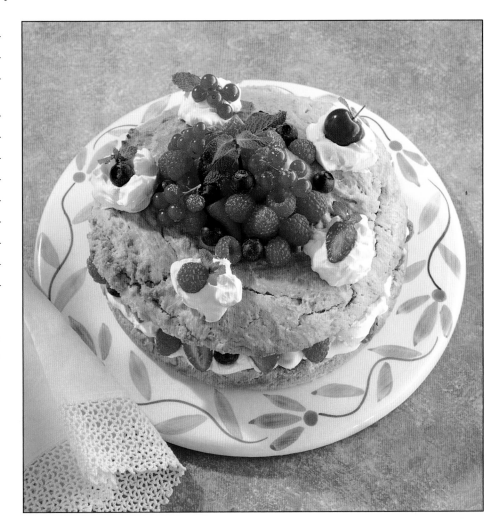

1 Preheat a 450°F/230°C/Gas 8 oven. Grease an 8 in (20 cm) round cake tin.

2 For the shortcake, sift the flour, baking powder and sugar into a bowl. Add the butter and rub in until the mixture resembles fine crumbs. Combine the milk and egg. Add to the crumb mixture and stir just until evenly mixed to a soft dough.

3 Put the dough in the prepared tin and pat out to an even layer. Bake for 15–20 minutes or until a wooden skewer inserted in the centre comes out clean. Leave to cool slightly.

4 ▲ Whip the cream until it starts to thicken. Add the icing sugar and continue whipping until the cream will hold soft peaks.

5 Put the berries in a bowl. Sprinkle with the caster sugar and toss together lightly. Cover and set aside for the berries to give up some juice.

6 ▼ Remove the cooled shortcake from the tin. With a long, serrated knife, split the shortcake horizontally into two equal layers.

7 ▲ Put the bottom layer on a serving plate. Top with half of the berries and most of the cream. Set the second layer on top and press down gently. Spoon the remaining berries over the top layer (or serve them separately) and add the remaining cream in small, decorative dollops.

MAKING YEAST DOUGH

Making bread is a very enjoyable and satisfying culinary experience – with no other preparation do you have such 'hands-on' contact. And from the kneading through to the shaping of the risen (or proven) dough, you are working with a living organism, yeast, not a chemical raising agent. You can use either fresh yeast or dried yeast, which is available in an easy-blend variety too.

Everyday White Bread
Sift 1½ lb (700 g) strong plain flour into a large bowl with 1½ teaspoons salt and 1 tablespoon caster sugar. Stir in 2 teaspoons easy-blend dried yeast. Make a well in the centre and add ¾ pint (450 ml) mixed warm water and milk and 1 oz (30 g) melted and cooled butter. Mix to a soft dough, adding more flour or liquid if necessary, then knead until smooth and elastic. Leave to rise until doubled in bulk. Knock back the dough to deflate. Divide it in half and shape each piece into a loaf, tucking the ends under. Put in 2 greased 8½ × 4½ in (21 × 11 cm) loaf tins. Leave in a warm place to rise for 30–45 minutes. Glaze the tops of the loaves with 1 egg beaten with 1 tablespoon milk. Bake in a 450°F/230°C/Gas 8 oven for 30–35 minutes. *Makes 2 loaves.*

1 ▲ If using ordinary dried yeast, put it in a small bowl, add some of the warm liquid (105–110°F/40–43°C) called for in the recipe and whisk with a fork until dissolved. Add a little sugar if the recipe specifies.

2 ▲ Sift the flour into a large warm bowl (with other dry ingredients such as salt). Make a well in the centre and add the yeast mixture plus any other liquid ingredients.

3 ▲ Using your fingers or a spoon, gradually draw the flour into the liquids. Mix until all the flour is incorporated and the dough pulls away from the sides of the bowl. If the dough feels too soft and wet, work in a little more flour. If it doesn't come together, add a little more liquid.

4 ▲ Turn the dough on to a lightly floured surface. Fold the dough over on to itself towards you and then press it down away from you with the heels of your hands. Rotate the dough slightly and fold and press it again. Knead until the dough looks satiny and feels elastic, about 10 minutes.

5 ▲ Shape the dough into a ball. Put it in a lightly greased bowl and turn the dough to grease all over. Cover the bowl with a towel or cling film. Set it aside in a warm, draught-free place (about 80°F/27°C).

6 ▲ Leave to rise until about doubled in bulk, 1–1½ hours. To test if it is sufficiently risen, press a finger about 1 in (2.5 cm) into the dough and withdraw it quickly; the indentation should remain.

7 ▲ Gently punch the centre of the dough with your fist to deflate it and fold the edges to the centre. Turn the dough on to a lightly floured surface and knead it again for 2–3 minutes. If instructed, shape the dough into a ball again and rise a second time.

8 ▲ Shape the dough into loaves, rolls or other shapes as instructed. Put into prepared tins or on to baking sheets. Cover and leave to rise in a warm place for ¾–1 hour. If the recipe instructs, glaze the loaves or rolls.

9 ▲ Bake in the centre of a heated oven until well risen and golden brown. To test, tip the loaf out of the tin and tap the base with your knuckle. If it sounds hollow, like a drum, it is fully cooked. Immediately transfer to a wire rack for cooling.

SHAPING ROLLS

A basket of freshly baked bread rolls, in decorative shapes, is a delightful accompaniment for soups or salads. After shaping, arrange the rolls on a baking sheet, leaving space around each roll for spreading, and leave to rise for 30 minutes before baking.

Working with yeast

Easy-blend (or fast-action) is the most readily available dried yeast. Unlike ordinary dried yeast, there is no need to mix it with liquid. Just combine it with the flour and other dry ingredients and then add the warm liquids.

If using fresh yeast, allow ½ oz (15 g) to each 1 tablespoon dried. Crumble it into a small bowl, add warm liquid and mash with a fork until blended.

If you are in any doubt about the freshness of ordinary dried or fresh yeast, set the mixture aside in a warm place; after 10 minutes or so it should be foamy. If it isn't, discard it.

1 ▲ **For Parker House rolls**: Roll out the risen dough to ¼ in (5 mm) thickness and cut out 2½–3 in (6–7 cm) rounds using a floured cutter. Brush the rounds with melted butter. Fold them in half, slightly off-centre so the top overlaps the bottom. Press the folded edge firmly. Arrange the rolls on a greased baking sheet.

2 ▲ **For crescent rolls**: Roll out the risen dough to a large round ¼ in (5 mm) thick. Brush with melted butter. With a sharp knife, cut into wedges that are 2½–3 in (6–7 cm) at their wide end. Roll up each wedge, from the wide end. Set the rolls on a greased baking sheet, placing the points underneath.

3 ◄ **For bowknot rolls**: Divide the risen dough into pieces. Roll each with your palms on a lightly floured surface to make ropes that are about ½ in (1.5 cm) thick. Divide the ropes into 9 in (27 cm) lengths. Tie each rope loosely into a knot, tucking the ends under. Arrange the rolls on a greased baking sheet.

Two-tone Bread

MAKES 2 LOAVES

1½ tablespoons dried yeast
4 fl oz (120 ml) warm water
2¼ oz (70 g) caster sugar
about 1½ lb (700 g) strong plain flour
½ tablespoon salt
1 pint (600 ml) warm milk
2½ oz (75 g) butter or margarine, melted and cooled
3 tablespoons treacle or molasses
10 oz (300 g) strong plain wholemeal flour

1 Dissolve the yeast in the water with 1 teaspoon of the sugar.

2 Sift 12 oz (360 g) of the white flour, the remaining sugar and salt into a large warm bowl. Make a well in the centre and put in the yeast, milk and butter or margarine. Gradually draw the flour into the liquids and mix to a smooth soft batter.

3 ▲ Divide the batter in half and put one portion in another bowl. To the first half add 10 oz (300 g) white flour and mix together to a soft dough. If necessary, add a little more flour or warm water.

4 Turn the dough on to a lightly floured surface and knead until it is smooth and elastic. Shape into a ball. Put it in a greased bowl and rotate to grease the dough all over. Cover the bowl with a towel or cling film.

5 ▲ To the second portion of batter add the treacle and wholemeal flour. Mix to combine well. Add enough of the remaining white flour to make a soft dough. Turn on to a lightly floured surface and knead until smooth and elastic. Shape into a ball, put in a greased bowl and cover.

6 Leave the dough to rise in a warm place for about 1–1¼ hours until doubled in bulk. Grease two 8½ × 4½ in (21 × 11 cm) loaf tins.

7 Knock back the dough to deflate it. Divide each ball in half. On a lightly floured surface, roll out half of the light dough to a rectangle about 12 × 8 in (30 × 20 cm). Roll out half of the dark dough to a rectangle of the same size.

8 ▲ Set the dark dough rectangle atop the light one. Roll up tightly from a short side. Set in a greased tin. Repeat with the remaining dark and light doughs. Cover the tins and leave the dough to rise for about ¾–1 hour until doubled in bulk.

9 Preheat a 425°F/220°C/Gas 7 oven. Bake the loaves for 30–35 minutes.

Cinnamon and Walnut Buns

MAKES ABOUT 24

2 tablespoons dried yeast
4 fl oz (120 ml) warm water
about 2 lb (900 g) strong plain flour
4 tablespoons caster sugar
2 teaspoons salt
12 fl oz (360 ml) warm milk
5½ oz (160 g) butter or margarine, melted and cooled
2 eggs, beaten
1½ teaspoons grated orange zest
6 oz (170 g) icing sugar, sifted
3–4 tablespoons orange juice

FOR THE FILLING

3½ oz (100 g) caster sugar
2 oz (55 g) walnuts, finely chopped
1½ teaspoons ground cinnamon

1 Dissolve the yeast in the water.

2 Sift the flour, caster sugar and salt into a large warm bowl. Make a well in the centre and put in the yeast mixture, milk, half of the butter, the eggs and grated orange zest.

3 Gradually draw the flour into the liquids and mix until the dough pulls away from the sides of the bowl. If the dough feels too soft and wet, work in a little more flour.

4 Turn the dough on to a lightly floured surface and knead until satiny smooth and elastic. Shape into a ball. Put it in a greased bowl and rotate to grease the dough all over. Cover the bowl and leave the dough to rise in a warm place until doubled in bulk. Grease two 9–10 in (23–25 cm) round cake tins.

5 With your fist gently knock back the dough to deflate it. Divide it in half. On a lightly floured surface, roll out one piece of dough to a 12 × 8 in (30 × 20 cm) rectangle.

6 ▲ For the filling, put the sugar, chopped nuts and cinnamon into a bowl. Mix the ingredients together until well combined.

7 ▲ Brush the dough with half the remaining melted butter. Sprinkle half of the filling evenly over the surface. Roll up tightly from a long side and pinch the seam to seal it.

8 ▲ With a sharp knife, cut the roll across into 1 in (2.5 cm) pieces. Arrange the pieces, cut side down, in one of the prepared tins. Repeat with the second portion of dough and the remaining melted butter and filling.

9 Cover the tins and leave the buns to rise in a warm place until very puffy, about 30 minutes. Preheat a 375°F/190°C/Gas 5 oven.

10 Bake the buns for 30–40 minutes or until golden. Transfer to a wire rack to cool.

11 Stir the icing sugar with enough orange juice to make a smooth icing of pourable consistency. Drizzle the icing over the buns and leave to set.

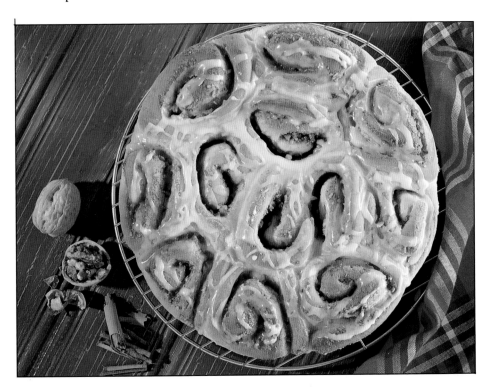

MAKING PIZZA DOUGH

The range of toppings for a pizza is virtually limitless. Although you can buy pizza bases, it's very easy to make your own at home, and takes much less time than you would expect.

MAKES A 14 in (35 cm) PIZZA BASE

2 teaspoons dried yeast	
6 fl oz (180 ml) warm water	
11½ oz (315 g) strong plain flour	
1 teaspoon salt	
1½ tablespoons olive oil	

1 ▲ Put the yeast in a small bowl, add 4 tablespoons of the water and soak for 1 minute. Whisk lightly with a fork until dissolved.

2 ▲ Sift the flour and salt into a large warm bowl. Make a well in the centre and add the yeast mixture, olive oil and remaining warm water.

Tomato and Mozzarella Pizza
Spread ½ pint (300 ml) tomato-garlic sauce (page 172) over the pizza base, not quite to the edges. Scatter 4 oz (115 g) grated mozzarella cheese evenly over the sauce (plus thinly sliced pepperoni or salami if liked). Sprinkle over freshly grated Parmesan cheese and then add a drizzle of olive oil. Bake in a 475°F/240°C/Gas 9 oven for 15–20 minutes.

3 ▲ Using your fingers, gradually draw the flour into the liquids. Continue mixing until all the flour is incorporated and the dough will just hold together.

4 ▲ Turn the dough on to a lightly floured surface. Knead it until it is smooth and silky, about 5 minutes. Shape the dough into a ball. Put it in an oiled bowl and rotate to coat the surface evenly with oil.

Food processor pizza dough
Combine the flour, salt, yeast mixture and olive oil in the processor container. Process briefly, then add the rest of the warm water. Work until the dough begins to form a ball. Process 3–4 minutes to knead the dough, then knead it by hand for 2–3 minutes.

5 ▲ Cover the bowl with cling film. Set aside in a warm place to rise about 1 hour until doubled in bulk. Turn the dough on to the lightly floured surface again. Gently knock back to deflate it, then knead lightly until smooth.

6 ▲ Roll out the dough into a round or square about ¼ in (5 mm) thick. Transfer it to a lightly oiled metal pizza tin or baking sheet. Add the topping as specified in the recipe. Bake until the pizza crust is puffy and well browned. Serve hot.

Goat's Cheese, Basil and Olive Pizza

SERVES 2–4

½ pint (300 ml) tomato-garlic sauce (page 172)

14 in (35 cm) pizza base

3 tomatoes, preferably plum-type, sliced

6 oz (170 g) firm goat's cheese, cut into small cubes or crumbled

½ oz (15 g) fresh basil leaves

18 large black olives, preferably Kalamata

2 tablespoons freshly grated Parmesan cheese

2 tablespoons olive oil

1 Preheat a 475°F/240°C/Gas 9 oven.

2 ▲ Spread the tomato sauce over the pizza base, not quite to the edges. Arrange the tomato slices on top.

3 Scatter the goat's cheese evenly over the tomato slices, followed by the basil leaves, torn if large, and olives.

~ COOK'S TIP ~

A stoneware pizza baking brick or stone will give a pizza a very crisp crust, similar to restaurant pizza. A flat terracotta tile will give the same result. The pizza is assembled on a semolina-dusted wooden paddle, and then slid on to the preheated stone for baking.

4 ▼ Sprinkle with the Parmesan and then the olive oil.

5 Bake for 15–20 minutes or until the pizza crust is puffy and well browned and the topping is golden brown.

~ VARIATIONS ~

For Tuna Pizza, spread with tomato-herb sauce (page 172), then add thinly sliced spring onions and 7 oz (200 g) drained flaked canned tuna. Make a lattice of anchovy fillets on top and put a black olive in each space. Sprinkle generously with grated Parmesan and Gruyère and drizzle with olive oil. For Mushroom Pizza, spread with tomato-garlic sauce and scatter 8 oz (225 g) sliced mushrooms on top. Sprinkle with 4 oz (115 g) grated mozzarella, plus Parmesan and olive oil.

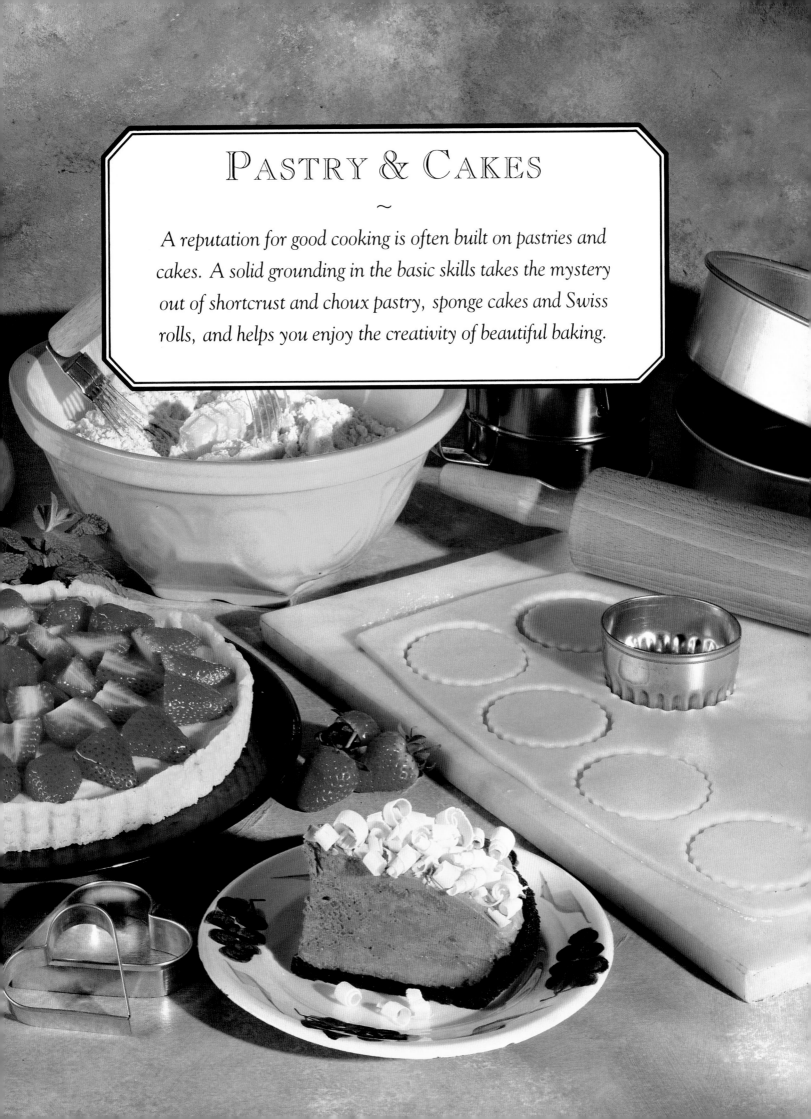

PASTRY & CAKES

~

A reputation for good cooking is often built on pastries and cakes. A solid grounding in the basic skills takes the mystery out of shortcrust and choux pastry, sponge cakes and Swiss rolls, and helps you enjoy the creativity of beautiful baking.

MAKING SHORTCRUST PASTRY

A meltingly short, crumbly pastry sets off any filling to perfection, whether sweet or savoury. The pastry dough can be made with half butter or margarine and half white vegetable fat or with all one kind of fat.

FOR A 9 IN (23 CM) PASTRY CASE

8 oz (225 g) plain flour
¼ teaspoon salt
4 oz (115 g) fat, chilled and diced
3–4 tablespoons iced water

1 ▲ Sift the flour and salt into a bowl. Add the fat. Rub it into the flour with your fingertips until the mixture is crumb-like.

2 ▲ Sprinkle 3 tablespoons water over the mixture. With a fork, toss gently to mix and moisten it.

3 ▲ Press the dough into a ball. If it is too dry to form a dough, add the remaining water.

4 ▲ Wrap the ball of dough with cling film or greaseproof paper and refrigerate it for at least 30 minutes.

Pastry making tips

• It helps if the fat is cold and firm, particularly if making the dough in a food processor. Cold fat has less chance of warming and softening too much when it is being rubbed into the flour, resulting in an oily pastry. Use block margarine rather than the soft tub-type.

• When rubbing the fat into the flour, if it begins to soften and feel oily, put the bowl in the refrigerator to chill for 20–30 minutes. Then continue making the dough.

• Liquids used should be ice-cold so that they will not soften or melt the fat.

• Take care when adding the water: start with the smaller amount (added all at once, not in a dribble), and add more only if the mixture will not come together into a dough. Too much water will result in tough pastry.

• When gathering the mixture together into a ball of dough, handle it as little as possible: overworked pastry will be tough.

• To avoid shrinkage, refrigerate the pastry dough before rolling out and baking. This 'resting time' will allow any elasticity developed during mixing to relax.

5 ▲ **To make pastry in a food processor:** Combine the flour, salt and cubed fat in the work bowl. Process, turning the machine on and off, just until the mixture is crumbly. Add the iced water and process again briefly – just until the dough starts to pull away from the sides of the bowl. It should still look crumbly. Remove the dough from the processor and gather it into a ball. Wrap and refrigerate.

Shortcrust pastry variations

• For *Nut Shortcrust*: Add 1 oz (30 g) finely chopped walnuts or pecan nuts to the flour mixture.

• For *Rich Shortcrust*: Use 8 oz (225 g) flour and 6 oz (170 g) fat (preferably all butter), plus 1 tablespoon caster sugar if making a sweet pie. Bind with 1 egg yolk and 2–3 tablespoons water.

• For a *Two-crust Pie*, increase the proportions for these pastries by 50%, thus the amounts needed for basic shortcrust pastry are: 12 oz (340 g) flour, ½ teaspoon salt, 6 oz (170 g) fat, 5–6 tablespoons water. For Nut Shortcrust, as above with 2 oz (55 g) nuts. For Rich Shortcrust, as above but using 9 oz (260 g) fat, 4–5 tablespoons water and 1 egg yolk.

Almond Syrup Tart

SERVES 6

3 oz (85 g) fresh white breadcrumbs
8 oz (225 g) golden syrup
finely grated zest of ½ lemon
2 teaspoons lemon juice
9 in (23 cm) pastry case, made with basic, nut or rich shortcrust pastry
1 oz (30 g) flaked almonds

1 Preheat a 200°C/400°F/Gas 6 oven.

2 ▲ In a mixing bowl, combine the breadcrumbs with the golden syrup and the lemon zest and juice.

3 Spoon into the pastry case and spread out evenly.

4 ▲ Sprinkle the flaked almonds evenly over the top.

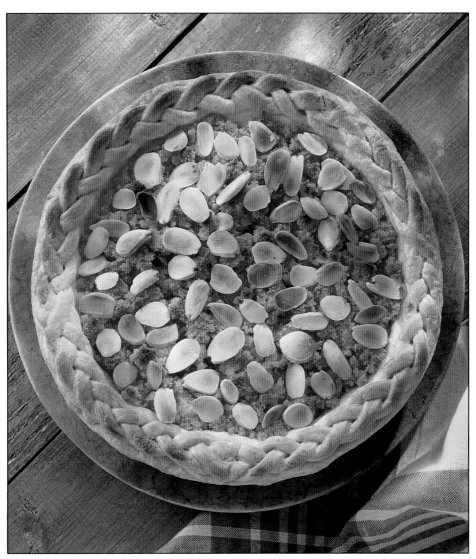

5 ▼ Brush the pastry with milk to glaze, if you like. Bake for 25–30 minutes or until the pastry and filling are golden brown.

6 Remove to a wire rack to cool. Serve warm or cold, with cream, custard or ice cream.

~ VARIATIONS ~

For Walnut Syrup Tart, replace the almonds with chopped walnuts.
For Ginger Syrup Tart, mix 1 teaspoon ground ginger with the breadcrumbs before adding the syrup and lemon zest and juice. Omit the nuts if liked.
For Coconut Syrup Tart, replace 1 oz (30 g) of the breadcrumbs with 1½ oz (45 g) desiccated coconut.

ROLLING OUT AND LINING A TIN

A neat pastry case that doesn't distort or shrink in baking is the desired result. The key to success is handling the dough gently. Use the method here for lining a round pie or tart tin that is about 2 in (5 cm) deep.

Remove the chilled dough from the refrigerator and allow it to soften slightly at room temperature. Unwrap and put it on a lightly floured surface. Flatten the dough into a neat, round disc. Lightly flour the rolling pin.

Rolling out and lining tips
● Reflour the surface and rolling pin if the dough starts to stick.
● Should the dough tear, patch with a piece of moistened dough.
● When rolling out and lining the pie or tart tin, do not stretch the dough. It will only shrink back during baking, spoiling the shape of the pastry case.
● Once or twice during rolling out, gently push in the edges of the dough with your cupped palms, to keep the circular shape.
● A pastry scraper will help lift the dough from the work surface, to wrap it around the rolling pin.
● Tins made from heat-resistant glass or dull-finish metal such as heavyweight aluminium will give a crisp crust.
● When finishing the edge, be sure to hook the dough over the rim all the way round or to press the dough firmly to the rim. This will prevent the dough pulling away should it start to shrink.
● If covering a pie dish, roll the dough to a round or oval 2 in (5 cm) larger than the dish. Cut a 1 in (2.5 cm) strip from the outside and lay this on the moistened rim of the dish. Brush the strip with water and lay the sheet of dough on top. Press edges to seal, then trim even with the rim. Knock up the edge with a knife.

1 ▲ Using even pressure, start rolling out the dough, working from the centre to the edge each time and easing the pressure slightly as you reach the edge.

3 ▲ Continue rolling out until the dough circle is about 2 in (5 cm) larger all round than the tin. The dough will be about 1/8 in (3 mm) thick.

5 ▲ Hold the pin over the tin and gently unroll the dough so it drapes into the tin, centring it as much as possible.

2 ▲ Lift up the dough and give it a quarter turn from time to time during the rolling. This will prevent the dough sticking to the surface, and will help keep the thickness even.

4 ▲ Set the rolling pin on the dough, near one side of the circle. Fold the outside edge of dough over the pin, then roll the pin over the dough to wrap the dough round it. Do this gently and loosely.

6 ▲ With your fingertips, lift and ease the dough into the tin, gently pressing it over the bottom and up the side. Turn excess dough over the rim and trim it with a knife or scissors, depending on the edge to be made.

FINISHING THE EDGE

1 ▲ For a forked edge: Trim the dough even with the rim and press it flat. Firmly and evenly press the prongs of a fork all round the edge. If the fork sticks, dip it in flour.

2 ▲ For a crimped edge: Trim the dough to leave an overhang of about ½ in (1.5 cm) all round. Fold the extra dough under. Put the knuckle or tip of the index finger of one of your hands inside the edge, pointing directly out. With the thumb and index finger of your other hand, pinch the dough edge around your index finger into a 'V' shape. Continue all round the edge.

3 ▲ For a ruffled edge: Trim the dough to leave an overhang of about ½ in (1.5 cm) all round. Fold the extra dough under. Hold the thumb and index finger of one of your hands about 1 in (2.5 cm) apart, inside the edge, pointing directly out. With the index finger of your other hand, gently pull the dough between them, to the end of the rim. Continue all the way round the edge.

Apple and Cherry Crumble Pie
Mix together 12 oz (340 g) peeled, cored and sliced Granny Smith apples, 10 oz (300 g) stoned cherries and 4 oz (115 g) soft light brown sugar. Put into a 9 in (23 cm) pastry case. For the topping, combine 4 oz (115 g) plain flour, 4 oz (115 g) soft light brown sugar and 1 teaspoon ground cinnamon. Rub in 3 oz (85 g) butter until the mixture resembles coarse crumbs. Sprinkle over the fruit. Bake in a 375°F/190°C/Gas 5 oven for about 45 minutes or until golden. *Serves 6.*

4 ▲ For a cutout edge: Trim the dough even with the rim and press it flat on the rim. With a small pastry cutter, cut out decorative shapes from the dough trimmings. Moisten the edge of the pastry case and press the cutouts in place, overlapping them slightly if you like.

5 ▲ For a ribbon edge: Trim the dough even with the rim and press it flat on the rim. Cut long strips about ¾ in (2 cm) wide from the dough trimmings. Moisten the edge and press one end of a strip on to it. Twist the strip gently and press it on to the edge again. Continue all the way round the edge.

MAKING A TWO-CRUST PIE

Two succulent pastry layers enveloping a sweet filling – what could be nicer? Use the same method for making small pies, such as mince pices.

American-style Apple Pie
Combine 2 lb (900 g) peeled, cored and thinly sliced Granny Smith apples, 1 tablespoon plain flour, 3½ oz (100 g) caster sugar and ¾ teaspoon mixed spice. Toss to coat the fruit evenly with the sugar and flour. Use to fill the two-crust pie. Bake in a 375°F/190°C/ Gas 5 oven for about 45 minutes or until the pastry is golden brown and the fruit is tender (test with a skewer through a slit in the top crust). Cool on a rack.

1 ▲ Roll out half of the pastry dough on a floured surface and line a pie tin that is about 2 in (5 cm) deep. Trim the dough even with the rim.

3 ▲ Roll out a second piece of dough to a circle that is about 1 in (2.5 cm) larger all round than the tin. Roll it up around the rolling pin and unroll over the pie. Press the edges together.

2 ▲ Put in the filling. Brush the edge of the pastry case evenly with water to moisten it.

4 ▲ Trim the edge of the lid to leave a ½ in (1.5 cm) overhang. Cut slits or a design in the centre. These will act as steam vents during baking.

5 ▲ Fold the overhang of the lid under the edge of the case. Press the two together gently and evenly to seal. Finish the edge as wished.

6 ▲ Brush the top of the pie with milk or cream for a shiny finish. Or brush with 1 egg yolk mixed with 1 teaspoon water for a glazed golden brown finish. Or brush with water and then sprinkle with caster sugar or cinnamon and sugar for a sugary crust.

7 ▲ If you like, cut out decorative shapes from the dough trimmings, rolled out as thinly as possible. Moisten the cutouts with a little water and press them on to the top. Glaze the decorations before baking.

Blueberry Pie

SERVES 6–8

| basic or rich shortcrust for a two-crust pie (page 222, shortcrust variations) |
| 1¼ lb (575 g) blueberries |
| 5½ oz (160 g) caster sugar |
| 3 tablespoons plain flour |
| 1 teaspoon grated orange zest |
| ¼ teaspoon grated nutmeg |
| 2 tablespoons orange juice |
| 1 teaspoon lemon juice |

1 Preheat a 375°F/190°C/Gas 5 oven.

2 ▲ Roll out half of the pastry and use to line a 9 in (23 cm) pie tin that is about 2 in (5 cm) deep.

3 ▲ Combine the blueberries, 5 oz (145 g) of the sugar, the flour, orange zest and nutmeg in a bowl. Toss the mixture gently to coat the fruit evenly with the dry ingredients.

4 ▼ Pour the blueberry mixture into the pastry case and spread it evenly. Sprinkle over the citrus juices.

5 Roll out the remaining pastry and cover the pie. Cut out small decorative shapes or cut 2–3 slits for steam vents. Finish the edge.

6 ▲ Brush the top lightly with water and sprinkle evenly with the remaining caster sugar.

7 Bake for about 45 minutes or until the pastry is golden brown. Serve warm or at room temperature.

MAKING A LATTICE TOP

A woven pastry lattice is a very attractive finish for a pie. Prepare shortcrust for a two-crust pie.

Roll out half of the pastry dough and line the pie tin. Trim the dough to leave a ½ in (1.5 cm) overhang all round. Put in the filling. Roll out the second piece of dough into a circle that is about 2 in (5 cm) larger all round than the pie tin.

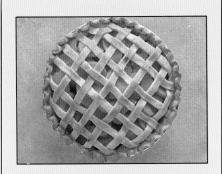

Apricot Lattice Pie
Toss together 2¼ lb (1 kg) peeled, stoned and thinly sliced apricots, 2 tablespoons plain flour and 3½ oz (100 g) sugar. Fill the pastry case and make a lattice top. Glaze with milk and bake in a 375°F/190°C/Gas 5 oven for about 45 minutes or until the pastry is golden and the filling is bubbling. Cool on a wire rack.

1 ▲ With the help of a ruler, cut neat straight strips of dough that are about ½ in (1.5 cm) wide, using a knife or fluted pastry wheel.

3 ▲ Fold back every other strip from the centre. Lay another strip across the centre, on the flat strips, at right angles to them. Lay the folded strips flat again.

2 ▲ For a square woven lattice: Lay half of the strips across the pie filling, keeping them neatly parallel and spacing them evenly.

4 ▲ Now fold back those strips that were not folded the first time. Lay another strip across those that are flat now, spacing this new strip evenly from the centre strip.

5 ▲ Continue folding the strips in this way until half of the lattice is completed. Repeat on the other half of the pie.

6 ▲ Trim the ends of the strips even with the rim of the pie tin. Moisten the edge of the pastry case and press the strips gently to it to seal. Finish the edge.

7 ▲ For a diamond lattice: Weave as above, laying the intersecting strips diagonally instead of at right angles. Or lay half the strips over the filling and the remaining strips on top.

Walnut and Pear Lattice Pie

SERVES 6–8

nut shortcrust for a two-crust pie (page 222, pastry variations), using walnuts

2 lb (900 g) pears, peeled, cored and thinly sliced

2 oz (55 g) caster sugar

1 oz (30 g) plain flour

½ teaspoon grated lemon zest

1 oz (30 g) raisins or sultanas

1 oz (30 g) walnuts, chopped

½ teaspoon ground cinnamon

2 oz (55 g) icing sugar

1 tablespoon lemon juice

about 2 teaspoons cold water

1 Preheat a 375°F/190°C/Gas 5 oven.

2 Roll out half of the pastry dough and use to line a 9 in (23 cm) tin that is about 2 in (5 cm) deep.

3 ▲ Combine the pears, caster sugar, flour and lemon zest in a bowl. Toss gently until the fruit is evenly coated with the dry ingredients. Mix in the raisins, nuts and cinnamon.

~ **COOK'S TIP** ~

For a simple cutout lattice top, roll out the dough for the top into a circle. Using a small pastry cutter, cut out shapes in a pattern, spacing them evenly and not too close together.

4 ▲ Put the pear filling into the pastry case and spread it evenly.

5 Roll out the remaining pastry dough and use to make a lattice top.

6 Bake for 55 minutes or until the pastry is golden brown.

7 Combine the icing sugar, lemon juice and water in a bowl and stir until smoothly blended.

8 ▼ Remove the pie from the oven. Drizzle the icing sugar glaze evenly over the top of the pie, on pastry and filling. Leave the pie to cool, set on a wire rack, before serving.

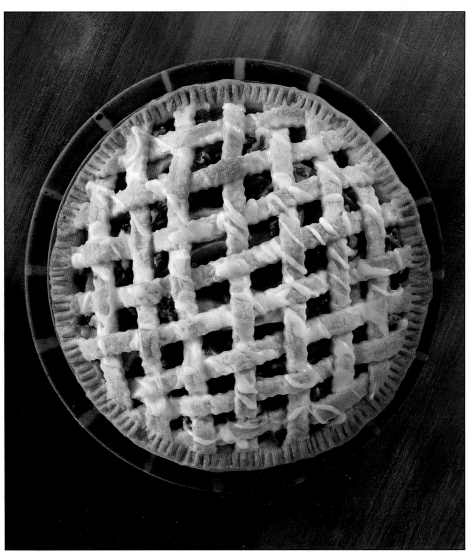

MAKING FRENCH FLAN PASTRY

The pastry for tarts, flans and quiches is made with butter or margarine, giving a rich and crumbly result. The more fat used, the richer the pastry will be – almost like a biscuit dough – and the harder to roll out. If you have difficulty rolling it, you can press it into the tin instead, or roll it out between sheets of cling film. Flan pastry, like shortcrust, can be made by hand or in a food processor. Tips for making, handling and using shortcrust pastry apply equally to French flan pastry.

FOR A 9IN (23CM) FLAN CASE

7oz (200g) plain flour
½ teaspoon salt
4oz (115g) butter or margarine, chilled
1 egg yolk
¼ teaspoon lemon juice
2–3 tablespoons iced water

1 ▲ Sift the flour and salt into a bowl. Add the butter or margarine. Rub into the flour until the mixture resembles fine crumbs.

2 ▲ In a small bowl, mix the egg yolk, lemon juice and 2 tablespoons water. Add to the flour mixture. With a fork, toss gently to mix and moisten.

3 ▲ Press the dough into a rough ball. If it is too dry to come together, add the remaining water. Turn on to the work surface or a pastry board.

4 ▲ With the heel of your hand, push small portions of dough away from you, smearing them on the surface.

Flan pastry variations
- For *Sweet Flan Pastry*: Reduce the amount of salt to ¼ teaspoon; add 1 tablespoon caster sugar with the flour.
- For *Rich Flan Pastry*: Use 7oz (200g) flour, ½ teaspoon salt, 5oz (145g) butter, 2 egg yolks, and 1–2 tablespoons water.
- For *Rich Sweet Flan Pastry*: Make rich flan pastry, adding 3 tablespoons caster sugar with the flour and, if liked, ½ teaspoon vanilla essence with the egg yolks.

5 ▲ Continue mixing the dough in this way until it feels pliable and can be peeled easily off the surface.

6 ▲ Press the dough into a smooth ball. Wrap in cling film and chill for at least 30 minutes.

LINING A FLAN TIN OR RING

A flan tin is shallow, with no rim. Its straight sides (smooth or fluted) give a tart or flan the traditional shape. The most useful tins have removable bases, making it very easy to turn out a tart. Flan rings are straight-sided metal rings that are set on a baking sheet.

In addition to flan tins and rings, there are porcelain quiche dishes and small, individual tartlet tins, both plain and fluted.

Pecan Nut Tartlets
Line six 4 in (10 cm) tartlet tins with flan pastry. Place 1 oz (30 g) pecan nut halves in each. In a bowl, beat 3 eggs to mix. Add 1 oz (30 g) melted butter, 10 oz (300 g) golden syrup and ½ teaspoon vanilla essence. Sift together 4 oz (115 g) caster sugar and 1 tablespoon plain flour. Add to the egg mixture and stir until evenly blended. Fill the tartlet cases and leave until the nuts rise to the surface. Bake in a 350°F/ 180°C/Gas 4 oven for 35–40 minutes or until a knife inserted near the centre comes out clean. Cool in the tins for 15 minutes, then turn on to a wire rack.

1 ▲ Remove the chilled dough from the refrigerator and let it soften slightly at room temperature. Roll out to a circle about 2 in (5 cm) larger all round than the tin or ring. It will be about ⅛ in (3 mm) thick.

3 ▲ With your fingertips, ease the dough into the tin or ring, gently pressing it smoothly over the bottom, without stretching it.

5 ▲ Roll the rolling pin over the top of the tin or ring to cut off excess dough. Smooth the cut edge and press it against the side of the tin or ring, if necessary, to keep it in place.

2 ▲ Roll up the dough round the rolling pin, then unroll it over the tin or ring, draping it gently.

4 ▲ Fold the overhanging dough down inside the tin or ring, to thicken the side of the pastry case. Smooth and press the side of the case against the side of the tin or ring.

6 ▲ For tartlet tins: Arrange them close together and unroll the dough over them, draping it loosely. Roll the rolling pin over the top to cut off excess pastry. Press into the bottom and sides of the tins.

BAKING BLIND

Baked custard and cream fillings can make pastry soggy, so the cases for these flans and tarts are often given an initial baking before the filling is added and the final baking is done. Such pre-baking is referred to as baking 'blind'. The technique is also used for pastry cases that are to be filled with an uncooked or precooked mixture.

The purpose of using weights is to prevent the bottom of the pastry case from rising too much and becoming distorted, thus keeping its neat shape.

Fresh Strawberry Flan
Make the case using sweet flan pastry or rich sweet flan pastry (page 230). Bake it blind fully, then cool. Beat 14 oz (400 g) full-fat soft cheese with 1¾ oz (50 g) caster sugar, 1 egg yolk and 4 table-spoons whipping cream until smooth. Fold in 1 stiffly whisked egg white. Pour into the case and spread evenly. Bake at 350°F/180°C/Gas 4 for 15–20 minutes or until the filling is softly set; it will set further as it cools. When cool, arrange halved strawberries on top in concentric circles. Melt 5 oz (145 g) redcurrant jelly and brush over the berries to glaze them. Leave to cool before serving. *Serves 6.*

1 ▲ Set the pie or flan tin, or flan ring, on a sheet of greaseproof paper or foil. Draw or mark around its base. Cut out a circle about 3 in (7.5 cm) larger all round than the drawn or marked one.

3 ▲ Lay the circle of greaseproof paper or foil in the pastry case and press it smoothly over the bottom and up the side.

5 ▲ **For partially baked pastry:** Bake the case in a 400°F/200°C/Gas 6 oven for 15–20 minutes or until it is slightly dry and set. Remove the paper or foil and beans. The pastry is now ready to be filled and baked further.

2 ▲ Roll out the pastry dough and use to line the tin or ring set on a baking sheet. Prick the bottom of the pastry case all over with a fork.

4 ▲ Put enough dried beans or baking beans in the case to cover the bottom thickly.

6 ▲ **For fully baked pastry:** After baking for 15 minutes, remove the paper or foil and beans. Prick the bottom again with a fork. Return to the oven and bake for 5–10 minutes or until golden brown. Cool completely before adding the filling.

Quiche Lorraine

SERVES 6

8 oz (225 g) smoked streaky bacon
  rashers, chopped

9 in (23 cm) flan case, partially baked
  blind

3 eggs

2 egg yolks

12 fl oz (360 ml) whipping cream

4 fl oz (120 ml) milk

salt and pepper

1 Preheat a 200°C/400°F/Gas 6 oven.

2 ▲ Fry the bacon in a frying pan
until it is crisp and golden brown.
Drain the bacon on paper towels.

3 ▲ Scatter the bacon in the
partially baked flan case.

4 In a bowl, whisk together the eggs,
egg yolks, cream and milk. Season
with salt and pepper.

5 ▼ Pour the egg mixture into the
flan case.

6 Bake for 35–40 minutes or until the
filling is set and golden brown and the
pastry is golden. Serve warm or at
room temperature.

~ VARIATIONS ~

Add 3 oz (85 g) grated Gruyère
cheese with the bacon. Replace
the bacon with diced cooked ham,
if desired. For a vegetarian quiche,
omit the bacon. Slice 1 lb (450 g)
courgettes and fry in a little oil
until lightly browned on both sides.
Drain on paper towels, then
arrange in the flan case. Scatter
2 oz (55 g) grated cheese on top.
Make the egg mixture with 4 eggs,
8 fl oz (240 ml) cream, 4
tablespoons milk, 1/8 teaspoon
grated nutmeg, salt and pepper.

MAKING A BISCUIT CASE

A biscuit case is one of the simplest bases to make, and the variations in flavouring are almost endless. Crumbs from any dry biscuit can be used, both sweet and savoury. You can also use breadcrumbs and cake crumbs. Most biscuit cases are sweet, to hold sweet fillings, but there are also unsweetened biscuit cases for savoury cheesecakes.

MAKES AN 8–9 IN (20–23 CM) CASE

8 oz (225 g) biscuits (see below), crushed

4 oz (115 g) butter, melted

3–4 tablespoons caster sugar (optional)

Biscuit case flavourings
- Use digestive biscuits. Sweeten with sugar to taste, if liked. Add 1 teaspoon ground cinnamon or ginger or mixed spice or ½ teaspoon grated nutmeg.
- Use digestive biscuits and sweeten with sugar to taste, if liked. Add 1 teaspoon grated lemon zest or 2 teaspoons grated orange zest.
- Use 7 oz (200 g) digestive biscuits and 1½ oz (45 g) ground or finely chopped nuts (almonds, hazelnuts, pecan nuts or walnuts).
- Use ginger nuts, shortbread, almond butter biscuits, amaretti biscuits or crisp almond macaroons. No sugar is needed.
- Use water biscuits or other cheese biscuits, without adding sugar, for a savoury filling.

Crushing the biscuits
To make fine crumbs, break the biscuits into small pieces. Put them, a small batch at a time, in a heavy plastic bag and roll over them with a rolling pin. Or grind them finely in a blender or food processor.

1 ▲ Combine the biscuits, melted butter and sugar, plus other flavourings, if using. Stir well to mix.

2 ▲ Turn the biscuit mixture into a buttered 8 in (20 cm) springform cake tin or 9 in (23 cm) tart tin. Spread it over the bottom and up the side.

3 ▲ With the back of a large spoon or your fingers, press the biscuit mixture firmly against the tin, to pack the crumbs into a solid crust.

4 ▲ According to the recipe, refrigerate the case to set it, usually at least 1 hour. Or bake the case in a 350°F/180°C/Gas 4 oven for 8–10 minutes; cool before filling.

Easy Chocolate Tart
Prepare the biscuit case using ginger biscuits and pressing it into a 9 in (23 cm) tin. Bake and cool. Melt 6 oz (170 g) plain chocolate with 4 tablespoons milk; cool. Whip ¾ pint (450 ml) double or whipping cream until thick. Fold into the cooled chocolate. Spread evenly in the case. Cover and refrigerate until firm. Just before serving, garnish with chocolate curls or grated chocolate. *Serves 6.*

Rich Orange Cheesecake

SERVES 8

1½ lb (700 g) full-fat soft cheese, at room temperature

7 oz (200 g) caster sugar

2 tablespoons plain flour

3 eggs

4 oz (115 g) butter, melted

1 teaspoon vanilla essence

1 tablespoon grated orange zest

8 in (20 cm) biscuit case, made with digestive biscuits and orange zest, chilled

4 sweet oranges, peeled and segmented

squeeze of lemon juice

1–2 tablespoons orange liqueur (optional)

1 Preheat a 300°F/150°C/Gas 2 oven.

2 ▲ Combine the soft cheese, sugar and flour in a bowl. Beat until the mixture is light and fluffy.

3 ▲ Add the eggs, butter, vanilla essence and orange zest and beat until smoothly blended.

4 ▲ Pour the filling into the biscuit case. Set the springform tin on a baking sheet.

5 Bake for 1–1¼ hours or until the filling is gently set (it will continue to firm up as it cools). If the top browns too quickly, cover with foil. Turn off the oven and open the door.

6 Leave the cheesecake to cool in the oven. When it is cold, cover and refrigerate overnight.

7 Mix together the orange segments, lemon juice and liqueur, if using. Serve with the cheesecake.

~ VARIATIONS ~

For Lemon Cheesecake, use 1½ teaspoons lemon zest instead of orange in the filling. For a lighter cheesecake, use a mixture of ricotta or curd cheese and full-fat soft cheese, worked in a food processor until smooth.

MAKING CHOUX PASTRY

Unlike other pastries, where the fat is rubbed into the flour, with choux pastry the butter is melted with water and then the flour is added, followed by eggs. The result is more of a paste than a pastry. It is easy to make, but care must be taken in measuring the ingredients.

FOR 18 PROFITEROLES OR 12 ECLAIRS

4 oz (115 g) butter, cut into small pieces

8 fl oz (240 ml) water

2 teaspoons caster sugar (optional)

¼ teaspoon salt

5 oz (145 g) plain flour

4 eggs, beaten to mix

Shaping choux pastry
- For *large puffs*: Use two large spoons dipped in water. Drop the paste in 2–2½ in (5–6 cm) wide blobs on the paper-lined baking sheet, leaving 1½ in (4 cm) between each. Neaten the blobs as much as possible. Alternatively, for well-shaped puffs, pipe the paste using a piping bag fitted with a ¾ in (2 cm) plain nozzle.
- For *profiteroles*: Use two small spoons or a piping bag fitted with a ½ in (1.5 cm) nozzle and shape 1 in (2.5 cm) blobs.
- For *éclairs*: Use a piping bag fitted with a ¾ in (2 cm) nozzle. Pipe strips 4–5 in (10–12 cm) long.
- For a *ring*: draw a 12 in (30 cm) circle on the paper. Spoon the paste in large blobs on the circle to make a ring. Or pipe two rings round the circle and a third on top.

Baking times for choux pastry
Bake large puffs and éclairs 30–35 minutes, profiteroles 20–25 minutes, rings 40–45 minutes.

1 ▲ Combine the butter, water, sugar, if using, and salt in a large heavy-based saucepan. Bring to the boil over moderately high heat, stirring occasionally.

2 ▲ As soon as the mixture is boiling, remove the pan from the heat. Add the flour all at once and beat vigorously with a wooden spoon to mix the flour into the liquid.

3 ▲ Return the pan to moderate heat and cook, stirring, until the mixture will form a ball, pulling away from the side of the pan. This will take about 1 minute. Remove from the heat again and allow to cool for 3–5 minutes.

4 ▲ Add a little of the beaten egg and beat well with the spoon or an electric mixer to incorporate. Add a little more egg and beat in well. Continue beating in the eggs until the mixture becomes a smooth, shiny paste thick enough to hold its shape.

5 ▲ While still warm, shape large choux puffs, éclairs, profiteroles or large rings on a baking sheet lined with baking parchment.

6 ▲ Glaze with 1 egg beaten with 1 teaspoon cold water. Put into a 425°F/ 220°C/Gas 7 oven, then reduce the heat to 400°F/200°C/Gas 6. Bake until puffed and golden brown.

7 ▶ When baked (see baking times, left) use the tip of a knife to make a slit in the side of each puff or éclair, or several around a ring, to let the steam inside escape. Return to the turned-off oven and dry out for 5–10 minutes. Cool on a wire rack. Shortly before serving, split the pastries open horizontally and fill as desired.

Fillings for choux pastry
● Fill sweet choux with sweetened whipped cream (page 160), ice cream or sweetened chestnut purée. Serve with bittersweet chocolate sauce (page 203).
● Fill savoury choux with cheese sauce or creamed chicken.

Hot Cheddar Puffs

MAKES ABOUT 28 APPETIZER PUFFS

2 oz (55 g) butter, cut into pieces

8 fl oz (240 ml) water

½ teaspoon salt

5 oz (145 g) plain flour

¼ teaspoon mustard powder

good pinch of hot paprika

2 oz (55 g) mature Cheddar cheese, grated

4 eggs, beaten

1 egg beaten with 1 teaspoon cold water, to glaze

FOR THE FILLING

8 oz (225 g) full-fat soft cheese, at room temperature

2 tablespoons spicy fruit sauce

4 tablespoons diced canned pimiento

2 tablespoons chopped black olives

1 Preheat a 425°F/220°C/Gas 7 oven.

2 Make the choux pastry, adding the mustard and paprika with the flour and beating in the cheese before the eggs. Shape into small puffs on a baking sheet lined with baking parchment. Brush with the egg glaze.

3 Put in the oven and reduce the temperature to 400°F/200°C/Gas 6. Bake for 20–25 minutes or until risen, golden brown and crisp.

4 ▲ Meanwhile, for the filling, beat the soft cheese with the spicy fruit sauce until well blended. Mix in the pimiento and olives.

5 Cut a slit in the side of each puff and return to the turned-off oven to dry out for about 10 minutes.

6 ▼ While the puffs are still warm, fill them with the cheese filling, piping or spooning it carefully into the slit cut in the side of each puff. Serve the Cheddar puffs warm.

MAKING CAKES BY THE CREAMING METHOD

The Victoria sandwich, with its tender crumb and rich, moist flavour, is always popular. It is delicious enough to be served plain, with just a dusting of sugar, or it can be filled and iced.

To make cakes by the creaming method, the fat and sugar are 'creamed' – or beaten – together before the eggs and dry ingredients are added. The fat (usually butter or margarine) should be soft enough to be beaten, so if necessary remove it from the refrigerator and leave it at room temperature for at least 30 minutes. For best results, the eggs should be at room temperature.

Mocha Victoria Sponge
Make the mixture using 6 oz (170 g) each butter or margarine, caster sugar and self-raising flour and 3 eggs. Divide between two bowls. To one add 1 tablespoon strong black coffee; to the other add 1 tablespoon cocoa powder mixed to a paste with 1–2 table-spoons boiling water. Place alternate spoonfuls of each flavour, side by side, in 2 greased and bottom-lined 7 in (18 cm) round sandwich tins. Lightly smooth the top. Bake at 350°F/180°C/Gas 4 for 25–30 minutes. Turn out on to a wire rack and cool. Sandwich the cakes together with coffee buttercream (page 242). Cover the top, or top and sides, with buttercream.

1 ▲ Sift the flour with the salt, raising agent(s) and any other dry ingredients, such as spices or cocoa powder. Set aside.

3 ▲ Add the sugar to the creamed fat gradually. With the mixer at medium-high speed, beat it into the fat until the mixture is pale and very fluffy. The sugar should be completely incorporated. This will take 4–5 minutes. During this process, air will be beaten into the mixture, which will help the cake to rise.

5 ▲ Add the dry ingredients to the mixture, beating at low speed just until smoothly combined. Or fold in with a large metal spoon.

2 ▲ Put the fat in a large, deep bowl and beat with an electric mixer at medium speed, or a wooden spoon, until the texture is soft and pliable.

4 ▲ Add the eggs or egg yolks, one at a time, beating well after each addition (about 45 seconds). Scrape the bowl often so all the ingredients are evenly combined. When adding the eggs, the mixture may begin to curdle, especially if the eggs are cold. If this happens, add 1 tablespoon of the measured flour.

6 ▲ If the recipe calls for any liquid, add it in small portions alternately with portions of the dry ingredients.

7 ▲ If the recipe specifies, whisk egg whites separately until frothy, add sugar and continue whisking until stiff peaks form. Fold into the mixture.

8 ▲ Pour the mixture into a cake tin or tins, prepared according to the recipe, and bake as specified.

9 ▲ To test creamed-method cakes, insert a metal skewer or wooden cocktail stick into the centre; it should come out clean.

MAKING AMERICAN FROSTING

This fluffy white frosting has an attractive gloss and a texture like meringue. It is a delicious filling and icing for sandwich cakes.

MAKES ENOUGH TO FILL AND ICE A 9 IN (23 CM) SANDWICH CAKE

10 oz (300 g) sugar
¼ teaspoon cream of tartar
2 egg whites
4 tablespoons cold water
1 tablespoon liquid glucose
2 teaspoons vanilla essence

1 ▲ Combine the sugar, cream of tartar, egg whites, water and glucose in a large heatproof bowl or the top of a double saucepan. Stir just to mix.

2 ▲ Set the bowl over a saucepan of boiling water. The base of the bowl should not touch the water.

Frosting variations

For *Orange Frosting*: Use orange juice instead of water and add 1 teaspoon grated orange zest. Reduce the vanilla to ½ teaspoon.

For *Lemon Frosting*: Use 2 tablespoons each lemon juice and water and add ½ teaspoon grated lemon zest. Reduce the vanilla to ½ teaspoon.

3 ▲ Beat with a hand-held electric mixer at high speed for about 7 minutes or until the frosting is thick and white and will form stiff peaks.

4 ▲ Remove from the heat. Add the vanilla and continue beating for about 3 minutes or until the frosting has cooled slightly. Use immediately.

Coconut Lime Gâteau

SERVES 8 OR MORE

8 oz (225 g) plain flour
2½ teaspoons baking powder
¼ teaspoon salt
8 oz (225 g) butter, at room temperature
8 oz (225 g) caster sugar
grated zest of 2 limes
4 eggs
4 tablespoons fresh lime juice (from about 2 limes)
3 oz (85 g) desiccated coconut
1 recipe quantity American frosting (page 239)

1 Preheat a 350°F/180°C/Gas 4 oven. Grease two 9 in (23 cm) sandwich tins and line the bottoms with greased greaseproof paper.

2 Sift together the flour, baking powder and salt.

3 In a large bowl, beat the butter until it is soft and pliable. Add the sugar and lime zest and beat until the mixture is pale and fluffy. Beat in the eggs, one at a time.

4 ▲ Using a wooden spoon fold in the sifted dry ingredients in small portions, alternating with the lime juice. When the mixture is smooth, stir in two-thirds of the coconut.

5 ▲ Divide the mixture between the prepared tins and spread it evenly to the sides. Bake for 30–35 minutes (test with a skewer).

6 ▲ Remove the cakes from the oven and set them, in their tins, on a wire rack. Cool for 10 minutes. Then turn out and peel off the lining paper. Cool completely on the rack.

7 ▲ Spread the remaining coconut in another cake tin. Bake until golden brown, stirring occasionally. Watch carefully so that the coconut does not get too dark. Cool.

8 ▲ Put one of the cakes, base up, on a serving plate. Spread a layer of frosting evenly over the cake.

9 ▲ Set the second layer on top, base down. Spread the remaining frosting all over the top and round the sides of the cake.

10 ▲ Scatter the toasted coconut over the top of the cake and leave to set before serving.

MAKING CAKES BY THE ALL-IN-ONE METHOD

Many cakes are made by an easy all-in-one method where all the ingredients are combined in a bowl and beaten thoroughly. The mixture can also be made in a food processor, but take care not to over-process. A refinement on the all-in-one method is to separate the eggs and make the mixture with the yolks. The whites are whisked separately and then folded in.

1 ▲ Sift the dry ingredients (flour, salt, raising agent, spices and so on) into a bowl.

2 ▲ Add the liquid ingredients (eggs, melted or soft fat, milk, fruit juices and so on) and beat until smooth, with an electric mixer for speed. Pour into the prepared tins and bake as specified in the recipe.

MAKING SIMPLE BUTTERCREAM

Quick to make and easy to spread, buttercream is ideal for all kinds of cakes, from simple ones to gâteaux. The basic buttercream can be varied with many other flavours, and it can be tinted with food colouring, too.

MAKES ENOUGH TO COVER THE TOP AND SIDE OF A 7–8 IN (17–20 CM) CAKE

4 oz (115 g) butter, preferably unsalted, at room temperature

8 oz (225 g) icing sugar, sifted

1 teaspoon vanilla essence

about 2 tablespoons milk

1 ▲ Put the butter in a deep mixing bowl and beat it with an electric mixer at medium speed, or a wooden spoon, until it is soft and pliable.

2 ▲ Gradually add the icing sugar and beat at medium-high speed. Continue beating until the mixture is pale and fluffy.

3 ▲ Add the vanilla essence and 1 tablespoon milk. Beat until smooth and of a spreading consistency. If it is too thick, beat in more milk. If too thin, beat in more sugar.

Buttercream variations
- For *Orange or Lemon Buttercream,* grate the zest from 1 small orange or ½ lemon; squeeze the juice. Beat in the zest with the sugar; use the juice instead of the vanilla and milk.
- For *Chocolate Buttercream,* add 4 tablespoons cocoa powder, beating it in with the sugar. Increase the milk to 3–4 tablespoons.
- For *Mocha Buttercream:* Warm the milk and dissolve 1 teaspoon instant coffee powder in it; cool and use to make chocolate buttercream, adding more milk if needed.
- For *Coffee Buttercream,* warm the milk and dissolve 1 tablespoon of instant coffee powder in it; cool before adding to the buttercream.

Chocolate Fairy Cakes

MAKES 24

4 oz (115 g) good-quality plain
    chocolate, cut into small pieces

1 tablespoon water

10 oz (300 g) plain flour

1 teaspoon baking powder

½ teaspoon bicarbonate of soda

pinch of salt

10 oz (300 g) caster sugar

6 oz (170 g) butter or margarine, at room
    temperature

¼ pint (150 ml) milk

1 teaspoon vanilla essence

3 eggs

1 recipe quantity buttercream, flavoured
    to taste

1 Preheat a 350°F/180°C/Gas 4 oven.
Grease and flour 24 deep bun tins,
about 2¾ in (6.5 cm) in diameter, or
use paper cases in the tins.

2 ▲ Put the chocolate and water in a
bowl set over a pan of almost
simmering water. Heat until melted
and smooth, stirring. Remove from
the heat and leave to cool.

3 Sift the flour, baking powder,
bicarbonate of soda, salt and sugar
into a large bowl. Add the chocolate
mixture, butter, milk and vanilla
essence.

4 ▲ With an electric mixer on
medium-low speed, beat until
smoothly blended. Increase the speed
to high and beat for 2 minutes. Add
the eggs and beat for 2 minutes.

5 Divide the mixture evenly among
the prepared bun tins.

6 Bake for 20–25 minutes or until a
skewer inserted into the centre of a
cake comes out clean. Cool in the tins
for 10 minutes, then turn out to cool
completely on a wire rack.

7 ▼ Ice the top of each cake with
buttercream, swirling it into a peak in
the centre.

MAKING A CLASSIC WHISKED SPONGE

The classic whisked sponge contains no fat and no raising agents – just eggs, sugar and flour. The light, airy texture of the finished cake depends on the large quantity of air beaten into the mixture.

Sometimes the eggs are separated for a whisked sponge and sometimes the cake is enriched with butter. American angel food cake uses egg whites only.

A whisked sponge can be simply dusted with icing or caster sugar, filled with sweetened whipped cream, a fruit jam or fresh fruit, or used to make a Swiss roll.

If you use a table-top electric mixer to beat the eggs and sugar, or if using separated eggs, there is no need to set the bowl over a pan of simmering water.

Whisked Sponge
Make the mixture using 4 whole eggs, 5 oz (145 g) caster sugar and 4 oz (115 g) plain flour. Pour into a greased, bottom-lined and floured 9 in (23 cm) round cake tin. Bake in a 350°F/180°C/Gas 4 oven for 25–30 minutes. Cool in the tin for 10 minutes, then turn out on to a wire rack and cool completely. Before serving, peel off the lining paper. Dust the top lightly with sifted icing sugar.

1 ▲ In a heatproof bowl, combine the eggs (at room temperature) and sugar. Set the bowl over a saucepan of simmering water; the base of the bowl should not touch the water.

3 ▲ Lift out the beaters; the mixture on the beaters should trail back on to the surface of the remaining mixture in the bowl to make a ribbon that holds it shape.

5 ▲ Sift the flour and fold it into the mixture, cutting in to the bottom of the bowl with a rubber spatula or large metal spoon and turning the mixture over, working gently yet thoroughly to retain the volume of the whisked egg and sugar mixture.

2 ▲ Beat with a hand-held electric mixer at medium-high speed, or a rotary beater or whisk, until the mixture is very thick and pale – about 10 minutes.

4 ▲ Remove the bowl from over the pan of water and continue beating for 2–3 minutes or until the mixture is cool.

6 ▲ Pour the mixture into the prepared tin or tins and bake as directed in the recipe. To test a whisked sponge, press the centre lightly with your fingertip: the cake should spring back.

Chocolate Orange Sponge Drops

MAKES ABOUT 14

2 eggs

2 oz (55 g) caster sugar

½ teaspoon grated orange zest

2 oz (55 g) plain flour

4 tablespoons fine shred orange marmalade

1½ oz (45 g) plain chocolate, cut into small pieces

1 Preheat a 400°F/200°C/Gas 6 oven. Line 3 baking sheets with baking parchment.

2 ▲ Put the eggs and sugar in a large bowl and set over a pan of just simmering water. Whisk until the mixture is thick and pale.

3 ▲ Remove the bowl from the pan of water and continue whisking until the mixture is cool. Whisk in the grated orange zest.

4 Sift the flour over the whisked mixture and fold it in gently with a rubber spatula.

5 ▲ Using a dessertspoon, put spoonfuls of the mixture on the prepared baking sheets, leaving space around each spoonful to allow for spreading. The mixture will make 28–30 drops.

6 Bake for about 8 minutes or until golden. Cool for a few minutes on the baking sheets, then transfer to a wire rack to cool completely.

7 Sandwich pairs of sponge drops together with the orange marmalade.

8 ▼ Melt the chocolate in a double saucepan over simmering water until smooth. Using a small spoon, drizzle chocolate over the tops of the sponge drops, or pipe it in fine lines using a small greaseproof paper piping bag. Leave to set before serving.

PREPARING CAKE TINS

Instructions vary from recipe to recipe for preparing cake tins. Some are simply greased, some are greased and floured, some are lined with baking parchment or greased greaseproof paper. The preparation required depends on the type of cake mixture and the length of the baking time. Proper preparation aids turning out.

Flavourful coatings
Some cake recipes specify that the greased tin be coated with sugar, cocoa powder or ground nuts. Follow the method for flouring.

1 ▲ To grease a tin: Use butter, margarine, or a mild or flavourless oil. If using butter or margarine, hold a small piece in a paper towel (or use your fingers), and rub it all over the bottom and up the side of the tin to make a thin, even coating. If using oil, brush it on with a pastry brush.

2 ▲ To flour a tin: Put a small scoopful of flour in the centre of the greased tin. Tip and rotate the tin so that the flour spreads and coats all over the bottom and up the side. Turn the tin over and shake out excess flour, tapping the base of the tin to dislodge any pockets of flour.

3 ▲ To line the bottom of a tin: Set the tin on the sheet of paper and draw round the base. Cut out this circle, square or rectangle, cutting just inside the drawn line. Press the paper smoothly on to the bottom of the tin.

4 ▲ To line the sides of a tin (for rich mixtures and fruit cakes): Cut a strip of paper long enough to wrap round the outside of the tin and overlap by 1½ in (4 cm). The strip should be wide enough to extend 1 in (2.5 cm) above the rim of the tin.

5 ▲ Fold the strip lengthways at the 1 in (2.5 cm) point and crease firmly. With scissors, snip at regular intervals along the 1 in (2.5 cm) fold, from the edge to the crease. Line the side of the tin, with the snipped part of the strip on the bottom.

6 ▲ For square and rectangular cake tins, fold the paper and crease it with your fingernail to fit snugly into the corners of the tin. Then press the bottom paper lining into place.

7 ▲ If the recipe specifies, grease the paper before you put it in the tin. If the tin is to be floured, do this after the paper is in place.

8 ▲ To line bun and muffin tins: Use paper liners of the required size. Or grease and flour the tins.

9 ▲ **To line a Swiss roll tin**: Cut a rectangle of paper 2 in (5 cm) larger all round than the tin. Grease the bottom of the tin lightly to prevent the paper from slipping.

10 ▲ Lay the paper evenly in the tin. With a table knife, press the paper into the angle all round the bottom of the tin, creasing the paper firmly but not cutting it.

11 ▲ With scissors, snip the paper in the corners, from top to bottom, so it will fit neatly into them. Grease the paper according to recipe instructions, unless using baking parchment.

USING SEPARATED EGGS FOR A WHISKED SPONGE

This version of whisked sponge is easier to make than the classic one that uses whole eggs, but the results are no less light and delicious. There is no need to set the bowl over a pan of simmering water for whisking, although if you are using a balloon whisk rather than an electric mixer or rotary beater you may want to do so to speed up the thickening of the egg yolk and sugar mixture and to increase its volume. Bowls and beaters used with egg whites must be scrupulously clean.

1 ▲ Separate the eggs, taking care that there is no trace of yolk with the whites. Put the yolks and whites in separate large bowls.

2 ▲ Add most of the sugar to the yolks. With a hand-held or table-top electric mixer, whisk at medium-high speed until the mixture is very thick and pale. Lift out the beaters: the mixture on the beaters should trail back on to the surface of the remaining mixture in the bowl to make a ribbon that holds its shape.

3 ▲ Whisk the egg whites until they form soft peaks (if not using a copper bowl, add a pinch of cream of tartar once the whites are frothy). Add the remaining sugar and continue whisking until the whites will form stiff peaks.

4 ▲ With a rubber spatula, fold the sifted flour into the egg yolk mixture, then fold in the whisked egg whites. Fold gently but thoroughly. Pour the mixture into the prepared tin and bake as instructed.

A Genoese sponge
This whisked sponge, made with whole or separated eggs, is more rich and trickier to make, as melted butter is folded in just before pouring into the tin.

MAKING A SWISS ROLL

A rolled sponge reveals an attractive spiral of filling when it is sliced. The filling may be sweetened whipped cream (page 160), ice cream (page 167), fruit jam or buttercream (page 242).

The whisked sponge mixture can be made using whole or separated eggs (pages 244 or 247), as preferred.

Line the tin with greaseproof paper or baking parchment, grease the paper and dust with flour.

Chocolate Ice Cream Roll
Make the sponge mixture using 4 eggs, separated, 4 oz (115 g) caster sugar and 4 oz (115 g) plain flour sifted with 3 tablespoons cocoa powder. Pour into a prepared 15 × 10 in (37.5 × 25 cm) Swiss roll tin. Bake in a 375°F/190°C/Gas 5 oven for about 15 minutes. Turn out, roll up and cool. When cold, unroll the cake and spread with 1 pint (600 ml) softened vanilla or chocolate ice cream. Roll up the cake again, wrap in foil and freeze until firm. About 30 minutes before serving, transfer the cake to the refrigerator. Sprinkle with caster or icing sugar before serving. If desired, serve with warm bittersweet chocolate sauce (page 203). *Serves 8.*

1 ▲ Pour the mixture into the prepared tin and spread it evenly into the corners with a palette knife. Bake as specified in the recipe.

3 ▲ Carefully peel off the lining paper from the cake. If necessary, trim off any crisp edges from the side of the cake.

5 ▲ Remove the towel and unroll the cake. Lift off the paper. Spread the chosen filling over the cake.

2 ▲ Spread a tea towel flat and lay a sheet of baking parchment on top. Sprinkle the paper evenly, as specified, with caster or icing sugar, cocoa or a sugar and spice mixture. Invert the cake on to the paper.

4 ▲ Carefully roll up the cake, with the paper inside, starting from a short side. Wrap the towel round the cake roll and leave to cool on a wire rack.

6 ▲ Roll up the cake again, using the paper to help move it forward. Sprinkle with sugar or ice the cake, as the recipe specifies.

Yule Log Cake

SERVES 8 OR MORE

4 eggs, separated
5 oz (145 g) caster sugar
1 teaspoon vanilla essence
pinch of cream of tartar (if needed)
4 oz (115 g) plain flour, sifted
8 fl oz (240 ml) whipping cream
10 oz (300 g) plain or bittersweet chocolate, chopped
2 tablespoons rum or Cognac

1 Preheat a 375°F/190°C/Gas 5 oven. Grease, line and flour a 16 × 11 in (40 × 28 cm) Swiss roll tin.

2 Put the egg yolks in a large bowl. Reserve 2 tablespoons sugar; add the remainder to the egg yolks. Whisk until pale and thick. Add the vanilla.

3 In another bowl, scrupulously clean and grease-free, whisk the egg whites (with the cream of tartar if not using a copper bowl) until they will hold soft peaks. Add the reserved sugar and continue whisking until the whites are glossy and will hold stiff peaks.

4 Gently fold half the flour into the egg yolk mixture. Add one-quarter of the egg whites and fold in to lighten the mixture. Fold in the remaining flour, then the remaining egg whites.

5 ▲ Spread the mixture in the prepared tin. Bake for 15 minutes.

6 Turn on to paper sprinkled with caster sugar. Roll up and cool.

7 Bring the cream to the boil in a small saucepan. Put the chocolate in a bowl, add the cream and stir until the chocolate has melted.

8 ▲ Beat the chocolate mixture until it is fluffy and has thickened to a spreading consistency. Spoon one-third of the chocolate mixture into another bowl. Mix in rum or Cognac.

9 Unroll the cake. Spread the rum and chocolate mixture evenly over the surface. Roll up the cake again.

10 Cut off about one-quarter of the cake, at an angle. Place it against the side of the larger piece of cake, to resemble a branch from a tree trunk.

11 ▼ Spread the remaining chocolate mixture all over the cake. Mark with the prongs of a fork to resemble bark. Before serving, add small Christmas decorations and sprigs of holly if liked, and dust with a little icing sugar 'snow'.

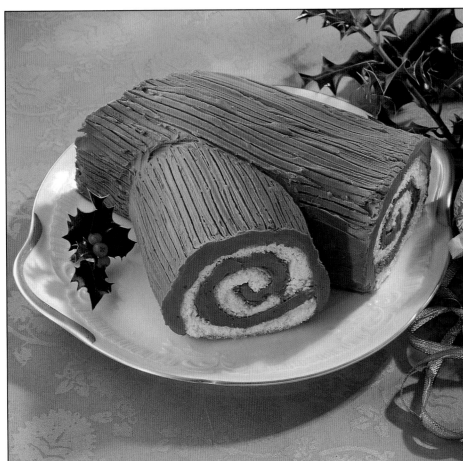

MAKING CAKES BY THE MELTING METHOD

Cakes made by the melting method are wonderfully moist and keep quite well. Ingredients such as sugar, syrup (treacle, honey, golden syrup) and fat are warmed together until melted and smoothly combined before being added to the dry ingredients.

Fruit Cake
Sift 8 oz (225 g) self-raising flour, a pinch of salt and 1 teaspoon mixed spice. Melt together 4 oz (115 g) butter or margarine, 4 oz (115 g) soft light brown sugar, ¼ pint (150 ml) water and the grated zest and juice of 1 orange. When smooth, add 4 oz (115 g) each sultanas, currants and raisins and simmer gently for about 10 minutes, stirring occasionally. Cool. Add the fruit mixture to the dry ingredients. Add 2 oz (55 g) each chopped glacé cherries and chopped mixed peel, 1 tablespoon orange marmalade and 2 beaten eggs. Mix thoroughly. Pour into a greased and lined 8 in (20 cm) round cake tin. Bake at 325°F/170°C/Gas 3 for 1½ hours or until firm and golden; a skewer inserted in the centre should come out clean. Cool in the tin for 30 minutes before turning out on to a wire rack.

1 ▲ Sift the dry ingredients (such as flour, raising agent, salt, ground spices) into a large bowl.

3 ▲ If recipe instructs, warm fruit in the syrup mixture. Remove from the heat and leave to cool slightly (if too hot, it will not combine well with dry ingredients).

5 ▲ If called for in the recipe, stir in fruit and/or nuts (if these have not been warmed in the syrup). Turn the cake mixture into a lined tin and bake according to the recipe.

2 ▲ Put the sugar and/or syrup and fat in a saucepan with any other ingredients specified in the recipe. Warm over a low heat, stirring occasionally, until the fat has melted and sugar dissolved. The mixture should not boil.

4 ▲ Make a well in the centre of the dry ingredients and pour in the cooled melted mixture. Add beaten eggs and any other liquid ingredients (milk, water, etc) and beat to a smooth, thick batter.

Maturing for flavour
Melting-method cakes taste best if they are allowed to 'mature' before serving. After the cake has cooled completely, wrap it in greaseproof paper and then over-wrap in foil. Keep it in a cool place for 1–2 days before cutting into slices.

Rich Sticky Gingerbread

MAKES AN 8 IN (20 CM) SQUARE CAKE

8 oz (225 g) plain flour
pinch of salt
1 teaspoon bicarbonate of soda
2 teaspoons ground ginger
1 teaspoon mixed spice
4 oz (115 g) butter or margarine
4 oz (115 g) golden syrup
4 oz (115 g) black treacle
2 oz (55 g) soft dark brown sugar
2 eggs, beaten
4 fl oz (120 ml) milk
4 oz (115 g) sultanas or chopped stem ginger (optional)
FOR THE ICING (OPTIONAL)
4 oz (115 g) icing sugar
about 4 teaspoons water

1 ▲ Preheat a 350°F/180°C/Gas 4 oven. Grease and line an 8 in (20 cm) square cake tin.

2 ▲ Sift the flour, salt, bicarbonate of soda and spices into a bowl.

3 Put the butter or margarine, golden syrup, treacle and brown sugar in a saucepan and warm over a gentle heat, stirring occasionally, until the fat has melted and the mixture is smooth. Remove from the heat and leave to cool slightly.

4 ▼ Make a well in the centre of the dry ingredients and add the melted mixture, the beaten eggs and milk. Beat with a wooden spoon until the mixture is smooth. Add the sultanas or ginger, if using.

5 Turn the cake mixture into the prepared tin. Bake for about 1 hour. To test if the gingerbread is done, press it lightly in the centre; it should spring back. Allow to cool in the tin for 5 minutes before turning out on to a wire rack to cool completely.

6 ▲ If icing the gingerbread, sift the icing sugar into a bowl and add 3 teaspoons of the water. Stir to mix, then add more water 1 teaspoon at a time until the icing is smooth and has a pouring consistency. Pour the icing over the gingerbread and leave to set before serving.

INDEX
~